Morning Dew and Roses

Folklore and Society

Series Editors

Roger Abrahams
Bruce Jackson
Marta Weigle

A list of books in the series appears at the back of the book.

A Publication of the American Folklore Society

New Series

General Editor, Patrick B. Mullen

Nuance, Metaphor, and Meaning in Folksongs

Morning Dew and Roses

Barre Toelken

University of Illinois Press   Urbana and Chicago

This book is printed on acid-free paper.

Library of Congress Cataloging-in-Publication Data

Toelken, Barre.
    Morning dew and roses : nuance, metaphor, and meaning in folksongs
/ Barre Toelken.
        p.   cm.
    Includes bibliographical references and index.
    ISBN 0-252-02134-7 (cloth)
    1. Folk poetry—History and criticism. 2. Folksongs—Texts—
History and criticism. 3. Metaphor. 4. Oral tradition.
    I. Title.
PN1341.T64   1995
398.2—dc20   94-13608
                                                                        CIP

For Albert B. Friedman
with gratitude and admiration

Contents

Preface

This project has taken me most of my life, although I was not aware of it until recently. As a boy in central Massachusetts, I was fascinated by the distinctly different ways in which my neighbors and friends responded to the song "Springfield Mountain," a brief narrative—sung most years at the Wilbraham reunion—which recounted the death of a local youth by rattlesnake bite in 1761. We had visited his grave, so we knew the story must be true, but we noticed that folks of our grandparents' generation (many of whom sang it to the tune of "Old Hundred," the common Protestant offertory song called the Doxology) tended to understand the song as a stern example of God's Providence in recent times, whereas we children thought it was a real howler whose most serious content might have been the avuncular warning, "Don't suck the poison out of a wound if you have bad teeth." The song and the words were the same, but they meant different things to different people. The puzzle was not clarified when our high school music teacher scripted a musical show in which several of us played a group of hayseed Jonathans going melodramatically through the whole story: mowing the hay with a wooden scythe, getting bitten, screaming for Molly to suck the poison out, and dying in each other's arms (far too slowly, it seemed to us) of snakebite, toothache, and teenage mortification.

I never did solve the discrepancy of meanings in "Springfield Mountain," but I did maintain my interest in folksongs, urged on by Lee Crabtree, that high school music teacher, and aided by several family members who sang or made and played instruments. My great grandfather, Edwin T. Kimball, was a fiddler and fiddle maker who believed that killing rattlesnakes and stuffing their rattles into a musical instrument helped to convert the wilderness into civilization. His scowling portrait on my wall reminds my family that he didn't get 'em all. Uncle Les Howland taught me to play the guitar he had made, and my cousin Dick Lee and I took it around to the homes of our various girlfriends in high school and made a clean-cut impression singing for their families. Then Burl Ives became famous, and we promptly dropped our family songs and began singing "Jimmy Crack Corn" and "On Top of Old Smokey."

Nonetheless, when I got to graduate school, I thought it might be rewarding to revive my memory of a few of the older songs I knew and see whether I could write a master's thesis about them. I worked on our skeptical department chair (who had told us that *Moby-Dick* might have made a good whaling novel had only Melville had left out every other chapter) and convinced him the project was legitimate, partly by promising not to bring in "extraneous elements" like music, and proceeded to write a thesis that used Robert Graves, James Campbell, Jesse Weston, Gordon Hall Gerould, and others to prove that English ballads were in actuality faded remnants of early European fertility myths, their gods and goddesses demoted to lords and ladies. By the time I was through with it, I didn't believe it myself, but by then I was on the eve of my orals and couldn't tolerate the thought of starting over. So I made the presentation to my committee (the toughest question was Nelson Ault's "What has all this got to do with the mythology of the Digger Indians?") and was through with it. I have since been chagrined to learn the thesis has been ordered numerous times on interlibrary loan.

At the University of Oregon, I had the great fortune to study with Arthur Brodeur, the distinguished medievalist who had retired from the University of California at Berkeley a few years earlier. He wanted to take on one last doctoral student in the ballad, and I was there at the right time. He was not only an excellent teacher—who seemed to know, in fact, did know, everything—but had also studied ballads with George Lyman Kittredge at Harvard, and Kittredge had studied with Francis James Child. Immodestly, I fancied myself in the fourth generation of an apostolic succession of ballad scholars and immediately set about expiating my Gravesean sins by writing a scholarly dissertation titled "Some Poetic Functions of Folklore in the English and Scottish Ballad" under Brodeur's stern supervision. This exercise was my first full exposure to current folklore scholarship, and it set the stage for virtually everything that followed in my professional career.

For several years after my doctoral work was completed, I tinkered with the dissertation, trying to make it into a book, and was finally well on the way to writing a final draft in the early 1970s when I attended a folklore conference at Freiburg University in southwestern Germany. One evening, sitting at supper with a jolly crowd including Lutz Röhrich and Jürgen Dittmar, I suddenly realized the Germans had been working in the same area of folksong poetics—both in German and in English. I clearly had several more years of reading to do before finishing my book, but the process was impeded by my increasing involvement with Navajo narratives, which—to put it mildly—resided in quite a separate fold of my brain. Now, after teaching some courses in ballad at Utah State University, and after noticing how Roger Renwick's *English Folk Poetry,* although dense in spots, has encouraged interest in poetic and metaphoric considerations in folksong, I feel emboldened to bring my studies forward.

In the process of putting these chapters together, I have many people to thank, and chief among them are my family—both those in the past who taught the songs to me when I was young and those now, my wife and children, who have sung along with me over the years, even in the most unlikely situations (such as a concert for deaf people in a retirement home). Whenever we have a family gathering, whether it be a wedding or a Thanksgiving dinner, we all sing, and this fact has provided me with the most persuasive personal arguments for the depth and power of vernacular expression.

Many colleagues have helped me understand the nature of folksong, but I especially thank Albert B. Friedman, who has argued with me about almost every paper I have ever given on folklore. At my very first American Folklore Society meeting, where as a fresh Ph.D. I had taken Friedman to task for writing that ballads had no unique poetic characteristics (not realizing, of course, that he would be in the audience), Thelma James strode up to me, shaking her finger, and warned me not to attack my betters. Friedman waited until others had left (and my eye had focused on his name tag) and said, "That was a fine paper, but it's all wrong. Shall we have a drink?" From that time forward he has been my most persistent and most honest critic.

I am also indebted to David Buchan and James Porter for their expert advice and ready help through the years, as well the members of the S.I.E.F. Kommission für Volksdichtung. In particular, Klaus Roth, Natascha Würzbach, Jürgen Dittmar, Lutz Röhrich, and Otto Holzapfel have provided useful responses and suggestions to particular segments of this book. Joe Hickerson of the Archive of Folk Culture in the American Folklife Center (Library of Congress) has provided rich perspective on all aspects of folksong.

One of my most valuable—and most reliable—sources of insight over the years has been Kenneth S. Goldstein, who has given his career to the study and understanding of ballad and folksong. His uncanny sense for folksong and his monumental memory (to say nothing of his monster collection, which he readily shares with colleagues) constitute a living treasure in the field of folklore. His comments and corrections on this book have been extremely helpful and have rescued me in advance from several faux pas. Close readings and generous commentaries on this work were also provided by Sandy Ives and Patrick Mullen, and although I did not take all their suggestions (my passion for the semicolon remains only slightly dampened), my thinking and final manuscript were vastly improved by their suggestions. Sandy and his virtuoso works have greatly encouraged my view that vernacular expressions cannot be fairly judged by whether or not they appear in print. Pat Mullen urged me to pay more attention the possibilities of gender differences in the perception of many of the central metaphors discussed in this book. In addition to the intellectual lift provided by these three colleagues, I feel a deep sense of pleasure that the perceptions of scholars I have admired so much have played a formative role in my work on this book.

A study of folksong would be nothing without the resources provided by singers, and I have tried to identify as many as possible in the notes. In particular, several people provided me with—or led me to—songs and materials that otherwise would not have become parts of this study: Norman Kennedy allowed me to use the words of his version of "The Wee Staggie"; Walter Bolton gave me the texts of two songs from his central Oregon area, "My Love Is a Rider" and "The Cowboy and the Maiden"; and Martin and Margot Kuske and Klaus Roth provided me with their verses of the north German (Plattdeutsch) song "Dat du min leevste bist." Bob Beers was also generous with his songs, and I will always be in debt to him for having shared his repertoire and expertise with me and audiences nationwide. Gary McMahon kindly gave permission for me to quote his poem, "The Two Things in Life That I Really Love."

My scholarly and personal obligation to Arthur Brodeur cannot be fully articulated but must be mentioned, along with my indebtedness to other deceased mentors: Wayland D. Hand, Albert Lord, and D. K. Wilgus gave generously of their time and perspectives, even though I was never formally a student of theirs, and Kester Svendsen, a Miltonist who believed folklore to be central to any consideration of literature—"the most articulate of all the arts."

Much of the work in this book has appeared in embryonic form in *Western Folklore, Journal of the Folklore Institute,* and *Jahrbuch für Volksliedforschung,* but all previous essays have been enlarged, modified, mixed, and enhanced by responses from colleagues. Some of my ideas have been strengthened, others thrown out or transformed by further discovery and (occasionally) good sense. As much as possible, I have tried to use perspectives gained through my own fieldwork, even though the necessary reference to ballad and song texts that others have collected has often made me work at an arm's length that I do not find comfortable and thereby focus more on text than on performance. For this reason, I urge readers to use my comments as suggestive and even provocative but to rely chiefly on observations of what people actually do and say when they sing. In the case of chapter 4, which focuses primarily on the traditional singing in an extended family in Austria, I have been able to be more extensive in my use of constant fieldwork and provide some description and judgment based on observations over a period of several years.

Although I have known the Koessner family and their many in-laws and singing friends for years, my first full year of intensive research on their singing was made possible by a Fulbright appointment to the Department of Folklore at Freiburg University. I am very much indebted to Lutz Röhrich, then director and professor of the Folklore Program, for his interest, encouragement, and advice during my stay in Germany. I must also acknowledge the help of Rolf Wilhelm Brednich, then head curator of the Deutsches Volksliedarchiv. He and his colleagues, Jürgen Dittmar, Barbara James, and David Engle, were gracious in sharing the inner sanctums of the DVA with me and providing advice on the project. My almost daily discussions with Hannjost Lixfeld and Gertraud Meinel allowed me to appreciate complexities of German folklore theory and practice that would otherwise have eluded me. My friend Michiko Iwasaka, then a doctoral student in the folklore and Japanese studies departments at Freiburg University, provided first aid to my rusty German and supplied practical and theoretical perspectives for the research.

Through the years, the students in my folksong and ballad courses have caused me to sharpen and clarify my approach to folksong metaphor, and I have benefited immensely from their patience and curiosity. During the actual writing of this book, my almost daily conversations with colleagues Barbara Walker and Leonard Rosenband have helped me see issues more clearly and plan my approach more intelligently. Without their engagement, the central thrust of the book would never have emerged so fully. Karen Krieger has not only taken part in these discussions, but she has also taken on the formidable responsibility of putting my primitive drafts where they belong, into the computer. My indebtedness to all these people is beyond description.

An unexpected bonus of publishing this book with the University of Illinois Press has been the privilege to work with manuscript editor Mary Giles, whose keen attention and good sense have rescued me from needless redundancies, infelicities in phrasing, and downright errors. If there are any of these left, they are the ones I insisted on keeping.

Morning Dew and Roses

1

"All concealed in the flap of his pants"
Metaphors and Vernacular Clarity

If it is true, as T. S. Eliot wrote, that "every revolution in [formal] poetry is apt to be . . . a return to common speech," then we can confidently claim that vernacular or folk poetry, as it occurs in the genres of folksong, is quite nonrevolutionary, for its tendency is not to stray from the living resources of common or everyday speech to begin with.[1] Geoffrey Leech notes that literary poets try to escape from banality, to avoid most kinds of redundancy, and to attempt bold, new—even audacious—formulations (poetic license being the positive view of a poet's right, perhaps obligation, to "ignore rules and conventions generally observed by users of the language").[2] Folksong poetry, on the other hand, thrives on familiarity, on repetition, and on the everyday conventions and usages of people who share close familial, social, and cultural ties.

This book examines the poetics of folksong, with special attention to lyrics and narratives in which everyday figurative usages are central elements of meaning. The total spectrum of vernacular song will not be discussed, for folksongs, printed broadsides, scribbled cowboy poems, and autograph book ditties—just as conventional formal poems—cover a vast and varied range of style, presentation, and quality. Unfortunately, this rich abundance of features has been partially obscured by folksong studies that have concentrated primarily on narrative structure, historical development, formulaic language, or stanzaic form. In this book, I will add to the ongoing discussion of figurative language on the informal—largely oral and aural—level of performative articulation, hopefully in tune with other recent works that have brought ballad and folksong study back to life by paying serious attention to their metaphorical language.

As noted in the Preface, my interest in folksong poetics came about in large part in response to Albert Friedman's statement that "any rare or subtle figurative expression in a ballad would make its genuineness suspect, for the language of ballads is a tissue of commonplaces, stock figures, stock symbols, and formulaic phrasing."[3] At first, this struck me as a resounding dismissal of those rare and subtle touches I had perceived, as well as an implied declaration that the ballads were lightweight poetry and not the powerful dramatic expressions I had found them to be. As I became acquainted with Friedman and had the benefit of arguing this topic with him over the years, I came to understand that his reference to "rare and subtle" expressions meant the identifiable conceits and devices used by individual art poets—those authors who develop their own recognizable styles by avoiding commonplace phrases and stock figures. Friedman held (and this is clear from other sentences in the same passage quoted) that the style and content of ballads, and other folksongs as well, derive from the distinctive ways in which ballads have been shaped by the eventually anonymous people who have polished them while performing them over the years. In this, we are in agreement; nonetheless, I have remained convinced that much of ballad and folksong poetry is indeed very subtle yet exceptionally powerful in its productive command of nuance and ambiguity, and thus I have tried to understand more fully how the highly charged and culturally meaningful phraseology of folksong "works," how it may be fairly apprehended and appreciated, and how it might be discussed more profitably.

After all, a song line like "I sowed some seeds all in some grove . . . there grows no green," unless it is to be understood as a silly or uninformed agricultural experiment, actually means something other than what it actually says; yet its meaning must be in some way consistent with the words, or the song would not make any sense. Cecil Sharp recognized the metaphorical nuances of lines like this, for as James Reeves points out, he and other collectors of folksongs routinely changed the wording or deleted verses altogether in the belief that they were too crude for print.[4] Yet the song is in no way pornographic (or even graphic, except in agricultural detail). How did Sharp and others perceive the greater complexities of meaning in such songs? Did they think the singers did not understand their own texts? Were they afraid of reading prurient images into otherwise innocent bucolisms, or did they recognize a powerful set of figurative uses that fit neither their Victorian constraints nor their preconceptions about primitive poetry? I suspect the latter is closest to the case, and perhaps we can feel lucky to be pursuing such a topic at a time in cultural history when we can discuss this imagery more openly and no longer feel inclined to think that rural and "primitive" people are too dull to create intentional poetic ambiguity. Beyond that, we can now capitalize on the advances made in linguistics, semiotics, and literary criticism and speak of decoding words, phrases, themes, customs, and gestures for their cultural and linguistic functions, which often run far beyond their lexical meanings or their manifest content.

Even so, the approach to metaphorical expression in folksong espoused in this study is not the theory- and jargon-ridden avenue of the semiotics field itself, although it is not—and cannot pretend to be—uninformed or uninspired by the rich insights that workers in that arena provide. Rather, my examination focuses on the available, normal, everyday figurative elements in the language that readers, like folksong singers and audiences, can readily recognize and apply; it is counterproductive to write about the richness and nuance of language in a vocabulary not suited to or illumined by the topic. Thus, my approach has more in common with that of George Lakoff and Mark Johnson in *Metaphors We Live By* than it has with the equally insightful works of Sausseure and his executors, for Lakoff and Johnson demonstrate the validity of their observations and illustrate their points with numerous examples taken from everyday speech.[5]

A complete overview of ballad and folksong scholarship is—and ought to be—beyond the scope of this book, but perhaps a characterization of some key issues would provide perspective on the subject. For fuller and more generous accounts of folksong scholarship, including the "ballad wars" of yesteryear, see *Anglo-American Folksong Scholarship since 1898* by D. K. Wilgus, as well as Jan H. Brunvand's introductory chapters (including full bibliographies) in *The Study of American Folklore: An Introduction* and Joseph Harris's informative introduction to *The Ballad and Oral Literature*.[6]

It is important to recollect that folksong scholarship has gone through several stages of growing up and that these have been parallel to the developmental increments in literary, historical, and anthropological analysis. The great anthology of ballads produced by Francis James Child, a scholar of eighteenth-century literature at Harvard University, and the earlier works of Scott, Motherwell, and others in the eighteenth and nineteenth centuries were essentially archaeological attempts to register and catalog oral antiquities for a cultural "museum" in printed form. The idea was to find, salvage, and print—and, to some extent, systematize—the faded remainders of a vanishing genre.[7] Sometimes several variants of a text were printed, but the modern folkloristic insistence on multiplicity of versions from oral tradition, as well as the contemporary recognition that folksong did not vanish in the face of literacy and general education, would have been illogical notions with little chance of practical application for those early scholars. In the succeeding generation of scholars, Child's former student and protégé George Lyman Kittredge, as well as a wide range of other literary scholars, including Louise Pound, Francis B. Gummere, and Andrew Lang, argued over the possible origins of a closed corpus of fossils.

Fortunately for the survival of folksong scholarship in academia, the next wave, from the early to the mid-twentieth century—perhaps folksong scholarship's golden age—was characterized by serious field collecting from live singers and by equally serious inquiries into prosody, structure, historical-geographical spread, and even meaning, all topics that attributed some kinds of intelligence and poetic awareness to the singers who had passed the songs on. Cecil Sharp and others traveled to areas where folksongs were still being sung and actually noted them down; Lowry Charles Wimberly studied the folkloric meanings of typical ballad motifs and themes; Albert Friedman could speak of the relationship between culture and folksong; Robert Winslow Gordon solicited folksong texts through newspapers and, along with his friend Arthur Brodeur (both of them students of Kittredge), collected and archived sea songs from skippers and sailors along the California coast—these and other songs becoming the embryo of the Archive of Folksong in the Library of Congress.[8] Scholars such as Holger Nygard, Edson Richmond, MacEdward Leach, D. K. Wilgus, and Roger Abrahams (not all of them the same age, but all working in the same cultural milieu) were establishing reputations for characterizing and discussing the genres of folksong in geographical, stylistic, and international frames.[9] Edward D. Ives, Helen Creighton, and Edith Fowke made large field collections and established standards and criteria for calling something a "folksong."[10] Those scholars were joined by numerous others, both scholars and faddists, who had become interested in folksong during the "folksong revival" of the 1950s and 1960s. University courses in folksong and ballad proliferated, and new collections were published. Probably the hottest critical issue of the day was James H. Jones's suggestion that Albert Lord's oral formulaic theories could be applied to ballads. Although Albert Friedman quickly pulverized this notion, it ushered in an era of closer scrutiny of ballad texts and language that dealt with folksong features as something more complex than could be accounted for by survival, illiterate redundancies, or rural mnemonics.[11]

More recent developments in folksong and ballad scholarship have followed this direction, with rich results. Under the encouragement of the Commission for Folk Poetry, a standing working committee of the International Society of Ethnology and Folklore, and with the strong involvement of the Deutsches Volksliedarchiv in Freiburg im Breisgau, folksong scholars from around the world meet regularly to discuss critical issues in understanding language, contexts, and meanings. Much of the work has involved a closer look at, and earnest reassessments of, how the structure and language of vernacular poetry and song is understood. It is in the spirit of this arena of analytical interest that this book is written.[12]

A beacon in folksong discussion has been Roger deV. Renwick's *English Folk Poetry: Structure and Meaning,* which considers the ways in which local frames of reference, local values, and local shared experiences create semantic fields in which certain phrases and topics attain a special intensity of meaning. Although some reviewers looked askance at Renwick's inclusion of vernacular written poetry and thus missed, or denied, his point about local semiotics existing on all levels of local discourse, the book is an exemplary articulation of where the discussion of folksong must go—into such questions as what we need to know about fields of cultural meaning and inference before we can know what culturally based songs mean to those who sing and hear them within their communities.[13]

Yet the recreation of semiotic systems recognizable to cultural outsiders is a formidable task. For example, providing a framework of understanding for the Navajo "Horse-riding Song," which has no words at all, would take a lengthy essay and still the reader would have little chance of getting a thrill of understanding, even if it were possible to be there in the desert late in the midwinter night, when fifty to a hundred men on horseback might sing it in falsetto on their way from one ritual location to another. Dealing with folksong in our own culture, on the other hand, at least yields some inside advantages in interpretation and cultural understanding, although it does not necessarily make the intellectual discussion of these matters any less delicate and demanding.

As an example, consider what can be brought out of a song from Euro-American culture through a consideration of the song's context, the comments and actions of its singer and the singer's family, and by other parallels from similar folksongs. It is Halloween 1971, and the occasion is a gathering of friends who enjoy traditional songs. They have met sporadically over several years in Eugene, Oregon, to teach each other the songs that have come down in customary channels in their own families. Bob and Evelyne Beers are in town to do a concert and have been invited to join in with their songs. The Beers, professional folksingers, have learned songs from a variety of sources and composed a number of their own, but Bob Beers especially recalls traditional songs that his grandfather, George Sullivan, a fiddler, sang and played.[14] After playing a few of George Sullivan's favorite fiddle tunes, Beers's face lights up, and he launches heartily into the following song, playing the tune through once before he sings. The verses are sung unaccompanied, but the chorus is sung while Beers plays.

Now you boys and you girls who inhabit this place,
Give an ear to this tale of the fiddle I plays,
For this fiddle of mine is a marvelous thing,
A finer and better one never did ring.

CHORUS: Whoop! dee dee dee dee dee dee
dee diddle dee diddle dee diddle dee dee;
whoop dee dee dee dee dee dee,
dee diddle dee diddle dee dee.

Now this fiddle of mine, when it was first tried,
'Twas as sweet as a lark and as soft as a bride;
This fiddle to see and its music to hear
Gave delight to the eye while it ravished the ear.

CHORUS

So let me tell of this fiddle's countree:
'Twas born and 'twas bred down in fair Italee,
In a town where a marshall, a proud man of France,
Brought it home all concealed in the flap of his pants.

(Prolonged laughter.)

CHORUS

Now having told of this fiddle's high birth,
I will tell of the fingers that give it such mirth;
For fingers so straight and so slim and so small

(Beers laughs heartily, holding up his right hand.)

Shall be sung by a poet or not sung at all.

(Beers laughs again; his own fingers are short and thick.)

CHORUS

And now having sung of the fiddle I know,
It would be no disgrace to sing of the bow,

(Pause: heavy laughter. Beers: "I can't go on with it!")

For heavenly [?] played has the virtue of such
That it wounded the heart if the ear it did touch.

(Laughter, prolonged.)

CHORUS

(Concludes in heavy laughter, then Beers: "I haven't thought of that for a long time [still laughing]. Grandpa Sullivan used to sing that one." Evelyne [laughing]: "He never sang it around the ladies, though.")

I think we can conclude that Beers's laughter at the end of the fourth verse is based on his acknowledgment that his own fingers are in ironic contrast with those described in the verse. But what of the laughter at the end of verse three and in the middle of verse five? And why didn't Grandpa Sullivan sing the song around the ladies? The answers to these questions are not supplied by the manifest content of the song but are triggered by something in the song that suggests another level of meaning. We could suppose that the curvaceous figure of a fiddle and the phallic design of the bow might have suggested something unmentionably erotic to George Sullivan (as they have to others), but he is not around to interview. What recourse is there but that of the text itself (surely the idea of a fiddle concealed in the flap of a man's pants is suggestive enough), the performance (with its laughter at key places), the knowing response of Evelyne Beers (who has heard her husband, but not her father-in-law, sing the song), plus the evidence obtainable from other similar references?

The problem with supporting evidence from the cultural background is that it is often most readily found in the printed collections of other folksongs and therefore usually lacks rich contextual and performance-sparked human responses. Yet it can be augmented by field collecting and personal experience. As an example of the latter, consider the common trick played upon young boys who forget to close the fly of their pants— "Hey! your violin case is open!"—followed, when the boy looks downward, with, "Oh, is that where you fiddle around?" The fiddle is also often referred to as the devil's own instrument, a nice pun in and of itself. According to Vance Randolph, not only did some Ozark fiddle tunes have crude or obscene titles, but a number of fiddle tunes were also perceived as bawdy.[15]

The fiddle was used figuratively in British broadside tradition, as in stanzas of "The Naughty Lord and the Gay Young Lady":

> His lordship loved the lady,
> And the lady she loved he,
> His lordship played by music,
> The tune called fiddle-de-dee.
>
> . . . .
>
> His lordship played the fiddle
> Down in Scotia's land, 'tis said,
> And his lordship must have fiddled well
> Both in and out of bed.[16]

In another broadside, "The Merchant and the Fidler's Wife," the merchant easily seduces the wife, and the fiddler laments:

> If I have lost my Fiddle,
> Then I am a Man undone;

My Fiddle whereon I so often play'd.
Away I needs must run.

The merchant consoles the fiddler by telling him "and thou shalt have thy Fiddle again, / But Peggy shall carry the case" and persuades the fiddler to play dance songs while he and the fiddler's wife make love.[17] In the broadside "My Thing Is My Own," a young woman is unsuccessfully courted by a sequence of men, one a musician, from varying professions:

A Master of Musick came with an intent,
To give me a Lesson on my instrument,
I thank'd him for nothing, but bid him be gone,
For my little Fiddle should not be plaid on.
 My thing is my own, and I'll keep it so still,
 Yet other young Lasses may do what they will.[18]

In "She Hoy'd Me Out o' Lauderdale," another broadside, a young fiddler is hoyed, that is, urged or incited, away from home by a woman who installs him in her bedchamber, but she apparently demands too much:

First when I came to Lauderdale
 I had a fiddle gude,
My sounding-pin stood [like] the aik (oak)
 That grows in Lauder-wood;
But now my sounding pin's gaen down,
 And tint (lost, broken) the foot forever;
She's hoy'd me out o'Lauderdale,
 My fiddle and a' thegither.

First when I came to Lauderdale,
 Your ladyship can declare,
I play'd a bow, a noble bow,
 As e'er was strung wi' hair:
But, dow'na do's come o'er me now,
 And your Ladyship winna consider;
She's hoy'd me out o' Lauderdale,
 My fiddle and a' thegither.[19]

The relatively consistent appearance of the fiddle image in sexual scenes in broadside ballads proves nothing directly about the use of the same image in oral tradition, but it does show that both oral and printed media used what appears to have been a common reference from the English vernacular. In other words, there is no indication here that the term *fiddle* is somehow a secret sexual term known only by those privy to an esoteric lingua franca (to use James Reeves's favorite term). Equally important, its use in these contexts does not mean that "fiddle" always means something sexual to all singers and audiences who speak English, an idea that might come from too rigid an application of the notion of a poetic or semiotic code. Rather, the fiddle and its bow have been used often enough, for reasons I will suggest, so they present some possibilities for metaphorical or metonymic word play in appropriate contexts.

In the song that Sharp (and Reeves) call "The Bold Grenadier," a young couple go out walking on a morning in May (one recalls here Renwick's convincing discussion about the semiotic and cultural dimensions of walking out together in May).[20] They sit down by the bank of a river:

> Where he softly clasped his arms around her middle
> And out of his knapsack he pulled out a fiddle
> He played her such a tune my boys that made the valley ring
> Hark hark said the fair maid how the nightingales sing.[21]

In "The German Flute," however, the instrument is not a fiddle, although it functions just as effectively:

> O it's on the banks of roses where my love and I sit down
> He pulled out his German flute and he played to her a tune
> In the middle of the tune O she sigh and she sing
> Lovely Johnny dearest Johnny do not leave me.[22]

And in "The Devil's in the Girl," a young gentleman who is staying overnight with a young woman offers to teach her a tune called "The Devil's in the Girl." Her response:

> Oh kind sir let me hear that tune
> If you your pipes can play
> I'll listen with attention
> So now play up I pray
> Oh the tune it is so beautiful
> And pleases me so well
> All night I'll lay, if you will play
> The devil's in the girl.[23]

Later, the sounds awaken the girl's mother, who rushes into the room, where "she spoiled this young man's music." When the young woman turns out to be pregnant—which must come as a curiosity to those who think the song is actually about music—her mother observes, "The music makes you swell / Why it's never good to play the tune / The devil's in the girl." In some versions like the following, the young woman asks repeatedly for more music until the boy, like the fiddler in the broadside, must plead that his instrument is overtaxed:

> "Oh now," says the soldier, "it's time I was gone,
> My peg is all slack and won't play one more song,

> The hair's off my bow and I can't find my string,
> Let's watch the water flow and hear the nightingale sing."[24]

In his comments on the lingua franca, Reeves notes that "many, if not most, references to music in traditional songs are directly or indirectly sexual. The 'flute' is a common male sexual symbol; the frequent use of 'fiddling' as a euphemism is probably due to the phallophoric suggestion of the fiddle-bow in action."[25] Here, I think, is the key to the metaphorical usage: Although form and motion may certainly be suggestive (and Freud would be pleased for us to notice it), the poetic function has more to do with a larger metaphorical frame. Making love is like making music, as in the phrase, "We could make such beautiful music together," and as in "she spoiled this young man's music," the line from "The Devil's in the Girl." The instruments used in the formulation of this metaphorical field function best if they are also appropriate in shape or in reputation, if they are common in slang (as is "skin flute" for penis), or if they are played by being blown, stroked, squeezed, or pounded. But the immediate reference for the instrument is not necessarily sexual if the song context doesn't call for it, for otherwise the imagery would be at odds with the understood meaning of the song instead of enhancing and foregrounding it. Reeves misses this point altogether when he refers to "fiddling" as a euphemism, for such usage is neither camouflage for the image nor an attempt to make it pretty or antiseptic. Rather, as in all good poetry, it is a way of intensifying deeper meaning in a recognizable and effective manner.

In the following American version of "The Bold Grenadier," the reference to "fiddle" is hardly a euphemism, for it focuses attention on the sexual situation that precipitates the girl's plea for the young man to stay with her. The song was sung by Walter Bolton, from Prineville, Oregon, as a response to Bob Beers's song. Bolton, who grew up in the ranch country of central Oregon, attended the University of Oregon and was a regular participant in the singing group, sharing his mostly western and cowboy-oriented songs. After the laughing had died down from Bob Beers's fiddle song, Bolton said, "While we're fiddling around, here's another one you might not want to sing in front of the women":

> One mornin', one mornin', one mornin' in May,
> I spied a young couple a-makin' their way;
> One was a lady and a fair one was she,
> And the other was a cowboy and a brave one was he.
>
> Said "Where are you goin' my pretty fair maid?"
> "Just down by the water, just down by the shade;
> Just down by the river, just down by the spring,
> To hear the wild ripplin' water, hear the nightingale sing."

They had not been there but an hour or so
When he pulled from his knapsack a fiddle and bow:
He tuned up his fiddle all on its one string,
And he played his tune over and over again.

(Whistles a verse.)

"Ah," said the cowboy, "I shoulda been gone."
"Oh no," said the pretty maid, "just play one more song.
I'd rather hear your fiddle and the touch of your string,
As to see the waters glidin', hear the nightingale sing."

"Oh cowboy, oh cowboy, won't you marry me?"
"Oh no, pretty maiden, that never can be;
I've a ranch and a family with babies three:
One cow ranch and a family is enough life for me."

"So I'll go back to Oregon and stay there one year,
And I'll spend all my money on whiskey and beer;
And if ever I return it will be in the spring
To hear your wild ripplin' water, hear your nightingale sing."

Walter Bolton's song is a western American variant of a well-known English song. It has made itself at home not only geographically but also culturally in an area where cowboys often describe themselves as more interested in romance and seduction than in expanded family responsibility. Features from earlier versions are retained as well, not only the by-now familiar musical metaphor, but also the mention of flowing waters and singing birds. Are these simply pretty scenery, or are they suggestions of the fluids and sounds of lovemaking? So far, I have found no singer willing to hold forth on the subject, but the following chapters contain an abundance of parallel examples.

Although not wanting to omit such considerations, I find some recurrent images provide more with which to work than others, and thus some possible directions of meaning will have to remain unpursued for the time being. Although I will try to use many song texts that have resulted from my own collecting, I will also mention songs that have appeared in the collections and publications of others; thus, the contextual details and the singers' comments will not always be available. In general, I use examples from the Anglo-American heritage, that is, songs from the English-speaking world, mostly from England, Scotland, and America, but a few examples from Germany and Austria also have strong parallels to the topics under discussion. The linguistic turf in this book, in other words, will be relatively familiar.

Moreover, this book will reflect the interdisciplinary interests in modern folklore research generally. Like social historians, folklorists look at the ways in which customs, rituals, songs, and vernacular themes illuminate and grow out of the historical constellations in which they are found. Like social anthropologists, folklorists want to know more about the relation of expressive behavior to cultural and social phenomena. Like literary critics, folklorists seek to establish the relationships between what is being said and how it is said as a central element of meaning. Like virtually all scientists, folklorists are suspicious of any single answer that pretends to account for a complex system; this is especially true of their approach to what has come to be known as oral literature. A story or a song almost never means just one thing, and thus scholars should not decide on a particular "correct" interpretation, but should explore the multiple aspects of a text to bring as many as possible forward into a conscious field of vision.

The term *folksong* is used herein to denote any song that has been shaped and given a cultural (rather than a personal, individualized) sense of meaning derived from the live, performative contexts of oral circulation. The term thus has little if anything to do with ultimate origins, antiquity, purity, quality, or political correctness. Some folksongs are old and some are quite recent, and although every song had to be made up by someone, folksongs as they are encountered in oral circulation are usually anonymous. The succession of singers who have sung them and the understanding of audiences modify and shape their wording, as well as their styles, structures, and meanings. When a composed song moves into oral circulation, its usage and meaning, its very articulation, become more and more related to the living cultural world in which the singers live and less tied to the particularized ideas of its original composer.

In this process of cultural interpretation and modification, a song may be changed considerably in some ways while retaining still other important features from the original. This can be illustrated by the myriad versions of the British broadside ballad "The Unfortunate Rake," which has descendants—among them "The Streets of Laredo" and "St. James Infirmary Blues"—that are not immediately recognizable without some elucidation. In other cases, as Renwick has ably demonstrated, a songmaker who belongs to a close-knit group (regional, ethnic, or occupational) may have the capacity to compose a song that so richly articulates the group's shared values and emotions that it is absorbed quickly—socialized perhaps—into the repertoires of other singers and reciters without much change. Edward Ives has discussed this important process at length in *Joe Scott, the Woodsman Songmaker.*[26]

Not all songs go into oral circulation, however. Some retain their identification with their composers and remain relatively stable in music and wording for years, often aided by print and copyright. Others lose their connection with their tunes and are later found in poetry collections, scrapbooks, and diaries. Others are preserved in, and may be composed for, the popular media. Indeed, performances by particular well-known stars make certain tunes and renditions so memorable that contemporary audiences are less inclined to make the songs "their own" by introducing variations than to sing them as the star does.[27]

But the existence of mass-media forms does not prevent a song from entering oral tradition. Ed Cray has claimed, for example, that most common folk ballads in the United States are also found in the most common broadside and written forms here as well, indicating the healthy interaction between oral tradition and writing in the transmission and perpetuation of vernacular songs, just as in the dissemination of contemporary legends.[28] Songs ranging from old hymns to new commercial jingles may also exist in printed, audio, or video formats until the possibility for parody arises. "The Battle Hymn of the Republic," while keeping its original contours in formal usage, becomes also the ironic basis for "Mine Eyes Have Seen the Glory of the Burning of the School," which is circulated orally among grammar school children.

Because it is possible for a song to be used in one set of circumstances in its printed, stable, and essentially conservative form although it is also used with dynamic variation in another situation in oral performance, it is indeed difficult—if not downright impossible—to say whether a particular song is or is not a folksong. On the other hand, when a number of clearly related but varying versions of a song owe their persistence through time to repeated singing by people who have learned it from each other, those can be said to be versions of a folksong whose original may be no more or less hypothetical than Plato's bed.

Substantive variation, persistent anonymity, and cultural, as opposed to individualized or idiosyncratic, meaning are probably the key elements in folklore, just as in biology.[29] Not all cats are tabbies, and not all tabbies are alike (even though they are all quite different from Siamese), but one can learn to recognize them from the accustomed range of their related but varying features. The reason for making the distinction is not that folksongs are somehow more pure or authentic than other songs or likely to be any better qualitatively, but that their manner of articulation—in which they have been shaped by many talented and, probably, untalented people rather than by one—will usually be recognizably different from that of other songs. It is to this important element of style and related considerations of meaning that current folksong studies address themselves. Themes and images in oral tradition may well be found in other formats in the same culture, however, as in the case of folksongs and broadsides.

There are several relatively distinct genres (lullabies, work songs, parodies, and love songs) among folksongs, but most fall into two large categories. One category (ballads) is made up of songs that portray the features of an event, or a related series of actions, with some kind of dramatic plot or narrative thread. The other category (lyrics) consists of songs that focus on a particular emotion or idea, usually without reference to a story line.[30]

It is handy to remember that there are several kinds of ballads, and because some are more metaphorical in their articulation than others, it is worth dwelling on their features. Some ballads were circulated first and foremost as printed items for sale. These broadsides (so-called because they were printed in the cheapest fashion on the broad side of a single page, rather than in quarto or octavo folded formats) are often characterized by a peculiar diction in which almost any word order is allowable in order for the poet to achieve an iambic meter and regular rhyme scheme and almost any term is usable for its impact, whether or not the word is used commonly. The plots are relatively simple but not especially compressed; indeed, their tendency is toward length, descriptiveness, and commentary.

When broadsides move into oral tradition, it is typical for them to undergo heavy editing by singers who want to perform something intelligible. For example, the extremely popular "The Children in the Wood," which appeared in printed versions of forty to fifty stanzas, was reduced to a very sentimental but spare lyric of three stanzas in its two-hundred-year tour through oral transmission.[31] Conversely, some broadsides remain lengthy and are apparently sung as tours de force by those stalwart enough of wind and volume to hold their audiences. Some long broadsides, for example, "Adam Bell, Clim of the Clough, and William of Cloudesly" (170 stanzas) and "A Gest of Robyn Hode" (456 stanzas divided into eight "fyttes") have an air of professional minstralcy: courtly descriptions, formulaic language, and not as much inverted word order as in the broadsides that have remained chiefly in printed form.[32] Instead of tortured verses like the following from "The Children in the Wood,"

> And in the voyage of Portugal
> Two of his Sons did dye;
> And, to conclude, himself was brought
> Unto much misery:
> He pawn'd and mortgag'd all his land,
> E'er seven years came about
> And now at length this wicked Act
> Did by this means come out.

"A Gest of Robyn Hode" has (in verses 317–18) a passage that contains some inverted word order yet appears singable even so:

> Lythe and lysten, gentylmen,
>> And herkyn to your songe;
> Howe the proude shyref of Notyngham,
>> And men of armys stronge,

> Full fast cam to the hye shyref,
>> The contre vp to route,
> And they besette the knyghtes castell,
>> The walles all aboute.

Other ballads that have been shaped even more by the moderating processes of oral tradition seem more normal in vocabulary and word order, but some, for example, "The Sweet Trinity" ("The Golden Vanity," Child 286), are largely narrational. The singer tells a story, giving descriptions and sequential details sometimes made more intense by lines of dialogue spoken by the characters depicted. Other ballads, like "Lord Thomas and Fair Annet" (Child 73), are more dramatic than narrational. In them, the singer conveys a dialogue in which characters speak for themselves. Listeners are forced to create an imaginary stage on which characters function, for the song contains very little information or attention to details of sequence. Rather, a dramatic enactment creates a traumatic event on the spot, about as far away on the narrative spectrum as one can get from the verbose details of the broadside even though both kinds may fairly be called narrative.

In dramatic ballads as in lyric folksongs, there is more latitude for metaphor, more room for variation, for it is the climactic moment and the shared experience of trauma rather than the detail of a coherent story line that seem to be the central concerns. Broadsides and narrational oral ballads use narrative structure for sequential coherence, whereas dramatic ballads seem to use narrative structure more as a framework for associated evocative images and metaphors, and it is the metaphors that provide focus or coherence. Of course, ballads that treat historical or historic-sounding events are tied more to the alleged action than those that deal with love or death.

Narrational ballads perform a narrative function very much like that of legend. They purport to convey a believable event, a musical kind of folk history. Dramatic ballads, on the other hand, are more like folktales or myths; their topics are universals like death, betrayal, sexuality, and assault. Often several of these issues are presented simultaneously in a complex mix of interwoven concerns that are not about the details of a story but about the responses of the characters. In this regard, the dramatic ballads have the sense of being literary-poetic rather than historical-descriptive. Metaphorical language is found throughout folksong and balladry, of course, but it is most prominent in lyrics and dramatic ballads, probably because the topics broached in these forms are complex and ambiguous for most people. On the basis of this much observation, I propose that the basic literary critical premise, that the way something is said is actually an important part of what is said, can and should apply to folksong as much as to formal written literature.

In most genres of folk tradition, how something is said features the richness and color of situations in everyday life, of word usage, cultural assumption, and custom, and is brought to life in appropriate phrasing by gifted people who know the resources of their culture well enough to be creative without transgressing boundaries of logic. The creative results of folk speech are familiar in the regional humor, hyperbole, and style found throughout vernacular expression. The New England epitaph "man goeth to his long home" counts on the live passerby to recognize a pun (long duration of death and a long box) and bring it together with "home" (a different kind of box, but also a long-term home in the grave or in heaven). The epitaph on the grave of a woman who died at eighty-seven, "I have come to my grave in a full age like a shock of corn fully ripe," suggests not simple old age and deterioration, but the kind of maturity that precedes burial (planting) and rebirth. In neither case does the audience get so confused as to suppose the first epitaph refers only to the length of a coffin or that the second one proposes a correspondence between the woman's physical shape and a shock of corn. Similarly, when in a folksong a young woman complains, "My virgin rose you stole away," or "It's he who has stolen my thyme," one is not even tempted to suspect that the references are to an early horticultural crime wave.

Admittedly, all the figurative expressions discussed in this book are not true metaphors in the narrowest sense, for they are not always direct equations, like "John is a pig." Some are metonyms, for they call things by an associative term, "thyme" for "virginity" or "cock" (rooster) for "cock" (penis), for example. But the figurative expressions to be discussed are basically metaphorical in that they bring up strong associations of value and response based on cultural correspondences and human experiences that relate a concrete pictorial image with its abstract referent, and these associations are usually not in the denotation or the manifest content of the word or phrase. Indeed, Lakoff and Johnson have argued that our entire language is by nature metaphorical and that we can make very little sense on any level—not just the vernacular—without using metaphor, for "metaphor pervades our normal conceptual system."[33] The extent to which language in general is basically metaphorical provides grounds for exciting speculation, but there is no doubt that ballads and folksongs use metaphorical language liberally.

Munro Edmonson cites such phrases as "don't horse around" and "monkey business" to demonstrate that we use sets of customary understanding in our figurative language. Such references are far more complicated than simple references to observed animal behavior would warrant, for the same animals may mean something different in other cultures. Where monkeys are sacred, for example, "monkey business"—if used at all—would suggest something far more serious than it does in English. An important dimension of folk metaphor is the cultural understanding of the figure being employed.[34] As with folklore generally, the person in the culture (or "folk group," any closely tied ongoing subculture) can accomplish the interpretation because he or she is an insider who has heard and used the reference (or others like it) so often and so consistently tied to particular contexts and constellations of meaning that there is no great intellectual gap between the figure and its field of reference. One could use the relatively simple signifier-signified equation so common in semiotics except that most of the figurative language to be discussed in this book is multilayered. There is seldom a single referent; rather, a rich field of related nuance is brought into play by a clever use of suggestive language.

A series of metaphors that suggest both death and sex, for example, can hardly be explained away as colorful ways of making a single abstraction a bit more available to the senses, for their result is not clarification but ambiguity. This delicacy animates many of what I have called the dramatic ballads. Although those inside the singer's culture may perceive these matters readily, they have not developed an analytical system for explaining the phenomena for outsiders, nor should they have. Just as we can make sounds without first understanding and expounding the international phonetic alphabet, just as we can speak without necessarily quoting all the grammatical rules that describe our language, just as we can run without naming all the engaged muscles, so we can use metaphors without articulating their principles intellectually. But just as we must run with the muscles we have and speak with the sounds and grammar learned from those around us, so we tend to use the metaphors supplied by the experiences and evaluations of our culture. Outsiders or scholars seeking to describe how these figures of speech work find the task of perception to be more conscious and intellectually ordered, and it takes more time. We must look for frequency and consistency of occurrence, for coherent usage in repeated expressive environments, and for meaningful parallels and reverberations with other expressive genres in the same or very similar cultures.

Insisting that "no metaphor can ever be comprehended or even adequately represented independent of its experiential basis," and that *"every* experience takes place within a vast background of cultural presuppositions," Lakoff and Johnson provide hundreds of examples from the English language to demonstrate such metaphorical logic as "good is up," "better is up," "the visual field is a container," and "time is a moving object."[35] Their categories cannot become clear until enough examples are at hand to suggest patterns, themes, and correspondences, and that is precisely the case with the metaphorical expressions to be discussed in this book. To inhibit reading some fortuitous meaning into songs and ballads, it is necessary to consult as many examples as can conveniently be brought into the discussion (a folksong scholar, however, can make no pretense of bringing in all possible texts).

A preponderance of the metaphorical references in Northern European and American folksongs operate in the semantic fields of death and sexuality. This is not a comment on metaphorical preferences in European cultures and languages, but it does reflect the heavy attention given to these arenas of human concern in the genres of folksong, as virtually all recent ballad scholars have noted.[36] If, for example, under the broad concept of sexuality we include those ballads from the Child collection that deal with courtship, seduction, adultery, incest, and rape (usually depicted in folksong and ballad as a sexual power play of male over female), and if we group under the rubric of death those ballads that focus on battle, homicide, suicide, and creative accident, all but eleven of the first fifty-three ballads treat these two subjects centrally. Indeed, at least nineteen deal with both areas at once. In the whole corpus of English-Scottish ballads it is hard to find one that depicts a happy marriage unless it is preceded by contest and seduction, as in "Captain Wedderburn's Courtship" (Child 46), or a natural death. Perhaps ideal occurrences have not been worth singing about, but even this tells something about cultural attitudes. In any case, the tendency among ballad singers has been to dramatize the traumatic, ironic, threatening, anxiety-provoking, and ambiguous dimensions of human experience rather than the stable, predictable, and mundane. The makers and singers of lyrics have also chimed in with laments, complaints, and gut-level responses to love, death, separation, and betrayal.

For the purposes of this book, the Child collection of ballads alone is not an adequate base for anything more than general observations on the heavy emphasis placed on the subjects of death and sexuality in narrative folksong. There is no reliable way to estimate how preponderantly the same topics are found in lyric (non-narrative) folksong or printed broadsides, but there are plenty of examples, and they will appear prominently in the coming discussion. Guided by the fact that the topics are indeed recurrent and widespread, and their textual examples bountiful, it is possible to inquire into this area of cultural metaphor without fear of a lack of vernacular evidence. This book will present a large enough body of this evidence to enable further appreciation of the dynamic ways in which figurative language animates lyric and narrative folksongs.

It is not my purpose, however, to uncover secrets, decode esoteric languages within languages, or even to discover complex structural principles in the songs discussed. Others have already taken these directions, some more profitably than others. My approach is better characterized by the line from Bob Beers's fiddle song. The flap of the pants does indeed conceal something, but it is perfectly clear to everyone just what is being concealed. The concealment itself is not a secret, nor is it a euphemism. It is a culturally meaningful way of playing with what everyone knows is there.

In many folksongs, certainly not all, the clever use of metaphor and metonym allows for the intensified perception of ideas that are "there" but not mentioned denotatively. In the final analysis, metaphors are not puzzles that block or confuse recognition as do riddles. Metaphors make meaning more rich, more colorful, and more fully experiential. Metaphors can be so open and bold that they come close to pornography, as in the case of many bawdy songs.[37] Others can be so delicate as to be virtually unrecognized by the young and naive, as in the case of "The Riddle Song" and others. Some are cute and simple, some are powerfully complex, some promote poetic clarity of feeling, others create puzzling and bothersome ambiguities. All use the resources of everyday language that everyday people share and therefore give vivid evidence of the range and sensitivity of poetry and song in the vernacular world.

Although we may make such claims for the power of everyday metaphor, however, even the most enthusiastic devotee of poetic language will note that the figures of speech discussed in this study do not work particularly well on their own. As with most metaphors, their influence on our understanding seems to derive in large part from how they are used within larger formations, whether narrative or lyric. And even then—as readers can quickly establish by trying to read a few ballads to someone else as our seventh-grade teachers used to do—folksong texts when spoken or recited do not often come across as great poetry. Moreover, both ballad stories and lyric expressions seem dull—even trivial—when summarized or paraphrased in objective, definitive terms. The reason, of course, is that in the singing of a song or ballad something unique happens—something more important than the production of sound waves or the act of entertaining—that does not happen when a text appears on paper. It also does not happen when only the words are conveyed, even by the most pleasant of voices. Perhaps scientific training toward visual acuity has predisposed us to accept the maxims that seeing is believing (or that a picture is worth a thousand words). We have not paused to notice that seeing focuses attention on detail, on precision, on what is there versus what is not there. Pictures and words on paper are not necessarily worth a thousand words, yet they are worth something, for they provide a particularized set of visual cues.

On the other hand, folksongs, dependent as they are on the styles, colorations, nuances, and ambiguities of spoken language and the ongoing creative variations of musical expression, thrive on the suggestiveness and multiplicity of possibilities inherent in culturally shared arenas of vernacular performance, negotiation, and discourse. Because so many levels of perception are simultaneously engaged, a folksong is worth a thousand pictures, for it expands our engagement with meaning beyond the visual plane. And yet, for this to be perceived and experienced with force, the song must be encountered in its unique reality—while it is being sung.

That simple fact notwithstanding, and for all my focus on live versions of songs from performative situations, I have not made music, the inevitable medium, a central issue of this discussion, primarily because of my own lack of expertise in the literary articulation of tonal features and their possible import. But music must be taken into account for its role in the shaping, maintenance, and delivery of folksong meaning. Even a listener who cannot understand the words to a song will note whether it is syncopated, jaunty, slow and romantic, or energetic and will have reason to believe that the tones and rhythms relate in some intimate way to the sensibility of the song. Because we know that different cultures have different assumptions about what is "jaunty" and what is "romantic," moreover, we must conclude that even the stylistic embodiments of those concepts in musical phrasing are loaded with unarticulated but nonetheless significant assumptions. Although a neat fit between musical phrase and metaphorical nuance may not always be discoverable, and even though recognizable tunes are known to migrate from one song to another, it is still profitable to consider that a tune is potentially far more central to, and important in, the establishment of meaning in a folksong than the terms *vehicle* or *accompaniment* would suggest. Whether a tune strikes us as beautiful, plaintive, cheerful, plain, or complex, the rhythm, tone, structure, and performance of a song is integral to its meaning. Mentioning a few important musical considerations will at least indicate the potential richness of the topic beyond the verbally metaphoric level on which most of this book concentrates.

First, the physical act of singing, even more than the physical act of speaking, requires a commitment of bodily energy, breath, and vocal tone. It demands, or perhaps creates, a more defined context than conversation or narration (try singing a ballad on an elevator or in a restaurant, for example). On the other hand, although singing thrives on an audience, it does not absolutely require one; we are more likely to sing to ourselves in the shower or while hiking alone than we are to talk to ourselves under those circumstances. A folksong is not simply a poetic utterance with a tune attached; rather, it is a unique kind of performative expression and seems to be the musical dimension that provides the incredible dramatic clarity that characterizes folksong and ballad. No matter how frugally the details of a ballad are presented, no matter how wonderfully ambiguous the metaphors may be, the music organizes the verbal materials into readily understood, intensely felt, and easily recalled units of cultural meaning. What accounts for this?

Beyond the physical engagement of the singer's lungs, vocal cords, and ability to carry a tune, basic qualities of folk music undergird and interact with the basic elements of language in a given song. For example, folk music is made up of repeated musical phrases that are not only redundant but also reflect on each other, rhetorically marking particular sections and subsections of song such as refrain-verse and opening and closing on a tonic chord. Moreover, in addition to the repetition of these smaller units, the whole tune usually repeats itself in each verse, just as the chorus is virtually always sung to the same tune each time. In some instances the tune phrases coincide exactly with verbal elements in the verse, as in Mrs. Parker's "Lovin' Henry," in which the lines carrying the woman's speech are sung to a different tune than those of the man's. The usual situation, however, is that the narrative or lyric statement unfolds lineally in the words while the music presents a circular, redundant counterpoint that mitigates and even slows the way a story progresses or intensifies the way a lyric develops. This means that in ballads especially, where descriptive detail is spare, the redundant tune creates an insistence on the relationships between each vignetted verse of the total montage.[38] The repeated tune also slows the lineal rush of cataclysmic events and thus allows for an intensified perception and savoring of the metaphorical language.

In folk lyrics, the same redundancy of tune conduces to a layering or distillation of images whose relationship may be suggested verbally, inferred from the repeated tune, or both. In both instances the redundancy is of poetic importance as much as it is of musical necessity, and therefore it can be seen as going beyond the practical functions of mnemonic device or delivery mechanism.

Indeed, in many cases, musical redundancy solidifies or intensifies the drift in a ballad's dramatic action. "Our Goodman" (Child 274) gains much of its depth and humor from repeated actions that in the aggregate take on ironic meaning. A husband comes home drunk several nights in a row and complains of seeing odd things about the house, details of which indicate the clear possibility that his wife is entertaining a lover. He sees a horse where his horse ought to be (see the discussion of horse imagery in chapters 2 and 7), a hat and coat where his ought to be, a boot under the bed, pants on the chair, a head on the pillow, and, in some versions, a penis as well, all where his ought to be. When his wife calls him a "drunken fool" or an "old fool and a blind fool" and tells him it's nothing but a milking cow, a blanket, a chamber pot, a bedpan, a dishrag, a cabbage, and, in some versions, a candlestick (or parsnip, rolling pin, or walking stick), the drunkard responds only that he has never seen a saddle on a cow, a feather on a chamber pot, spurs on a bedpan, or ballocks on a candlestick. Neither have we, and we cannot help wondering at his continued naiveté as he continues to come home drunk. If he is indeed so suspicious, everyday logic requires us to ask, "Why doesn't he stay home?" Of course, traditional narrative logic requires that he continue on his course of blind drinking, otherwise there would be no story and no point to the song.

The effect on the listener is a subtle shift of empathy. We view the man first as the victim of cuckoldry, but as he persists in coming home drunk he earns the appellations ("blind fool") thrown at him by his wife, for he is more and more certainly blind to what is going on and is made a fool by his repetitious and willful drinking. Yet we never discover whether the wife is really enjoying the attentions of a romantic visitor. We have only the redundancy of blind actions, foolish confusions, and the subtle progression from stable to hall to bedroom to bed, all intensified by the redundancy of the music (which suggests an intimate connection between all the repeated actions) and the repeated refrain, "You old fool, you blind fool, can't you plainly see?" The audience assumes he is being hoodwinked and eventually comes to enjoy the irony of his discomfiture, especially when he thinks he sees someone else's penis in the place of his own. Clearly, whether it is a candlestick, a parsnip, or a visiting lover, the equation is the same: The husband is not discharging his marital duties and cannot see his own predicament.

The partnership between repeated words, parallel action, and redundant tune functions so powerfully that the song is understandable even if the progression from barn to bed is scrambled (as it is in the version sung by Hattie Presnell);[39] or if the last verse contains no suggestive words at all, as in the case of my great grandfather Edwin T. Kimball's version in which the key lines were played on the fiddle; or Uncle Clel Spivey's version, which I heard in 1952 in Buckeye Cove, North Carolina, in which the suggestive lines featured a fast guitar run; or the unaccompanied version sung to me in Eugene, Oregon, by T. J. Easterwood, who hummed the second, fourth, sixth, and eighth lines of the last verse while slapping his thighs.

The whole song is one of suggestion rather than clear definition, and the use of music rather than a specific anatomical reference in the last verse is an option that maintains—even intensifies—the ambiguity and suggestiveness while providing a euphemistic decorum about as innocent and antiseptic as "the flap of his pants." The result is to make an audience laugh even more than they would at something more explicit. And the fact that they do indeed laugh means that the music is effective in carrying meaning without the use of words, that the audience understands what is implied but not expressly articulated, and that the device is not just a puritanical way of avoiding sexual reference. Indeed, the use of a fiddle or a guitar run or knee-slapping seems to signal that the words could have been explicit, or at least that the audience clearly understands the situation. Thus the song ends less ambiguously than it started, the audience now assuming the wife very well could have been engaged in something other than concern for the homecoming of a drunken husband.

That said about "Our Goodman," we should not overlook the other cultural structures provided by the range of sexually oriented folksongs, for these structures in the aggregate create a field of meaning in which musical codes make sense. Renwick says that daytime is the common time for sexual intercourse in English songs of seduction and calls attention to the usual settings: outdoors, out and away from house and village, in springtime. Romantic visits that take place inside and at night seem invasive and are attended by the hazards of discovery—by parents in the German night-visit songs and by the husband in ballads like "Little Musgrave" (Child 81). The inversions in "Our Goodman," then, are several. The focus is on the husband entering his own home rather than on the lover making a night visit; the opening signal is "I came *home* the other *night*" rather than "as I went *out* one May *morning*"; the husband is not only incapable of sex, but also represents no hazard to the presumed male intruder. In this comic situation, it would be difficult to empathize with the husband, and it would be easy to play with the sexual overtones by humming of fiddling phrases rather than singing them because the overall metaphorical field is so recognizable. The ballad is an exemplar of the rich and complex ways in which cultural attitude, ambiguous language, and appropriately meaningful music can be integrated into the performance of effective vernacular songs.

Other important elements of potential meaning also arise from, or are expressed in, various kinds of musical structure: marches, lullabies, work songs, games and play parties, and hymns all have recognizable features of rhythm, tone, volume, and style that affect us in meaningful ways not dependent on manifest content. In fact, in some cases, the music and the words may function on quite different levels simultaneously, as Bess Lomax Hawes showed in her study of American lullabies in which the tunes are designed to lull the baby and the words are expressive of parental fears and concerns.[40] And when a musical style or a tune becomes so well known that it carries an automatic load of assumptions and responses, it is ripe for parody, as illustrated by the various versions of "Dakota Land" or "Nebraska Land" (which feature ironic contrasts to the bucolic optimism of the hymn "Beulah Land"), or "Mine Eyes Have Seen the Glory of the Burning of the School," or the wide range of early labor songs like "Pie in the Sky," "Hallelujah, I'm a Bum," and "Keep Your Hand upon the Dollar and Your Eye upon the Scale."

The parodic element simply does not exist unless the listener can register the disjuncture between the pious tune and the sarcastic words. On a more serious level, when early New Englanders sang "Springfield Mountain" to the tune of the Doxology ("Praise God from Whom All Blessings Flow"), no one could have escaped the implied parallel between the biblical Garden of Eden and the young Massachusetts couple in their "New Eden" being brought low by a snake, a sequence loaded, moreover, with the Puritan concept of God's Providence (rattlesnake bite equaling "amazing Providence"). Similarly, for early Mormons there must have been a pleasant rush of triumph to hear new hymns being sung to the tunes of recognizable drinking songs, a species of musical conversion whose force has been overlooked.

The Kiowa Gourd Dance Society is made up principally of veterans, who often dance in battle fatigues and carry captured enemy weapons from the Korean and Vietnam wars. It is said that during their battles on the Plains with the U.S. army, Kiowas developed the "game" of capturing a cavalry bugler and bringing him back to camp to play the call for charge as they did their victory dance. If he played particularly well (one wonders how a bugler could blow any note at all under those circumstances), he would be set free. The irony of hearing the bugler impotently calling for a charge while warriors sang and danced, celebrating their safe return from battle, must have had complex effects on Kiowa listeners. Was it a serious conversion of a symbolically aggressive piece of music to their own ritual use? Was it a seizing of the enemy's power? Or was it done just to provide a good laugh by putting the bugler on the spot? Whatever the immediate impetus, the custom has been carried forward, and now that modern Kiowas have themselves served in the Armed Forces (including armored cavalry units), the combination has deepened in meaning. One can hear the bugle occasionally at Kiowa gourd dances and on a record edited by John Bierhorst, *A Cry from the Earth*.[41] The striking juxtaposition of the bugle notes with the Kiowa drumming and singing is impressive enough; one need not be able to articulate precisely why listening to this eerie combination is a thrilling experience to appreciate its reach and depth for Kiowas, who must hear in it an eloquent musical phrasing of their cultural history. Its very suggestiveness, its wild creative ambiguity, says more musically than one could ever explain rationally, which means that the song is, in its own right, a matchless cultural poetic expression.

This and so much more can—and must—be said of the musical dimension of vernacular song. Nonetheless, the present study addresses itself principally to the metaphorical elements produced by the careful and creative use of culturally charged words and phrases. It is important to remember, however, that still other nuances—indeed, many of them—await the attentive eyes and ears of other commentators. Because the following chapters discuss issues and songs that overlap considerably, my discussion will not follow a neat, single-stranded approach; rather, like the songs themselves, the chapters are meant to be cumulative and mutually reflective, like the petals of a maturing rose.

2

"One morning in May"

Our Engagement with Vernacular Imagery

The encounter between a printed text and its audience has been characterized in a great number of ways, ranging from pleasant entertainment to intellectual enlightenment to emotional catharsis to rigorous dialectic—often according to the current intellectual or academic fashion. In Northern Europe and America in earlier times, the serious literary audience was thought to be in need of a classical education in languages, history, and literatures before the most basic approach to a literary work could be made. For the New Critics during the forties and fifties, one only needed the text itself, one's reading glasses, an adequate lamp, and perhaps a drink within arm's reach. Not long afterward, at least for the structuralists and the semioticists, the text disappeared into a galactic fog of comparative hypothetical constructs or disappeared out of peripheral range of the scholarly microscope while constituent molecules emerged as the center of focus and were given names more precise and certain than the works of which they formed a part. In several contemporary fashionable approaches, such as deconstructionism and postmodernism (the latter an arrogant term suggesting there will be no further modern developments), the text is often seen as a provisional construct dependent on its audience for much of what can be said about its meaning. No matter how passionately we embrace or vilify these approaches, and the many others that have inhabited the critical field, all have provided insight into the nature and power of that most articulate of all the arts, literature. And no matter how these critical fashions have held sway or have vanished, literature—the artistic use of words—has remained central to the human condition in spite of its oddly anachronistic name, which unfairly links it to the narrow limitations of visible letters.

At the same time, each approach has had the tendency to focus on the written expressions of unique authors and assume that the keenest perceptions about them will be found on the informed, educated, intellectual level of scholarly conversation among critics. Ironically, this has left the field of other options open to specialists of other orientations; indeed, it has been the folklorists, the anthropologists, and more recently the social historians who have called attention to the proposition that the capacity for powerful expression is grounded in the culture (in its shared symbols, worldviews, mores, and assumptions), alive in the social fabric, and thus to a large extent available to everybody, not just the educated few.

Language and all its capacities for articulation grow outward from the people who speak it, not downward from those who study it. Approaching literature and language from the intellectual, formal level is not fruitless, of course, but it yields only partial (and problematic) results, much like those of Henry Nash Smith's *Virgin Land,* a well-known attempt to characterize the experience of the American frontier. Smith looked at the written works of relatively elite authors who used the West as a topic or setting and did not seek out the vernacular everyday expressions (the folksongs, tales, jokes, customs, proverbs, beliefs, and crafts) of those who actually lived and died off the land.[1] Had he paid attention to the real expressions from the real people who had shared the real experience of the frontier, he might have written somewhat less about the patriotic, optimistic "yeoman-farmer," forging his way bravely westward, and a good deal more about the frustrated, impoverished sodbuster who lamented in song, "We do not live; we only stay; / We are too poor to get away."[2]

Everyday literature has enjoyed a tremendous longevity, mainly in oral tradition. It usually comes to us in multiple variants, none of which can be called "the" text; it is usually sung, sometimes recited, sometimes found in print or in handwritten notes. The words are not completely stable, nor are the tunes. Calling such a form "folksong" pays more attention to its musical dimension than to its words; calling some of the texts "ballads" and "lyrics" lets us know that there are varying focuses but ignores the plain fact that many examples are so close to the generic line that the distinction is hard to make; calling this material "vernacular poetry" focuses attention on its poetic element but downplays its vocal or musical aspects. The German term *Volksdichtung,* literally "folk poetry" or "popular poetry," encompasses all these possibilities, including folksong. Clearly, the world of scholarship is hard-pressed even to name what we talk about. Nevertheless, for convenience I use the general terms *folksong* and *vernacular poetry* and then qualify them as needed.

In order to avoid the intellectual bias of the Smith approach to history, however, folksong and vernacular poetry should be seen as expressive not of single intellectual visions but of native categories, values, and talents. Like a tree, expression not only has many roots, but it is also constituted of nutrients supplied by supportive soil. Like a tree, a folksong is not unique unto itself, but exemplary of a type, one among many, a variant with its own constituent characteristics but a variant nonetheless. The folksong—like the tree—may also be said to have meanings that proceed in part from the attitudes of the "audience": the logger, the forester, the silviculturist, the firefighter, the artist, the naturalist, and the conservationist. Particularly in the case of folksong—compared to formally authored poetry—there are meanings that are not unique to the tree itself but rather derive from the local climate, elevation, soil base, and so on. They are elements of meaning for which a particular tree is an indicator, one of many possible articulations.

This simile cannot be carried far enough to do more than suggest the orientation of the argument. We view vernacular expression not from the crown downward, but from the soil upward. The texts of songs are articulations that may or may not have a heavy load of manifest content, but in every case grow out of and provide reference to the value-laden assumptions—the nutrients—of the cultures in which they function. Rather than possessing meaning in themselves, folksongs touch off or excite culturally shared meanings in listeners. Among other things, we must explore the extent to which the makers and singers of folksongs use their cultures in poetic expressions. Thus the critical task requires taking the everyday level of culture seriously enough to consider it as a matrix for literary discussion. In turn, this occasions a certain inversion of scholarly custom, for here empirical evidence from everyday poetic behavior enjoys the same standing as abstract theory. Sex is as important as genetics, language as important as linguistics, ethnic food as important as dietetics, telling jokes as important as narrative theory, singing as important as musicology, and talking as important as communication or information theory.

Vernacular poetry gives voice to the recurrent, traditional, or striking activities and values that continue to animate everyday life. In doing so, the text of a folksong combines recognizable human actions into constellations of foregrounded meaning, into concrete dramatizations of cultural abstractions. The language used is the language of the everyday community and not the refined or specialized or private language of unique individuals. A fuller appreciation of the range and depth of vernacular expression leads to a greater comprehension of shared meanings in everyday life, just as knowing what songs and jokes were being shared around the campfire at Valley Forge would tell more than we now know about the texture, meaning, and "feel" of that historical occasion for those who experienced it, not in terms of data or political theory but in terms of human dynamics.

As Michael Bell has fully demonstrated, the study of folksong (and particularly of ballad) was for many years the province of romanticist antiquarians.[3] Later, it was a haven for hardworking comparatists who, using the historic-geographic method, sought to answer questions of date, spread, provenience, and origin, questions which, as one can well imagine, were not of much interest to the singers themselves.[4] Francis James Child and his colleagues, contemporary and subsequent, energetically suppressed, destroyed, or expurgated anything of an erotic nature, so that the corpus available to most of us has been incomplete and atypical, and hundreds of the poetically most powerful items have remained under the table. Indeed, the difficulty of printing "off color" or suggestive songs has until recently spawned formulaic complaints about expurgation and censorship in the introductions of virtually every scholar in this arena, from James Reeves, Ed Cray, and Gershon Legman to Guy Logsdon.[5] Moreover, folksongs were often dealt with as if they were but paltry leftovers from better times (chapter 1).

Naturally, Child and his colleagues were products of their time, and aside from what they often refer to as their "disgust" at crudeness, they were probably not willfully slashing and burning their cultural patrimony; at least they would not have seen their attitudes as destructive. Nonetheless, the effects of their method have been profound. Throughout the various hurricanes of the ballad wars and up to the 1960s, few scholars were interested in dealing with folksongs as poetry. Instead, ballads and folk lyrics were reminders of a vanished age, vehicles for primitive thought or superstitions, examples of ethnic interchange, records of historical perspective, forerunners of "real" poetry, and vestiges of "ancient" poetry.[6]

Since the 1970s, however, folksong and ballad scholars have begun to insist that there are poetic elements in vernacular poetry that can be addressed profitably in an analytical way. There is no longer a hesitance to speak of complexities in folksong (compared with cataloging the commonplaces, noting the stanza forms, and counting variant texts). David Buchan has demonstrated the importance of the subcategories of role and action among the dramatis personae; James Porter has investigated the complexities of tune and performance as elements of meaning; Eleanor Long has examined how textual comparison can reveal not only a folksong's genetic heritage but also its essential meaning; and Roger deV. Renwick has probed the semantic reference systems in specific locales and occupations.[7]

These and other approaches suggest that the questions in folksong scholarship are no longer those of geographical spread, historical development, or antiquity, but rather those which come up naturally in the study of any good literature: What does it mean? How is the meaning phrased? What is the relationship between phrasing and meaning? and How do we know? I will proceed from the assumption that further careful questions of this sort, based on the folksongs themselves and informed by the values of those who have sung them, will lead to fruitful insights into the nature and meaning of vernacular expression. This approach accepts Porter's sensible theorem that "culturally shared meanings are of primary interest in discovering the meaning system of a traditional singing community."[8]

The recurrent phrases and images in folksong indicate a relatively consistent field of shared experience, for, as the anthropologist Edward T. Hall has pointed out, shared experience and attitude among members of high-context groups foster figurative or indirect expression, because people already know a lot about, and do not require explicit comment on, topics that are pleasing, enticing, or shocking.[9] A basic working premise (which I believe experience well illustrates) is that folksongs tend to exist most readily in high-context groups, those groupings that most scholars recognize as "folk groups." These are not large national or racial groups usually, but the intensely felt groupings in which we spend the most intimate parts of our lives: family, occupational, age, gender, neighborhood, religious, and ethnic groups. Most people belong to more than one of these, and when they sing traditional songs, it is usually in the company of one of these groups, with the family in the car, with age-mates in summer camp, with other rugby team members, with buddies in the service, or with chums around the campfire. In some singing societies, it might be with the men in coffee shops, with neighbors in local pubs, with men and women weavers *waulking* their bolts of woolen cloth, or with nearby farmers after the harvest. In many cases, the occasion centers on an older person who knows "all the songs." In all these instances, the typical song is one that everyone already knows, a song that has stood the test of time in content and phrasing.

Such songs tend to be repetitive in language and image and tend to borrow heavily from each other. It is partly to this matter of culturally recurrent phrasing that we will orient ourselves. But I do not suggest using the concept of "oral formula" for these redundancies, for they strike me as less concerned with metrical or technical aspects of oral composition than they are with situational and contextual relationships having to do with the coherence of dramatic ideas. Nor am I concerned with the technical world of semiotic discussion, in which the relationship between signified and signifier exists in far more solid correlation than the ambiguity of folksong metaphor allows.[10]

Renwick and others have explored the area of semantic domain thoroughly, and although I refer to their observations, my interest is in exploring the relatively more variable and rich dimensions of metaphor and connotation in folksong for what they may add to poetic understanding. For example, if we note that an everyday process like combing hair seems to appear with great regularity in certain contexts in folksongs, we are justified in wondering whether the action is used for more than its apparently practical or decorative possibilities. If it is a commonplace, it may have become commonplace or persistent not because it is a code or because singers are too dull to think of anything else, but because it projects an idea appropriate to the cultural meaning of the song.

In the criticism of so-called elite or authored literature, redundancy is treated as a kind of flaw, a sign of inventive flabbiness (unless it is part of a clever structure, as in a Shakespearian sonnet). Thus the "commonplaces" and "clichés" of folksong were formerly treated as intellectual weaknesses, as charming marks of poetic naiveté, as aids to the memories of crude farmers, and as characteristics of the leveling process of ongoing oral tradition (as opposed to the elevation achievable by a single composing genius). But just as a joke will not be repeated unless it continues to satisfy or articulate something shared by both performer and audience, so a slang term, a figure of speech, a custom, a gesture, or a dialect phrase will not remain in use unless there is some function, understanding, or savoring of it among the members of the closely related group. In this consideration lies one of the greatest differences between vernacular and formal literature. In formal, or elite, literature, the works of a particular individual can be preserved visually and are usually read by strangers in the privacy of their own rooms. Vernacular expressions are preserved by the fact that people keep doing them, live, for people close at hand. Traditional singers sing primarily for their friends, families, and social colleagues more than they do for strangers. It should be no surprise that many of the phrases are used over and over, like slang, not because of a weakness in the singer's creative ability, but because they are living tokens of live interchange between performer and audience in that model folklorists have discussed since the seventies as the "performative scene" (never mind that postmodernists are just now inventing it and the "intertextuality" it naturally implies).[11]

Reeves argues that the kind of phrasing that animates folksong, far from being weak and full of ignorant fluff, was pregnant with special meaning, and he laments that Cecil Sharp destroyed or altered so much of it in his efforts to produce national songs that could be put before proper British school children.[12] Although I share Reeves's complaint about Sharp, and although this book indeed supports the idea of poetic richness in folksong language, I do not believe there was anything special or esoteric about the matter, either in earlier days or now. The common redundancies are one indication. As in the examples discussed in chapter 1, folksongs do not use a secret language of the sort Robert Graves argued for the druidic poems of Wales.[13] Rather, folksongs participate in the local, functional, connotative systems that exist in the everyday lives of any group (for example, students, women, soldiers, or farmers). If it were not so, the songs would not have attained such a wide currency and would not have maintained coherent meanings over time. In addition, of course, there is danger in using Reeves's own system as a strict measure or predictor of metaphors in folksong, as S. Richards has noted.[14]

Vernacular language articulates, not explains, the shared values, assumptions, logic, and the sense of the normal and the discrepant that constitute any culture's system of meaning. In a situation where a phrase continues to exist only as long as people keep using it, a connotative commonplace is important *because* it is common. As Renwick points out, a cliché may reveal the "deepest" aspects of language, for its longevity in usage may derive from the cultural load it carries.[15] Naturally, if a lot of contextual and historical information is available about a group, we can perhaps perceive the richness of the group's connotative commonplaces more fully. But even when we have comparatively little live context, as with the texts found in many folksong anthologies, the very redundancy of a commonplace image, when it recurs in similar or parallel story situations, implies or reveals something about the shared system being used. In the case of songs still being sung, we can ask the singers and get their impressions, as well as make fuller use of empirical observation; in other cases, like many of the ballads, we have mainly the printed texts (and redundancy itself) as evidence.

The first method should not be counted on too heavily, nor should the second deter us, for it is possible for a singer to perform a powerful song without (and without any interest in) explicating it. Buck Fiske, a cowboy in Kayenta, Arizona, sang a song to me in 1955 that included the lines, "I've wandered up, I've wandered down, / I've wandered this wide world all around." When I commented on the great amount of alliteration in the stanza, his response was, "Huh?" And when I explained what alliteration was, he contemptuously dismissed my academic attempt to make something out of nothing. Well and good; perhaps Fiske was unaware of it, but the fact remains that the stanza is full of alliteration. My mistake was in using the scholarly term *alliteration* and not asking something like, "Why are there so many wa- wa- wa- sounds in there?" The stanza was his favorite, and he often sang it by itself. Because one cannot argue that the alliteration just fell into the stanza from the sky, one could surmise that the sounds had something to do with Buck Fiske's enjoyment of that verse—something he must have shared tacitly with other singers of the song, a version of "The Tenderfoot." I did not have the talent to elicit that factor from Buck Fiske himself, but the text still constitutes a basis for continuing puzzlement. In cases where there is abundant contextual and performer information, we will perhaps have more to account for and discuss, but in all cases the remaining text will have to form the focal point of the discussion in order to note the coherence between metaphor and story.

For this reason, I suggest that the text is not an end in itself, but a fossil. To paraphrase and contradict D. K. Wilgus, the text is not *the* thing, but the text is *a* thing, an arrested event—like a photograph—that we can use for a topic of discussion.[16] Fossils are important not so much for what they are physically (unless we are in the oil or souvenir business), but for what their suspended forms tell about the live animals in their live contexts. As in the study of fossils, much of our interpretive exercise is conjectural, more in the nature of what Jungians call "amplification" than of definition. But in the study of folksongs, the "animal," the song, is still alive, and its live context—human performative interaction—is still available for scrutiny.

Considering the continual availability of folksong, considering all the many hours of field collection done by hundreds of folksong students, considering the vast corpuses of amassed folksong texts, it is indeed odd to note that so little has been written about the poetic aspects of this dynamic form of expression. I agree with Renwick that the language of folksong rests not on unconscious factors, but on tacit, implicit assumptions, and that the discussion of these codes lies not so much in the direction of Freudian or Jungian psychological analysis (although these approaches might also open dimensions of meaning), but rather toward illumination of the code systems. Yet, because I feel it is counterproductive to see the poetic language of folk poetry in terms of a puzzle, I would rather not refer to "textual decoding" as much as to amplification of poetic performance.[17] After all, the original cultural scene is a live, performative interaction between people who understand each other.[18] The perception of a metaphor, along with its coherent role in a performance, may sometimes be puzzling, especially for someone who was not there, but it still does not require the intellectual guessing game of "What's *really* meant?" Quite the contrary. Because metaphors and other connotative references ask us to register more than one level of meaning at a single moment, they have the capacity to bring several "loaded" referents together into a vivid articulation or dramatization of meaning that should need no decoding.[19]

What is the point of using metaphor after all? Like a pun, it allows for—demands—the perception of two or more relatable concepts at once. It sets up a reflective ambiguity. The connection between the two ideas might not be obvious on the denotative level (hence the ambiguity), but in the framework of a song or story the two concepts are shown reflecting on or interacting with each other in a creative way that produces a flash of understanding. Moreover, one concept is often an abstract idea not so easy to articulate, whereas the other is often a concrete dramatization, a provisional embodiment of the first. Herrick, advising young women to make the most of time before age ruined their beauty, could have started the poem "To the Virgins, to Make Much of Time" with the phrase "make hay while the sun shines," for denotatively it means the same as "gather ye rosebuds while ye may." But the hay image lacks the connection of rosebuds with virginity that folk tradition supplies (virginity equals abstraction, rosebud equals metaphorical embodiment). It also suggests a sweaty, roll-in-the-hay attitude not in key with the delicacy of the poem. Herrick could have maintained the delicacy with "gather ye primroses while ye may" (and thereby would have achieved a more regular meter), but he would have lost the implication of virginity. Similarly, Blake, in "To a Sick Rose," could have written "oh pansy, thou art sick," but it would have been at the expense of a highly suggestive vaginal metaphor. The point is that although all metaphors pull the abstract into the palpable range, vernacular folk metaphors usually do so by using images drawn from a rich supply of customary ideas that participants in the culture already share. Many writers, from Herrick, Donne, Blake, Chaucer, and Shakespeare to Barth and Malamud, have found folk metaphors to be a rich source of poetic impact. Why, then, has there been hesitation to notice their function in the traditional genres where they are so lively and at home? Perhaps because doing so entails dealing with a whole culture rather than with a single author; perhaps because academics have harbored the silent prejudice that everyday people are not bright enough to use metaphor powerfully or coherently. A close look at folksong metaphor should illustrate that this view is narrow and wrong-headed, for the facts contradict it overwhelmingly.

To be sure, we cannot let enthusiasm for vernacular expression carry us off to what George Lyman Kittredge called "the cloud-cuckoo land" of scholarly fantasy. We will not want to read meaning into a song, but rather attempt to read meaning out by carefully noting—as Renwick demands—the relationship of the metaphor to the assumptions in its culture and by charting its coherent relationships to the song in which it appears.[20]

Thus it is immensely helpful to be guided in vernacular encounters not only by suggestions in collected texts, but also by the comments, attitudes, and gestures of those who sing the songs. Perhaps subsequent collectors will keep their recorders running and so provide at least some account of the situational and conversational matrix in which a song is embedded. In reality, however, most available folksong texts come to us with little more than dates, names, and geographical contexts, so at least part of our engagement with vernacular—as far as conscious discussion is concerned—must be built on textual comparison and cultural analogies within reasonable frames of reference. And because it is also true that many singers perform songs for friends without making any comment at all, sensitivity to the range of metaphorical possibilities within the singers' cultures is necessary in order not to miss the obvious but unstated use of figurative language. Another cowboy song sung by Walter Bolton of Prineville, Oregon, provides an example. Bolton sings "My Love Is a Rider" readily in mixed company, but it is clear by the smile on his face that he does not consider it to be most meaningful as a song about riding horses to impress the ladies.

> My love is a rider, wild horses he breaks,
> But he promised to give it up just for my sake.
> One foot he ties up, and the saddle he puts on,
> With a swing and a jump he is mounted and gone.
>
> The first time I seen him was early in spring.
> He was ridin' his bronco, a high-headed thing.
> He tipped me a wink as he gaily did go,
> For he wished me to look at his buckin' bronco.
>
> He gave me some presents and one was a ring,
> But the present I gave him was a far finer thing:
> 'Twas my young maidenhead, and I'll have you all know
> That he won it by riding his buckin' bronco.
>
> It was in the dry canyon he first laid me down.
> He was dressed for the roundup and I wore a gown;
> Then he wiped off his chaps so the stains wouldn't show,
> And then turned and rode off on his buckin' bronco.
>
> So come all you young maidens where'er you reside:
> Don't love those cowboys that swing their rawhide.
> They'll hug you and love you, then one day they'll go
> In the spring up the trail on their buckin' bronco.[21]

Clearly, the song is more about dalliance than it is about rodeoing. Bucking broncs are not used for casual trips into canyon country, for example, so the overriding "feel" of this song is that the bronco image is being used to suggest sexuality rather than that eroticism is being forcibly inserted into an otherwise straight bronco-riding song. "Mounted and gone," in the last line of the first verse, the theme of the song, is underlined by the ease with which the young rider gains his goal and then departs. "Highheaded" is a term used in reference to women as well as to horses, but if "bronco" here is the metonymic equivalent of penis—as the rest of the song implies—the "high-headed thing" would be the erect penis. By the time he winks and wants her to look at his buckin' bronco, we are pretty well into a seductive sequence, whether the singer actually says so or not. The references to the woman's maidenhead in verse three and to the cowboy wiping off his chaps in verse four leave no doubt. We have crossed from suggestive metaphor to open denotation, and only the buckin' bronco remains figurative, as does the reference to "those cowboys that swing their rawhide" in the last verse (compare "his sickle of leather" in the discussion of riddle songs in chapter 6). The line virtually always brings knowing smiles and laughter from listeners, who patently do not respond to it as if it were a reference to the way someone handles a lariat.

The song (which is sometimes known as "The Buckin' Bronco") has other verses that are equally metaphoric. In the Fife Archives, one version has the verse:

> My love had a gun that was sturdy and long,
> But he wore it to visit the lady gone wrong,
> Though once it was strong and it shot straight and true,
> Now it wobbles and it buckles and it's red, white and blue.[22]

Gun-penis imagery is, of course, common in male folklore; one recalls the military jingle—if it can properly be called that—"This is my rifle, this is my gun; this is for fighting, this is for fun." It is found in other cowboy songs as well, as in bawdy versions of "The Old Chisholm Trail":

> Well, I went to the doctor 'cause my gun was sore,
> "Good Lord," said the doctor, "same damn whore.
> You can put away your holster, you can put away your gun,
> Your barrel's been breached and your shootin' is done."[23]

But the effect of such figurative language is that of bawdy wordplay rather than the multiple ambiguity of many other folksong metaphors. The figurative possibilities thus range from almost explicit metonymy to complex suggestive metaphor. Moreover, in a number of instances at both ends of the spectrum the metaphor conveys more than one level of meaning, as in the cowboy examples. In the gun-penis figure, there is a simultaneous reference to potential death and sex, for example. And in the customary usage of the horse-riding image the horse may represent the stallionlike capacities of the male protagonist in one song, whereas in others it suggests the female character being ridden. As a verse from the same version of "The Old Chisholm Trail" goes, "Well, I rode her standin' and I rode her lyin' / And if I'd had wings, I'd rode her flyin'."

Equine terms for women are not uncommon in vernacular English. Alongside male terms for other males like "stallion" and "old horse" are phrases indicating that men prefer "young fillies" to "old nags." Although such figures may seem particularly at home on the western ranges among the cowboys, they are actually quite old, having been well and consistently used by Chaucer and Shakespeare. Chaucer's Monk, for example, rode fine horses and "loved venerie"; see also Eric Partridge's entries under *horsemanship, manage, vault, pace, ride,* and *rider* in *Shakespeare's Bawdy.*[24]

One of the oldest and most resilient humorous tales told in virtually all European—as well as contemporary American—societies is "The Taming of the Shrew," Aarne-Thompson tale type 901, which is usually known in the United States by its punchline: "That's once!"[25] In it, an independent (read "noncompliant") wife is "broken" when the male character threatens to give her three chances, after which he'll kill her as he has killed their horse. The parallel between woman and horse—both requiring breaking or taming by a man—is obvious and still causes laughter among Americans, many of them women, who would never consciously accept the underlying theme (one brings women into line by treating them like horses) but may laugh because the narrative triggers a recognition of the cultural saturation of the whole view. A joke circulating among Utah cattle ranchers describes a young farmer who goes home at lunch time to "have some romance" with his wife. While the couple is making love, their four-year-old son comes in and wants to "ride the bronco." After unsuccessfully trying to get the boy out of the bedroom, the man pulls him up and places him on the woman's shoulders while continuing to have sex. When the woman becomes especially aroused and "gets kinda athletic," the boy yells, "Ya better get a good ear-hold on 'er Dad; this is where she bucked me and Uncle Bob off yesterday!"

On a 1983 gravestone in the Logan, Utah, city cemetery, is the following inscription:

> Two things I love most,
> Good horses and beautiful
> Women, and when I die I hope
> they tan this old hide of mine
> and make it into a ladies riding
> saddle, so I can rest in peace
> between the two things I love
> most.

We can well imagine that in a small, conservative town like Logan, such a tombstone must have been commissioned and paid for in advance. The attitudes thus represented—in this case by a quote from an older cowboy poem—were important enough and recognizable enough to have been worth inscribing in stone. The currency of these phrases is illustrated in a published poem by Gary McMahan, "The Two Things in Life That I Really Love":

> There's two things in life
> That I really love:
> That's women and horses,
> This I'm sure of.
> So when I die,
> Please tan my hide
> And tool me into
> A saddle so fine.
> And give me to a cowgirl
> Who likes to ride,
> So in the hereafter
> I may rest
> Between the two things
> That I love best.[26]

Gene Wiggins, in his admirably full study of Fiddlin' John Carson, presents a song that begins:

> I rode seven horses clean to death;
> I rode them till they had no breath—
> Wore five saddles to the tree,
> And none of the girls won't marry me.
> Sing fa lie riddle aye day.[27]

Although Wiggins takes the verse at face value, that is, as an index of how hard the young man has ridden his horses in his attempts at courting, the song itself dwells on how sleepy the man is from so much courting and how content he is to keep the girls up until it's almost day and then sleep in a barn on his way home—all to maintain his bachelor's status. But surely the metaphor is based on the same set of assumptions as found in the widely traveled stanza "I ain't no rider, nor no rider's son, / But I'll set in your saddle till the rider comes."[28]

More openly exploitative of the ambiguities of overlap between sex and riding is the story told in Arizona about the preacher who decides to give a sermon using the metaphor of riding horses. His wife feels he should lecture on something he's more familiar with and finally decides not to attend. At the last minute, the preacher changes his subject to sex and preaches a powerful sermon. When one of the congregation tells the wife of the wonderful sermon, she replies, "I don't know why he insisted on preaching about that subject. He doesn't know much about it; why, he's only done it twice—once before we were married and once afterward—and both times he fell off."[29]

Can it be fairly said that all of these ancillary "texts" are present in Walter Bolton's mind, or those of his audience, when he sings "My Love Is a Rider"? Is he consciously trying to separate out the proper codes for bronco-penis from those suggesting horse-woman? Do all who sing this song necessarily know about all these references and the many more like them? Although we do not know, we must acknowledge the general consistency of the references, which should indicate that they are not entirely coincidental or random. The more fully we can perceive the vernacular system from which the song grows and in which such references make sense, the more we will realize that there is not a strict code of any sort, but rather a field of metaphorical possibility, a pool of culturally recognizable resources in the language and in everyday jokes and formulations. Some singers use these resources more than others; some perhaps use them more coherently than others; some use them less or may employ them only because they have memorized a song the way someone close to them sang it without regard to its diction. The same metaphors are not in every version of a given song, but it is possible to judge the effectiveness of a song in its performative moment in part by noting the appropriateness of its metaphors.

Considering the other animals mentioned prominently in folksong yields an impressive range for metaphoric usage. The animals are usually those which are not only likely to appear in everyday experience but also carry other connotative loads. In addition to horses, folksongs make heavy use of hounds, cats, and birds. For example, in many ballads a bird carries the news of a murder or takes a message of importance to someone. Both functions are so common in everyday folklore that it would be foolish to overlook their well-known application (a bird flying in the house presages or announces a death; "a little bird told me"). But bird imagery has other, more complicated possibilities that can be discovered by closer scrutiny of local beliefs and legends about birds in areas where bird images have appeared in ballads. For example, the lark is often associated with dalliance in the fields, and in some amorous songs the girlfriend of the "plowboy"—the term is hardly coincidental (chapter 6)—is actually described as a lark rising from the fields. In "Young Hunting," a bird appears after a murder that takes place in an amorous context, a fine example of the multivalence in ballad metaphor.[30] Aggressive birds like hawks appear in stories featuring both sex and death, as does the domesticated cock, which functions as a warning both to visiting revenants and illicit nocturnal male visitors.

Another category of metaphorical possibility lies in color values. As Renwick points out, bright colors other than blue were not common in the villages we often associate with the nineteenth-century social context of ballad singing. Why, then, are green and red so common in ballads? Only because they are bright, and the same people who would never wear them for fear of being unseemly would be willing to sing about them out of class envy or primitive love of bright colors? It is possible, of course, yet green is considered a bad luck color in England. Renwick notes this, and green is mentioned in collections of popular belief as a color that ought not be worn to weddings. When we consider that virtually every time someone gets dressed up in green in a ballad that person is dead by the end of the story, and that accidentally pregnant young women are often "green as any grass" or "glass," we could argue for a fairly consistent vernacular usage of the color green for connotative effect. The connection is too consistent, too insistent, to be merely a matter of coincidence or to reflect merely a favorite color cliché of ballad singers. Commonplace it may well be, but hardly meaningless or unpoetic.

Images and items suggesting agricultural fertility comprise yet another set of suggestive possibilities almost always employed with reference to human sexuality. Actions like plowing, seeding, mowing, reaping, threshing, and grinding, along with the tools for such activities (plows, sickles, scythes, or mills), will be prominently discussed in subsequent chapters, as will the related images of gardening and gleaning, which include scenes in gardens and actions like plucking and gathering boughs, buds, flowers, berries, nuts, and fruits, which occur outside the home context. Closely associated are the many references to dew, rivers, wells, and springs that also occur most heavily in songs of seduction and murder.

Flemming Anderson has argued convincingly that actions and gestures once thought of as formulaic commonplaces are seen on closer inspection to occur not just anywhere a lily-white hand is required, but primarily in consistent situations where seduction, betrayal, and death are involved. Thus, sewing, giving someone a lily-white hand, mounting someone on a steed, or a woman combing her hair, all suggest certain dramatic implications within the narrative of a ballad. For example, the hair-combing image usually occurs just before a suitor appears and would seem to indicate readiness for marriage or willingness to be courted or approached. In several ballads where a woman loses her lover, she vows that a comb will never go through her hair again, suggesting the other, consistent aspect of the image: lack of availability. Beyond this, hair is often associated in folklore with various aspects of sexuality. There are inferences of sexual engagement in these tragedies that we may easily miss simply because they are not named specifically.

Particular items like knives (and sometimes their sheaths), swords, bows, and arrows come into play not only in narrative folksongs about famous battles, but also, and even more often, in accounts of tragic love affairs. Candles are used not only to locate the bodies of drowning victims, but also figure prominently in songs of seduction. In some versions of "Young Hunting," Lady Margaret tells the protagonist that there is a candle "burning free" and invites him to stay overnight. In a well-known bawdy song, a woman asks her lover to blow the candles out. In some versions of "Our Goodman," the man spies "a thing within the thing where my thing ought to be" and is told by his wife that it's a candlestick. Freud notwithstanding, is there a traditional field of reference based on candles, flames, and fires being extinguished to which it would be worth paying more attention?

Some particular plants—notably the rose—are found with great consistency throughout the range of folksong. I proposed in 1967 that the image of a rose entwined with another plant occurs in traditional ballads primarily at the end of stories about lovers separated by such negative factors as bad parental advice, war, or travel.[31] The reuniting of the plants over the graves of the young couple provides a physical union not allowed them in the action of the story. The custom of grafting two rose plants together over a grave is still found in northern Germany, and it would be worth knowing whether this suggests a cultural parallel for such ballads. The "true love's knot" tied by fishermen is also a well-known cultural expression accomplished to suggest a couple in intercourse.

In these ballads, the rose almost always grows on the woman's grave and the briar (or some thorny plant or a tree) typically grows on the grave of the male protagonist. Considering the extensive connection in folk speech and slang between the rose and female sexuality, the vagina, and virginity, it seems ill-advised to overlook it as a powerful way of foregrounding the physical, sexual, reunion of the couple. And in some versions, the briar is roughly uprooted or cut down by an angry father or a shocked priest, surely further indication that this is not seen as a quaint pictorial ending to a sad story. Further, the appearance of the motif at the end of some versions of "Barbara Allen" indicates that for some singers the gender connections of the plants are less important than their use as evaluators of human actions. Here the female villain often gets the thorn, and the innocent male victim is awarded the rose. Thus, although gender is not central, the image still fulfills a distinctly metaphorical—or at least heavily connotative—function.

Time and direction are still two further areas for vernacular cultural assumptions. Renwick has pointed out how powerful the meaning of "out" must have been in rural England, where being "in" (surrounded by family, co-workers, and other villagers) meant a lack of privacy. When a couple walks out—away from confinement and prying eyes—and does so in the seductive month of May, the erotic suggestion is so strong that it defines the song's plot. Other times of year are rare, although some versions of "Little Musgrave" (Child 81) begin with a Christmas church service during which Lady Barnard entices Little Musgrave to come visit her at home in her husband's absence, a nice irony in that the young man is seduced during a mass for the newborn Christ child.

Structural devices can also have certain fields of meaning in their employment, and Olrik's Law of Three is a prominent example.[32] In "Babylon" (Child 14), for example, three sisters encounter a man who knifes them one at a time while the others stand and watch, a series of actions more ritualistic than real. Why doesn't at least one of them run for help? Beyond the obvious (that there would then be no story), three murders make the story more intense, especially when the dramatic progression leads to the surprise revelation that the murderer is the victims' brother (rather than revealing it early on, where it would have created quite a different story of intentional sibling murder). The sexual overtones of the story—a man entering women's bodies with a knife (the term *vagina* is from the Latin for *sheath,* a phallocentric view of sex consistent with the action)—are reinforced by the triple repetition of the red rose image in version A, the refrain "among the broom" in C, wiping his knife along the dew in D, and pulling the rose and lily in version E.

The Law of Three does more than just saturate: It allows for structural development and intensification of a key issue and for even greater intensity when it is used as the vehicle for suggestive imagery. In one version of "Sir Hugh" (Child 155), for example, the Jew's daughter offers the little boy three traditionally seductive gifts—a mellow apple, a ring, and a "cherry as red as blood"—in order to entice him into her garden. The association of cherry with virginity (the boy's, no doubt), strengthened by other images often associated with sexual enticement, not only underscores three times the seductive nature of the Jew's daughter's role but also foregrounds that subtle but common suggestion of sexual threat often encountered in association with interracial or interethnic conflict. The triadic progression—enticement (apple), involvement (ring), loss of virginity/loss of life (cherry/ blood)—is a deliberate presaging of what is in store for Sir Hugh. His murder "down in the cellar," parallel to the pit in Chaucer's Prioress's Tale, provides a vertical image suggestive of debasement and murder that extends the third element (cherry/blood) of the sequence.

Similarly, when Lord Barnard asks his page, "My castles burnt? My tenants robbed? My Lady with baby?" in "Little Musgrave," the listener, who already knows what is happening in Lord Barnard's home, hears him equate adultery with others' losses and calamities while ironically naming (in the key third position) what is actually the case, for in some versions he discovers that his wife is pregnant by angrily dissecting her with his sword. I cannot believe that such delicate consistency of image, sequence, and meaning, such fit of connotative structure, is fortuitous.

The songs edited by James Reeves and Frank Purslow provide rich examples of the ubiquity of these fields of metaphorical potential. In his edition of the manuscripts of Sabine Baring-Gould, H. E. D. Hammond, and George B. Gardiner, Reeves provides texts for well over a hundred British folksongs.[33] Number 6, "The Barley Rakings," features a couple "playing" during the haying and barley raking season; twenty weeks later, she is pregnant and he is gone. In number 26, "Cupid and the Plough-boy," cupid is described "in the tilling field," plowing deep furrows. He sows seeds, uses a "coulter sharp and keen," and later the girl laments, "O Cupid was that ploughing boy / Who caused me all my pain." In number 30, "Deep in Love," a girl plucks a rose, pricking her finger, whereas in number 34, "Died of Love," a girl picks flowers until her apron is full (the full apron is used in several folksongs as an image for pregnancy). "The Furze Field," number 47, is the scene of an invitation to sexual encounter (offered by a woman persona). The song is full of hunting metaphors that function—as they do in *Gawain and the Green Knight*—as suggestive of sexual pursuit. In "Gathering Rushes," number 48, a girl gathers rushes, spreads her morning gown because of the dew, and worries about being in trouble. "I Sowed Some Seeds," number 72, focuses on a man who sows his seeds "in yonder grove" but cannot stay to reap the crop. In "I Gave My Love an Apple," number 73, the singer wants to give his love an apple without a core (compare the cherry without a stone, discussed in chapter 6, and as well the insulting tag, "There's an apple in me pocket and you can have the core"). "The Lark in the Morn," number 81, is set in May and features a ploughboy, a lark that rises, meadows mowed, and "the grass all cut down." Not surprisingly, twenty weeks later the girl is "thickened in the waist." When lovers take poison and die in number 88, "Maria and William," a cock crows in the last verse. In the humorous accumulative anatomical song "Mathew the Miller," number 89, each verse ends "where Mathew the miller the corn grinds in." In "The Molecatcher," number 93, a cuckolded husband says to a young farmer, "I will make you pay dear for tilling my ground," quite an opposite impression from the more virtuously titled "One Man Shall Mow My Meadow," number 100. In song number 107, "The Queen of the May," a maid gathers armfuls of may, is propositioned by a boy, and then refuses him, whereupon he grabs her, lays her down, and "gath'red his arms full of may." "The Seeds of Love," number 116, features a garden, thyme, a tree, rose and thorn, a ploughboy (in version C), and a reference to "Dead Man's Land" (version E). In number 123, "The Sprig of May," a girl gathers may in a flowery field in May, and "one sprig of May made her belly swell."

At least as old as an Anglo-Saxon riddle (number 44 in Krapp and Dobbie's edition of the *Exeter Book*)[34] is the central figure in number 125, "Strawberry Fair":

> O I have a lock that doth lack a key,
> O I have a lock, sir, she did say.
> If you have a key then come this way
> As we go on to Strawberry Fair.

The unfortunate young woman rues the day later on and laments that had her lock been a gun, she could have shot the blacksmith. In "Three Maids a Rushing," number 132, a girl becomes pregnant while out "rushing" (of course in May). In version B, she says, "There I met him in the dew of a May morning." In number 137, "The Wanton Seed," the title of which is used as a near-pun with "wanting," "All she wanted [in the sense of both "lacked" and "desired"] was the chiefest grain," and she asks the young man to sow her meadow with the "wanting seed." Later on, quite naturally, "under her apron the seed did grow."

In Appendix 2 of *The Everlasting Circle,* Reeves provides a text of "The Keeper," another of many songs that use the metaphors of the hunt to suggest "venereal" pursuits. Reeves's promotion of a lingua franca among ballad singers and their audiences, along with the attendant assumption of a homogeneous society with homogeneous ideas, has come under fire from later critics, but I have seen no refutation of the overwhelming evidence he presents for a pervasive and consistent metaphorical system of erotic reference in folksong. Indeed, Gerald Porter has used the coherence of metaphorical reference to gardens, dew, blood, and water to argue convincingly that the origins of "Sir Hugh" (Child 155) lie in an earlier ballad of love and death.[35]

In Purslow's *The Wanton Seed,* many of the same songs are presented, as well as a few more examples of the same range of metaphor. In "All under the New Mown Hay," a young woman has a baby nine months after a tryst; in "Blow the Candles Out," the young woman is pregnant and nine months later the young man leaves her. In "The Buxom Lass," the girl asks the boy to mow her field of grass: "My grass is in good order, I long to have it in." He observes that her grass is "well-watered by the spring which makes it grow so fast," but after some energetic mowing his scythe gets bent, and he has to quit the field. In "Catch-Me-if-You-Can," the scene is early spring; small birds are singing, and boy meets girl by the riverside. Nine months later she has a son. In "Down by the Woods and Shady Green Trees," a young woman laments, "Don't trust a young man in any degree, / For when they've enjoyed the fruits of your garden, / They will go and leave you as he has left me." In "Haymaking Courtship," a sailor meets a girl who is raking hay; he seduces her, and nine months later she regrets having gone with him. The seducer in "The Hostess's Daughter" says, "In yonder grove I sowed my seed." Later,

> The seeds of love they grew apace,
> The tears were ever on her face,
> All for to reap it I could not stay . . .
>
> Now when this pretty babe is born,
> Oh she must keep it, it is her own,
> And reap the seeds which I have sown.[36]

Unquestionably, as both Reeves and Purslow have fully demonstrated, the language of many English folksongs is laced with vernacular metaphors, and it is certainly not simply to rehearse their observations that I provide the preceding overview. When these images are seen in the aggregate, we become more aware of the body of consistent reference that singers use, whether or not they are all keenly cognizant of all the implications, as the Reverend Sabine Baring-Gould, a Victorian folksong collector and bowdlerizer, perhaps naively, doubted.[37]

Finding so many good examples in Reeves and Purslow is no surprise, because both works were produced, as was Reeves's *The Idiom of the People,* to redress the Victorian suppression of such songs by bringing out more honest texts from collectors' own notes and manuscripts. There is no certainty that the existence of all these fine examples proves that the songs or their metaphors were typical or in greater circulation than regional, occupational, or household songs, but their obvious imagery does indicate that the metaphors are abundant, that they are consistent, and that they have directly to do with the action of the song and are not just pretty decorations. Otherwise, pregnancy and abandonment would not so often result. This is only one area of metaphorical expression, and others more appropriate to home, regional, or occupational usage are likely, as in several of the mining songs Renwick discusses, in which human workers are compared to, or put in competition with, machines.

Nonetheless, because the arena of all these metaphors is sexuality, an important aspect of meaning is bound to reside in the varying gender perspectives of men and women. Granted that both men and women sing these songs, we also know that many men will not sing some of them in female company. We also know—or should know—that the very nature of such themes as seduction will be registered differently by men than by women because the action of the song means something different to each gender. Unfortunately, although there has been much commentary on language in feminist theoretical debate, there has been little work on the female perception of such metaphors. Shari Benstock discusses the semiotic and Freudian aspects of women's being in ancient Greek, thought of as coming from an earlier chthonic concept (woman equals earth), later interpreted metaphorically as woman being a field to be plowed and cultivated. Mary Field Belenky and her colleagues have shown voice itself as a powerful metaphor especially appropriate to women, particularly in respect to having a voice, being silenced, and in terms of voice as a metaphor for a sense of mind and self. Yet much of the attention to women's language has been placed on such matters as male-female variances in vocabulary, phonology, syntax, pacing, and interaction (like interruption) rather than on the use and perception of metaphor itself.

Most helpful to me as I have dealt with the gendered possibilities of folksong metaphors have been works by Joan Radner and Susan S. Lanser, Debora Kodish, and, in particular, Polly Stewart. Stewart argues that women appear prominently in those ballads that feature a male-female relationship, and that the women characters usually achieve success (if they do so at all) by clever use of words. Even in songs where women lose their lives or their loves, the very singing of the song can stand as an example of the dangers women may encounter. As Stewart observes, "What are the lessons women might learn from these ballads? That a man will take from a woman what he can and will punish her for being his victim . . . that, for a woman, stepping outside the house is a dangerous act. . . . By horrible example, a woman learns how not to get killed."[38] These are registers quite different than the male's vicarious enjoyment of seduction and power.

Vernacular imagery requires seeing the range of expressive devices not as an obligatory, memorized, closed system, then, but as a field of poetic opportunity in which skilled singers operate. In order to have a better sense of how and why some of the choices are made, a speculative inquiry at best but certainly worth the effort, we must go further into the details of song contexts (chapter 3). Still, vernacular imagery must be appropriate to the assumptions of the culture in which it thrives. We are not dealing so much with independent artists (which is not to say that traditional singers are neither independent nor artistic), but with community-oriented artists (which is not to say that singers are always models of community decorum, either). The resultant songs, if they survive, ring true to people beyond the immediate composer who participate in the culture's sense of worldview. Although this may have the sound of lofty philosophy, it is, in fact, the observation that shared cultural tastes have an impact on the traditional songs we sing, and the songs in turn provide articulate reference points to those tastes. The two cowboy songs provided by Walter Bolton are admirable examples.

Bolton's song "One Mornin' in May" is metaphorical in its reference to lovemaking, whereas his version of "My Love Is a Rider" is more metonymic in its use of "bronco" to suggest the untamed athleticism of the cowboy's penis. The first song is more subtle, the second more overt, but neither is prurient or pornographic, neither is obscene, neither is overt and denotative in the main. Yet both songs are quite understandable to speakers of the English language who know anything about cowboys and who have any experience with traditional love imagery. Both songs are figurative in that their language adds emotional, evaluative, occupational, and situational dimensions of shared meaning to an otherwise biological or social event. Both songs, seen from the perspective of gender politics, dramatize male conquests, and most of those sharing in the assumptions of this dimension will be male (or perhaps females who accept the domination factor as normal or even flattering).

Part of the metaphorical thrust of the songs is connected with cowboy culture, and part of it is connected with the culture as a whole, in which male aggressiveness toward females has been an assumed mode of behavior. Because of the fit between these various levels of cultural understanding and the action of the songs, the function of the figurative language in these cases is not to lend color but to establish and savor culturally valid meanings. Whether or not we agree with them intellectually, they have the ring of familiarity, normality, everyday validity, and fidelity to cultural assumptions and values. Moreover, similar clusters of vernacular imagery with similar functions are found in folk songs from all over northern Europe and America. To refuse engagement with this mass of rich vernacular expression would be to ignore a significant portion of our poetic heritage.

3

"It's dabbling in the dew
where you might find me"

Some Contexts of Folksong Metaphor

What are the "cultural scenes," the live contexts, in which—and perhaps because of which—figurative vernacular expressions exercise a liveliness beyond the denotative arena? If it is true that vernacular expressions are by their very nature saturated with connotative power based on shared cultural values, we will expect them to lend depth and cultural evaluation to actions and situations that might otherwise seem quite mundane or trivial. Not to recognize the connotative force of culture-based language would be to overlook some of the most compelling reasons for discussing folksongs. To read too much into them or to interpret them according to arbitrary systems would be to denigrate the facility with expressive language that those who perform the songs demonstrate.[1]

The various contexts in which vernacular songs have had meaning for those who sang (or sing) them are important, for usually the words themselves do not carry the metaphorical meaning, but rather the skilled application of the words in particular culturally recognizable situations. For example, in everyday English language, *nut* can mean the seed of a particular tree, something that goes on a bolt, a crazy person, a testicle, a zealous hobbyist, or a lovable person who does zany things at a party. We perceive the differences and register the connotative meanings chiefly by context and cultural experience and not by simple reference to denotation or by what Freud might have said about round objects.

The act of registering connotation appropriately is a complex cultural matter (surely, a non-English speaker would be puzzled by the possibilities for understanding "nut"), but it occurs every day in virtually every conversation; indeed, it has been argued that connotation sets humans apart from other animals. Munro Edmonson observes, "In a sense what the other animals lack is connotation. And connotation is intrinsic to human speech." Edmonson's argument is that connotation is almost always based on shared cultural values and provides the richest insights into the real nature of human thought and tradition. All humans use connotation, yet all cultures arrange it and understand it according to their individual worldviews. According to Edmonson, "Since the innovation of speech, man's fate has been to live uncertainly between connotation and denotation."[2] Perhaps all powerful metaphors can be judged by how fully they manipulate or express this uncertainty, yet although a metaphor might thrive on uncertainty and ambiguity, the effect of an appropriate metaphor in a culturally recognizable context is not confusing for someone who participates in the culture.

Luisa del Giudice has provided an impressive demonstration of the ways in which everyday denotative terms (*bird, horse, flower, garden, dew, river, fig, night, hair, drum, purse, door,* and *pistol,* for example) function with consistent connotative power in the story contexts of erotic Italian songs.[3] Some of these terms become metaphoric, of course, because of obvious analogies. Mills, chimneys, guns, and snakes have often been used for their suggestive parallels to human parts or functions. But words like *bird, dew, sea, pilgrim,* or *horse* must—like *nut* in English—depend on cultural attitude for their meanings in poetic situations. It may be, as del Giudice suggests, that such metaphors are important because they help to veil or avoid taboo or sensitive subjects. They also allow for a deeper response to a taboo idea by enabling the audience and singer to savor it poetically. Thus, the topic is made more palpable than avoidable and, among other things, allows listeners to play with forbidden themes.

Because some metaphors allow for two apparently opposed concepts to be brought together (death-sex, illness-romance, and weapons-love tokens), there is—as del Giudice points out—the kind of apparent ambiguity found in riddles, in which a unique quality or evaluation emerges from the juxtaposition of the terms. It isn't likely that every Italian listener would perceive the metaphors and their implications in exactly the same ways. Yet, because the connotative uses are regular enough—and have been used long enough—to be recognizable, they are available to someone familiar with the culture.

As Sol Tax has observed, "Metaphoric behavior is operationally defined as that which is not self-explanatory, because it requires previous knowledge. Even in the society to which the metaphor is native, its understanding can only be relative to the age and sophistication of individuals."[4] Where do we obtain this sophistication and previous knowledge? By paying attention to the nuances of the culture around us—and some pay more attention than others. A person who is culturally well situated is in position to savor the fit between a simple word and its metaphorical context. Is there anything in balladry more delicately fit than the beautiful young Mary in "The Cherry-Tree Carol" asking the old Joseph for the only possible fruit that could suggest both her pregnancy and her virginity?[5] Is there anything in ballads so humorously ironic as when Joseph, summoning all the bitter cleverness available to a cuckold, says, "Let the father of your baby get your cherries for thee"? What a mouthful! And it is susceptible to understanding only by listeners well situated enough to know who the characters are, what their theological identities are supposed to be, what the sudden food craving of a woman means traditionally, and what a cherry symbolizes—and only as listeners register all of these apparently disparate elements as figuratively related in a consistent constellation of meaning.[6]

David Buchan has correctly insisted that the formulas and connotative units in folksong not be abstracted from their contexts, a position not only basic to a holistic conception of song performance but also of utmost importance to a fair and rewarding analytical approach to folksong poetics. Cultural and performative contexts provide levels of meaning that simply cannot be discovered or accounted for by structural, historical, or textual approaches alone. In folksong, as in folklore generally, articulation exists in a number of contexts: cultural, generic, performance, family, poetic, historical, scholarly, and musical. It is important to understand, however, that these contexts are provisional, overlapping, interactive, and difficult, if not impossible, to separate from each other.

One of the most important considerations is cultural context, the shared system of customs and values that animate or give rise to stories and those cultural codes of meaning through which any story or utterance makes poetic sense to the culture that tells or sings it. Cultural context operates on at least two levels: the locally referential (allusions to ways of life, local customs, weather, social and historical detail, ethnographic and biographical matters, occupational customs, and the like) and the metaphorical (clear use of images for suggestive rather than denotative capacities but in terms recognizable to and familiar within the culture, through traditional usage, what Buchan calls "received traditional diction").

An example of reference to local custom and weather would be the role the month of May plays in British love songs. As Renwick points out, May is a time in England when agricultural chores shift from intensive indoor winter work to the onset of strenuous outdoor involvement. People think about going "out," and thus the line "I went out one May morning" has local urgency and currency. May, coming after a long, dark winter, also has overtones of excitement, warmth, fertility, and new beginnings. Moreover, probably because of all these factors—as well as whatever associations might still accrue to it from the various May celebrations of earlier times—the month is often the time of wooing, dalliance, and seduction.

The reference to May could hardly have produced anything but expectation of an amorous narrative, or at least one with amorous possibilities. Irony, or perhaps surprise, is achieved when a murder or rape occurs in a figuratively amorous setting. But this irony is possible only when an appreciable number of the audience shares the figurative possibilities of the language being used. The cultural context category is simply a reminder that much of the field of reference comes from the realities and the connotations of everyday life in the community (chapter 2).

Because these shared attitudes and connotations are learned and passed on in many folksongs, ballad and lyric folksong genres may in themselves be contexts for the functioning and dissemination of figurative language; thus another category: generic context. To use another aspect of the May morning figure, recall Renwick's suggestion that May, being a ritualized threshold period between important indoor and outdoor activity, functions in ballads and folksongs as other thresholds do. Water edges, riversides, forest margins, and bridges provide dramatic settings understood to be fraught with implications of tension, danger, and vulnerability.

It is likely that a talented folk singer would be aware of such recurrent figurative settings that augment and make clear the emotional and cultural dimensions of song. So many of these thresholds occur in so many folksongs in so many analogous positions that it is more difficult to argue for coincidence than for a consistent body of poetic usage. The figure of speech or its functions may come from other ballads, but it will be applied according to the conventions of the genre, as well as its consistency with cultural reality and its fit to the particular song within its own immediate folksong context. For the constellation "one morning, one morning, one morning in May / I seen a young couple a-taking their way" to be meaningful, these references must be interdependent and largely consistent with others like them, just as these contexts themselves are functionally interdependent. In current terms, they would be examples of intertextuality and intercontextuality.[7] In folk lyrics as well, the reference to May sets up an expectation for dalliance and romance, even though a dramatic narrative does not ensue.

Two other examples show how the figurative information available within a generic context is important. In the common line "as I went out one May morning" is still another commonplace suggestion. Renwick notes that "out" indicates movement away from the confines and conventions of the culture (exactly appropriate for a song about illicit sexual liaison). But "out" need not take place only in a commonplace line with "May" and "morning." One thinks of all the other ballads where someone, most often a young woman, goes "out" and plucks flowers, nuts, branches, or the like. Of course, there are different ways of being "out" and away from the confines of town and farm. Gypsies and travelers have always been "out," which perhaps explains the popular stereotypical assumption that they are out of control and potentially dangerous to established order. Often the ballad character—especially a woman—moves out from a situation clearly suggestive of protection to one of the marginal areas that present the possibility of vulnerability to attack. In "Babylon,"

> There were three sisters lived in a bower,
> fall alee and a lonely-o;
> They went out to pick some flowers,
> by the bonny, bonny banks of the Virgie-o.[8]

Leaving aside the possibility that the river's name might be suggestive of virginity (not all versions use the same name), the words present the standard figure for a ballad of rape and murder. Going out to pluck any fruits or flowers is an action so ineluctably connected to the subsequent drama that it must be dealt with as a metaphorical part of it. Just as dressing in green marks a ballad character as heading for death or doom (but without telegraphing the audience how it will happen), so plucking fruits, nuts, and flowers, especially by a river or forest out and away from the limits or protections of society, virtually always sets the stage for the plucking of a maidenhead, or a life, or both.[9]

If out is a condition where women are at the mercy of men, what does the genre tell us about being in, at home, where women are more likely to be not only safe but also in control? Often, being in can be disastrous or embarrassing for men. In "Our Goodman" (Child 274) the man comes home nightly to see signs that he is being cuckolded. In "The Baffled Knight" (Child 112), the would-be seducer brings the intended victim to her home, where she quickly slips inside and declares, "Now I am a maid within, and you are a man without," a nice pun in addition to its positional reversal. Men visiting women in their homes are often killed in bed, or at least discovered there by the woman's family. These situations and descriptions are both common and commonplace; they are so consistent that they argue for further refinement of folksong poetics, a matter to which Flemming Anderson has devoted years of study.

The performance context is the live situation in which a folksong is actually performed by a singer to an audience, often a group of closely related people who know the song already. Because various conditions might affect the way in which the text actually comes forth, however, (male singer to a mixed-gender audience versus male singer to an all-male audience, for one example), the actual performance takes place within contextual realities that can create a particular cluster of meanings. A vivid example for me came in 1952 while I watched a large family gathering in western North Carolina. There, in an audience of pious Southern Baptists, I heard an engaged couple sing "The "Riddle Song" ("I gave my love a cherry that has no stone"), alternating lines in such a meaningful way that it was quite clear they were metaphorically expressing a common courtship sequence in the mountains: cherry, egg, ring, baby.[10] The audience was completely aware of this meaning, and there were meaningful glances and smiles that indicated that only the smaller children were innocent of the full meaning. I also have heard the song in other social contexts where it was equally clear that the singers and the audiences meant to sing (and hear) a statement about love and family stability expressed in homey, rural figures. In a case like this, it seems evident that the figurative meaning cannot reside entirely within the text as a part of its manifest content, but somewhere between the performed text and the shared body of assumptions and associations triggered when the singer performs the song before an audience.

The metaphorical possibilities in the performance context may be enhanced or intensified even more by particular factors shared by those in a group who engage in the same occupation or belong to the same family. Personal experience with tools and procedures has the tendency to add a dimension of familiarity that underscores metaphorical usage; thus, when a sailor sings of "climbing up in her riggin'," or a cowboy sings of "swinging the raw-hide," or a farmer sings of asking a young woman to see how his "thrashing machine" works, or a mother sings of all the defective toys that papa has brought home (as in "Hush Little Baby"), listeners not only perceive the poetic "meaning" of the song but also share the sense of personal involvement. The triggers for full response are only partly in the text and can only be brought forth or amplified by close attention to contextual features.

In what I would term family context, the features can only be discovered through conversation with the participants, although they may sometimes come out voluntarily in the comments of a singer, such as when Clarissa Judkins of Eugene, Oregon, sang "The Girl with the Striped Stockings On" to me and followed it with the remark, "My brothers and I always knew that a woman who wore striped stockings would be the lightfingered sort." An extended example of meaning in family context would be the custom in at least one New England family of singing a particular whaling song immediately after their Thanksgiving dinner. The family descends from a grandmother whose forebears were fishermen and whalers out of Rockport and Gloucester, Massachusetts. One of the oldest houses on Cape Ann is named after the family, and contemporary members of the family are contemptuous of the people who inhabit the house today, for the residents demand genealogical papers as identification for any family member who wants to see the house. Up until the 1940s, it was the tradition in this family for males, when they reached twenty-one, to have a ship under full sail tattooed on their right shoulder, with the inscription "Rolling Home" under it. It is the firm conviction of this family that the song "Rolling Home," which they sing after Thanksgiving dinner, was a whaling song sung by their ancestors. They sing it now not as an actual sea song (only one person in the family has gone to sea willingly since the turn of the century), but as a memorial to all those in the family who went down at sea and, by extension, to all departed relatives on that side of the family. The term *rolling home,* in other words, has come to mean something in this family like going "home" to heaven, although virtually no one in the family has any particular beliefs about the existence of heaven. On the less spiritual side, the song itself uses the term *rollin' home* in its normal seaman's description of the sideways motion of a sailing ship on the high seas, and the men in the family still recall brief phrases that allegedly made the best of the lurches: "Roll, roll, you son of a bitch—the more you roll the less you'll pitch" and "pitch, pitch, goddamn your soul—the more you pitch the less you'll roll," indicating that these natural but sickening (and dangerous) motions were not considered especially graceful, let alone worth memorializing in a song to be performed at the dinner table.

Beyond these interpretations of the old song lies still another set of meanings considered bothersome by the women in the family but seen as humorous by the men. "Rolling home" also seems to describe the drunken gait of amorous ancestors who visited the beautiful ladies of the South Seas during their layovers for provisioning. Moreover, the word *spent* in the following verse is understood by the men in the family to mean male ejaculation. Thus it is that the men dare each other before dinner to include the two "dangerous" verses, while the older women especially show their disapproval by facial expressions on those occasions when someone actually sings them. Because everyone feels obliged to join in the chorus, however, no one leaves the table, and so there exists an unspoken but palpable tension between the men's vicarious recollection of their forefathers' dalliance and the women's exasperation at being reminded of their grandfathers' romances and the possible existence of relatives in Hawaii. Everyone remembers that some sea captain in the family had explained that the phrase "leaving your best wishes" meant having left a young woman pregnant. Other verses of the song are typical of its many published versions. The two that carry heavy family meaning are:

> Good-bye, you fair Hawaiian ladies,
> We must bid you all adieu,

But we'll recall these pleasant hours
That we've often spent with you,

CHORUS
Rollin' home, rollin' home
Rollin' home across the sea,
Rollin' home to old New England
Rollin' home, dear land, to thee.

We will leave you our best wishes
As we leave your rocky shore;
We'll be sailin' home to Rockport,
And you won't see us anymore,

Rollin' home, . . . etc.[11]

The way the men in the family move smoothly from the last line of the verse into the phrase "rollin' home"—which they do not do on the other verses—indicates that they see a rhetorical connection: "These hours that we've spent with you, rollin' home," and "you won't see us anymore, rollin' home," the former a suggestion of sexual movement (considering their understanding of "spent"), and the latter a suggestion of staggering back to their lodgings.

The extent to which other seafaring singers of "Rolling Home" have understood the text in the same fashion is difficult to establish, but the family feels that its understanding of the words is valid enough, considering that they have inherited the song from those who are thought to have believed these things and used these words. Thus, for the family, just singing the song is a physical act of vicarious involvement with ancestors and with their values. The "meanings" thus derived and assumed are not foreign to the text and do not represent a wrong-headed insertion of "new" meaning. On the other hand, now those meanings are clear and functional within the context of a family and not an occupation. I suspect that many songs—regardless of their topics—are performed within high-context groups like families and thus cannot be fully understood in their figurative dimensions without recourse to the family's critical system.

The song text itself also provides a poetic context with its own highly focused constellation of images or dramatic interaction, dialogue, and plot. It may be, as Lucy Broadwood suggested in the early 1900s, that "The Bold Fisherman" (Laws O 24) is full of Gnostic elements, but surely the continued coherent performance of the ballad by singers who knew nothing about such matters is, as Renwick suggests, due to the fact that the song has developed an understandable plot of its own and presents a well-known, popular set of metaphors and structural formulas about returned lovers.[12]

The song's metaphors are judged more by their coherence with the narrative drama in the ballad than with any outside system. Considering Broadwood's Gnostic parallels—however closely they may have been connected with the ballad's earliest history—leads us away from the performative meanings of the ballad in its current live context in favor of hypothetical textual connections in the now-moribund past or the active mind of scholars. Clearly, the performative approach to folklore that Dell Hymes and Richard Bauman (among others) advocate should not encourage us to denigrate or avoid textual studies or the historic-geographic method or historical analysis.[13] It does ask that we look at the dynamic aspects of the folk performance as part of the meaning, for one element of folksong performance must always have been the internal coherence of the song itself.

D. K. Wilgus suggested yet another possibility: the historical context. Calling attention to Eleanor Long's thorough study of the twining branches, he suggested that knowing about the diverse and often complicated literary and cultural history of certain texts, commonplaces, and clusters of meaningfully related actions should be another way of perceiving the depth of ballad meaning.[14] I find no quarrel with this view, although it seems to me that it is addressed more to scholars who have access to such history than to singers and audiences who may not know about the details of a symbolic or metaphoric development. But scholars are indeed a substantial part of the audience for folksongs, and this dimension ought not to be put to one side. We should be willing to reexamine, for example, Lucy Broadwood's intellectual history of "The Bold Fisherman" to see whether it provides some possibilities of meaning that might have been ignored. Or we will want to wonder about the extent to which early Germanic heroic legend might have influenced the employment of the twining branches motif in a way that bears on the image level of "Barbara Allen." These possibilities are no more farfetched than is Freudian psychology, for they ask us to be always willing to amplify (not invent) possible nuances and implications that might otherwise be overlooked.

For these reasons, we might want to add still another context: the scholarly context, the aggregate of study, research, comparative scholarship, argument, and the like that has gone into the diachronic discussion of a particular folksong. To this might be added (also suggested by Wilgus) the musical context, that family of tunes and tones through which a song reaches articulation and the melodic codes through which scholars recognize and classify what is occurring during the folksong performance.

It is in the nature of figurative expression in folklore that there would seldom be a metaphor that makes sense only in the folksong in which it appears. That would be more likely to happen in written poetry, as when a poet develops a conceit or a specially invented and unique way of expressing an abstraction. A folksong in which a young woman asks a young man to find her fallow field, plow it, seed it, and gather in its produce, all within a dialogue suggestive of amorous play, does not require listeners to notice that all these actions are widely found in English sexual metaphors in order to understand their figurative functions in the ballad. However, if an audience could recognize that these references were consistently used metaphors, and if they had noted the appearance and registered the meaning of these elements in a number of other ballads of similar import, would it not provide a richer, more powerful set of connotative references? Strange if it were not the case. Buchan argues convincingly that in a ballad society such language as this, used through generations of singers, acquires and develops ever richer connotative reverberations.[15] Given the evidence, I cannot believe that traditional singers have ever been innocent of these matters. They may have lacked a professional jargon for the intellectual discussion of ballad characteristics, but then they have never had to read papers at professional meetings, either.

On the other hand, traditional singers live in communities where recurrent human activities require no special explanation because they are so self-evident, even though the particulars in which they are acted out are by no means unambiguous. Courtship is one example. The culture "expects" a certain deportment during courtship, but individuals are often pleased to stretch the "rules." In Austria, where unmarried girls often slept in second-floor rooms with grillwork over the windows to prevent entry, the custom of *Fensterln* or *Gasslgang* (windowing or going along the alleyway) developed. In the hill country of the Tennengau and Pongau areas of Austria, thoughtful fathers would make sure that ladders were available along the side of houses should enterprising young men wish to make secret night-time visits. In several areas where I collected mountain songs and yodels from families, nearly all the older generation (people in their sixties and older) admitted courting through windows. They told astounding and hilarious accounts of acrobatics on ladders and shared reminiscences of the wide range of activities that can be accomplished through metal grillwork. Two women even admitted that they had become pregnant by *Fensterln* and had borne children before marriage, and several reminded me of the earlier custom of the *Probenacht* or *Probe-Ehe,* seeing whether both parties could engender children before making final plans for marriage. Yet even though most people did these things, and believed that their parents had done them, they nonetheless insisted that their parents had disapproved and that their own children would be prevented from doing them if at all possible. Clearly, here is an instance of ambiguity in cultural values and behavior, and it would be surprising if there were no jokes, legends, anecdotes, and songs about it.

Indeed, Röhrich and Brednich provide several examples under the category "Fenstergang und Fensterstreit" that have essentially the same characteristics. The male petitioner stands outside the window and asks to be let in; in some instances he is successful, in others he is rejected and must leave. In one, he says, "I'm not coming back to you anymore, you're going to have a small baby."[16] The traditional singers of the Klappacher and Fuchsberger families in Niederalm, Austria, sing the following "window song," which they call "Rosengarten" (Rose garden):

> Geh nur eina in Rosengarten
> Schöne Bleamal wachsn drin.
> Brock nur ab zwoa, drei rote Roserl,
> Trags zum Dianei ihrn Fenster hin.
>
> Dianei schläfst du, oder wächst du,
> Oder bist du denn gar nit drin?
> Na, i schlaf net, na i wach net,
> nur zu dir steht mir mei Sinn.
>
> (Just go into a rose garden
> beautiful flowers grow therein.
> Break off only two or three red roses,
> Take them to the girl's window.
>
> "Young lady, are you asleep or awake,
> or are you not even in there?"
> "No, I'm not sleeping, nor awake,
> I'm thinking deeply only of you.")[17]

In an Austrian-Bavarian dance called the *Ländler,* one of the figures forms a window with the partners' arms, through which they can flirt.

A favorite song in northern Germany describes the romantic night visit. Almost everyone knows it, especially the old-timers, who sing it with happy tears in their eyes in remembrance of the older agrarian life that formed the matrix for much of the north German sense of normality. Like their Austrian counterparts, however, singers became uncomfortable when I suggested that their children would do the same thing. The song is sung and is presented in Plattdeutsch, the dialect spoken along the flat lowland coast of northern Germany. One reason for the maintenance of the dialect may be to force a geographic as well as a cultural contextualizing of the song:

a. Northern German farms were and are large and cannot be managed without considerable help; hiring people is expensive, thus having a large family is the real answer to maintaining a thriving farm.

b. There is no point, therefore, in marrying a woman who cannot conceive easily or a man who cannot engender children;

c. the *Probe* (test, experimental try) is one way to find out; however

d. the church and all good Christians frown on premarital sex, so it cannot be done in the open.

Ideally, then, the night visit entails the young suitor making a late-night appearance outside the girl's window which, unlike the Austrian custom, is not barred and is situated conveniently on the ground floor along a *Gang* (passageway) leading off from the central hall (*Diele*). The young man identifies himself (after all, the young woman might be dealing with several hopefuls) and is let in or given instructions on how to get in. The entry is to be quiet enough so that it does not attract the attention of the parents, who are not to be forced into open cognizance of what is going on. The visitor leaves before dawn so as not to be discovered by the parents or seen by the neighbors. If and when the girl becomes pregnant, the couple, ideally at least, begins planning their wedding.

Everyone in the region recognizes the custom although not countenancing it within their own families, whether or not it actually occurs. In fact, the custom is rare today but lives on in the continued singing of songs like the following and in related customs like the one in the area around Bremen that requires men who have not married by thirty to dress in a top hat and long-tailed coat and sweep the steps of the cathedral while friends make merry, drink, play organ-grinder music, and heap refuse on the church steps. A major context for this song is, then, a mixture of regional and cultural custom.

> Dat du min leevste bist,
> dat du voll weest;
> kumm bi de nacht, kumm bi de nacht,
> seg wo du heest.
>
> Kummst du um middernacht,
> kummst du klock een;
> vadder slept, modder slept,
> ick slap aleen.
>
> Klop an de kammerdoor,
> fat an de klink;
> vadder meent, modder meent
> dat deit de wind.
>
> Kummt dann de morgenstarn

kreiht de ool hahn;
leevste min, leevste min,
denn must du gahn.

Sachen den gang entlang,
lies op de klink;
vadder meent, modder meent,
dat deit de wind.

(That you are my dearest
that you know full well;
come by night-time, come by night-time,
say what your name is.

Come at midnight,
come at one o'clock;
father will be sleeping, mother will be sleeping,
I'll be sleeping alone.

Knock on the chamber-door,
grab the latch;
father will think, mother will think,
the wind is doing it.

When the morning star comes
the old cock will crow;
my dearest, my dearest,
then you must go.

Sneak [?] down the hallway,
let up the latch;
father will think, mother will think,
the wind is doing it.)[18]

On first reading, this song seems to leave out, or imply as obvious, the actual sexual liaison itself, and perhaps because of this apparent ellipsis some other singers add humorous directions for the suitor. The folklorist Klaus Roth, who grew up in northern Germany, sings the following two verses between verses three and four (note how the extra syllables in lines three and four call attention to them as additional material):

Kumm in de kammer rin,
liesen un still;
links steiht 'n schapp, rechts steiht 'n schapp,
in de Mitt steiht dat bett.

Kumm op dat bett hinto,
liesen un still;
unner liggt 'n deck, boben liggt 'n deck,
in de mitt, dat bun ick.

(Come into the chamber
quiet and still;
on the left is a closet [a tall clothes chest], on the right is a closet,
in the middle stands the bed.

Come up to the bed,
quiet and still;
underneath lies a blanket, on top lies a blanket,
in the middle, that is I.)

Another version gives even more explicit information to the apparently naive night visitor, but so far I have been able to find only the line "rechts liggt 'n bein, links liggt 'n bein" (on the right lies a leg, on the left lies a leg). From its cultural context, we can conclude that the song is meant to suggest behavior not countenanced openly, but rather savored secretly. It allows for the expression of something relatively taboo on one level, relatively common (at least in reminiscence) on the other. The song's performance creates a stage in the minds of northern German listeners, who bring to the event their knowledge of history, customs, and beliefs that animate the vicarious—and ambiguous—experience of the story. It is likely that the song has remained in oral tradition because it has continued to foreground a complex cluster of local attitudes and values.

Northern Germans also savor other elements of the song, not the least of which is the use of Plattdeutsch itself, with its distinctive pronunciations and local vernacular terms (*klock een* for *ein Uhr, fat* for *anfassen, klink* for *Klinke,* and *sachen* for *schleichen,* for example). The several closely related dialects of the northern German flatland—hence the term *Flat German,* sometimes called *Low* (i.e., lowland) *German*—are discouraged in polite conversation, but the vernacular is proudly maintained by people who use it to savor their locale. One finds books of local stories and poems published in Platt, Radio Bremen features regular news broadcasts in the dialect, and even some banks display a placard at tellers' windows that proudly proclaims *ik snakk Platt* (I speak Platt). Maintaining the language in the song undergirds the sense of local identity and local values in which the actions of the song make local sense, even though it is equally true that its singers do not openly condone premarital sex.

The wording of the song also concentrates attention on finer points of protocol within this delicate and ambiguous situation. The action is predicated on duping the parents into thinking that any stray sound is really the wind, but at the same time—although the girl tells the boy that he is her dearest (*leevste*)—she also tells him to identify himself by name when he comes, indicating that perhaps she is "interviewing" several possible candidates for the kind of marriage that will stabilize and perpetuate the family farm. Again, as with so many of the meaningful details derived from contextual situation, these elements are not actually articulated by the song text, but rather are retrieved by the text in the minds of culturally active listeners in the home context of the song.

Thus, cultural context provides one set of meanings that any text references in its performed articulation. But there are other sets as well, including the scholarly. The song, for example, falls into the generic category of the *aube* or *aubade,* songs and poems that focus on the night visit of a suitor to his lady. In an early article on the form, Charles Read Baskerville argued that *aubade* falls into two distinct groupings: those that focus primarily on the arrival of the lover (and his secret entrance into the lady's room, usually), and those that concentrate mainly on the predawn departure of the young man.[19] But, as Frances Cattermole-Tally demonstrates, the genre is much broader and far more complex than Baskerville realized.[20] The scholarly context provides several more considerations. First, through the extensive criticism available, we can see that the form is found across Europe and is from an early date. There are close parallels in Germany, England, and France, and—without the hesitation that normally comes in comparing items from different cultures—we can, provisionally at least, enlarge our sense of range for the *aubade* and use a number of good examples of the available possibilities. This does not allow us to assume, of course, that any one singer must have known any or all of them.

The second consideration, as Cattermole-Tally points out, is that if we examine the cluster of motifs or actions that typify the genre, we will be forced to conclude that a great number of the so-called revenant ballads also belong in the same category. This scholarly observation can be applied to representative texts to see whether two larger questions can be approached through generic context: (1) Does anything about the typical structure and sequence of the folk *aubade* suggest metaphorical meanings that might account for the continued fit of the song? and (2) Why should a sequence associated with courtship and sex also be appropriate to songs having to do with death? Is there a metaphorical interplay between sex and death, the understanding of which might enhance our ability to understand the songs?

Cattermole-Tally believes that one part of the puzzle lies in the historical custom of the night of love before a knight rode off to battle, leading to a reasonable expectation that such a tryst might actually take place just before death, and that the ghost of the lover might reasonably be described as returning to prove his undying love. Another possibility might lie in the older beliefs found throughout Northern Europe about the relationship between death and fertility, a topic about which there is much evidence but precious little clarity. Perhaps there is a hint of Christian death and revival as applied to love-making. In one German love song, God takes pity on the two lovers, and "er tet die zwai erquicken, / er weckt si baide von dem tod (he brought the two to life, he woke them both from death)."[21] The figure is common enough in Renaissance literature, where the "little death" is used as a metaphor (perhaps in polite society, a euphemism) for orgasm. Indeed, critics normally treat the expression as a conceit, a self-consciously developed poetic figure, but Shakespeare's use of it (for example, in *Lear* IV:201, "I will die bravely, like a smug bridegroom") indicates that it was within easy reach of theater audiences. As is often the case with Shakespeare, figures of speech and even plot details closely parallel—or even derive directly from—folk tradition and speech.[22] Taken together with the wide spread of themes in folksongs, we may at least speculate that the field of reference is of some antiquity and broad vernacular provenience.

But whether they derive from Christian imagery, from Northern European assumptions about the natural cycle (in which death and fertility are reciprocally associated), from the amorous customs of knights or soldiers going off to wars, or even from a belief in the possibility of interchange between the worlds of the living and the dead, how do metaphors create something palpable for singers or audiences as songs come down to more recent times? It is the same dilemma that Renwick faced in the case of "The Bold Fisherman." Even if the originals stem from Gnostic tradition, what do they mean to those who have sung them subsequently? *Aubades* have survived only by chance (which would make the multiple versions in several European languages difficult to account for), or by sheer dint of ongoing memorization of an ancient idea (which makes the variety of good poetic expression hard to explain), or else there has been some sense to the songs that people have savored and passed along. Taking the principal contexts seriously and enlarging our understanding of their possibilities by reference to analogous versions, it is possible to account for the sense and function of a complicated metaphor.

The main elements of the night-visit song "Dat du min leevste bist" correspond with those found in a great number of analogues: (1) the arrival of the lover, often guided or precipitated by an invitation from the young woman; (2) his entry into her house, chamber, or bower; (3) a reference to a cock crowing a warning of impending dawn (sometimes in the German versions the cock is replaced by a watchman); and (4) the retreat of the lover, usually without being detected by the girl's family. As Cattermole-Tally points out, the cock plays more than a merely practical role in this drama, for *cock* (*Hahn* in German) is one of the most common English metaphorical terms for penis, and both terms carry heavy implications for fertility and agricultural plenty.[23]

Taken together with the familiar metaphor of a man entering a woman's chamber or garden, a scene found widely in folk and elite literature since medieval times, the song text does not leave out any important action, but rather suggests it through a rich interplay of metaphor and context. In unpoetic terms, there is invitation and negotiation, entry into a woman's chamber, cock-crow, and exit from chamber—more explicitly, verbal foreplay, sexual entry, ejaculation, and withdrawal. The brief narrative is itself a metaphor for sexual union, as is the following fifteenth-century British lyric:

> I have a gentil cock   crowyt me day
> he doth me rysyn erly   my matyins for to say
> I have a gentil cock   comyn he is of gret
> his comb is of red coral   his tayl is of jet
> I have a gentil cock   comen he is of kynde
> his comb is of red sorel   his tayl is of inde
> his leggs ben of asor   so gentil and so smal
> his spors arn of sylver whyt   in to the wortewale
> his eynyn arn of cristal   lokyt al in ambyr
> and every nygt he perchyt hym   in my ladyis chamber

> (I have a gentle [genteel] cock who crows for me when it is day;
> He makes me rise early to say my prayers.
> I have a gentle cock, he is of great [lineage];
> His comb is of red coral, his tail is of jet [black].
> I have a gentle cock, he is a native [or: He comes from the same group as I]
> His comb is of red sorrel, his tail of indigo [blue]
> His legs are azure, so gentle and slender;
> His spurs are of silver white into [up to] the root.
> His eyes are of crystal, locked all in amber,
> And every night he perches in my lady's chamber.)

In his notes to this poem in *Medieval English Lyrics,* R. T. Davies observes the similarity to the nursery rhyme "Goosey, Goosey Gander, whither do you wander? 'Upstairs, downstairs, in my lady's chamber'" but does not comment on the sexual suggestion of the male bird in the lady's chamber.[24]

As with most of the examples used in this book, the effect of the metaphor is neither to disguise sexuality nor to make it prurient. Rather, the metaphor allows for the perception of other important elements in the equation. People knew how to accomplish the sexual act, presumably; the ambiguous part was the social situation that required secrecy in an event that everyone nonetheless recognized as normal. Moreover, when a young woman might have had more than one suitor, when one or more young men in the community might have been going off to war (or later to work in the towns), when pregnancy might turn out to be either a blessing or a tragedy (depending on whether or not the man would be there), and when religious teachings insisted that sex led to death and torment, small wonder that the prevailing metaphors were the ones that suggested the maximum range of anxieties and ambiguities.

Another rationale for the death implications of some songs might be the common image, found in Europe from the Middle Ages to the present, of the Dance of Death. People from all walks of life, dressed in everyday clothes, are shown dancing together, almost in ecstasy. Leading the dance is the Grim Reaper, a skeleton in monk's clothing. Often, several people in the dance are shown as starting to turn into skeletons, apparently without realizing it. The image illustrates the medieval Christian idea that we are dying even as we are in the midst of life. Because the dance metaphor was also used widely for sexual engagement (referring to the Wife of Bath's sexual expertise, for example, Chaucer says, "For she knew of that art the olde daunce"), it is difficult to escape the added sense that as we enjoy the physical expressions of life, even the sexual ones, we are simultaneously in the grip of physical and spiritual death.[25]

This matter of romance and death is found in all the revenant ballads in English. In "Proud Lady Margaret" (Child 47), the suitor who answers the lady's riddles and thus puts himself in position for more serious courtship (chapter 6) turns out to be the ghost of her brother. "Sweet William's Ghost" (Child 77) starts with a typical night-visit negotiation; the young man knocks and is invited in by the girl, but he refuses, revealing the fact that he is dead. The ballad finishes with an ironic reversal in which she tries to get into his chamber—his grave. In "The Twa Brothers" (Child 49), it is the bereaved lover who with wonderful hyperbole grieves so much that she cries, harps, pipes, or sings her true love out of the grave (versions B and C). In "The Unquiet Grave" (Child 78), the surviving lover still wants to kiss the corpse, and the ongoing urge—which might be called pathological grief (or unextinguished sexual passion) today—is enough to summon the ghost of the dead partner. In "The Cruel Mother" (Child 20), the murdered babies, born illegitimately of a love affair, come back to curse their mother-murderer, and in "Sir Hugh" (Child 155), after a seductive murder scene, the ghost of the murdered boy wanders or sings out until his demise is discovered. "Willie's Fatal Visit" (Child 255) features an almost standard *aubade* sequence: identification of the lover's identity, the lover makes noise at the latch and is admitted to girl's chamber, the cock crows (too early), and the lover departs. Death comes to him on his way home in an odd addendum that describes a ghost who dismembers him for not having uttered a prayer for safety during travel. "The Grey Cock" (Child 248), which might be the original for Buchan's version of Child 255, describes just the night visit and premature cock-crow without the grisly epilogue. In version A of "Young Benjie" (Child 86), the lovers quarrel, and she declines to let him into her chamber when he visits at night. When he threatens to leave, she rushes outside to him (remember that "out" is where women are vulnerable), and he kills her. When her brothers later try to find out the murderer's identity, it is at cock-crow that her body begins to squirm and writhe ("thaw"), not with sexual passion but with accusation and punishment for her lover-murderer.

The one problematic ballad in this grouping is "The Wife of Usher's Well" (Child 79). Although it contains both the revenant motif and some of the night-visit elements, little romance seems to be involved, for the woman is described as the mother of the three men. Her sons have died abroad, and in grief or madness she wishes or prays that they would come home to her. When their spirits do come, she sets the table and makes the beds for them, common motifs in many songs in the *aubade* genre. When the cock crows (in the English and in some American versions), the spirits depart, in one version bidding farewell both to their mother and the "bonny lass" who is the mother's maid. Like "The Twa Brothers" and "The Unquiet Grave," the ballad features someone whose passionate grieving calls back the dead. But unlike those ballads, the passionate one in this ballad is not a lover, but a mother. The time of year in Child's version A is Martinmas, when conviviality to guests is stressed in English tradition. In other versions, the season is Christmas, equally a time for feasting, entertaining, and drinking. Most American versions (for example, versions A, B, C, and F in the *Brown Collection*), all more complete in detail than the two given by Child, mention Christmas specifically and describe the serving of cake, bread, and wine.[26]

In "The Wife of Usher's Well" there is, as in no other ballad, an insistence on a religious season and on a mother—rather than a lover—bent on receiving and providing food, drink, and bedding for male visitors. Because of the suggestiveness of the night-visit components, we cannot dismiss the amorous possibilities, but given the ballad's insistence on a close connection between the sons' spirits and the Savior "a-standing so near," we should be hesitant to insist that the ballad presents a metaphorical Oedipal scene. A more likely possibility is that different versions were sung for different reasons, some foregrounding the intensity of the mother's love for her dead sons and paralleling that passion with the rich implications of the Mary and Jesus story, some exploiting the ironies inherent in the suggestion of incest (chapter 7). In regard to the first possibility, the song functions metaphorically like the medieval poem "I Syng of a Mayden," which depicts the entry of Christ into his mother's bower and uses the traditional imagery of romantic love songs, in which bowers or gardens are normal scenes of sexual encounter, and dew usually suggests virginity.[27]

I syng of a mayden
that is makeles:
Kyng of alle kynges
to here son she ches.

He cam also stille
ther his moder was.
as dew in Aprille
that fallyt on the gras.

He cam also stille
to his moderes bowr
as dew in Aprille
that fallyt on the flowr.

He cam also stille
ther his moder lay
as dew in Aprille
that fallyt on the spray.

Moder and mayden
was nevere non but she:
well may swich a lady
Godes moder be.[28]

A number of medieval poems to Mary use the erotic devices of love poetry, as do a number of love poems intensify lovers' passions by metaphorically phrasing the lady-love in terms of Mary's virtues. In "The Wife of Usher's Well," the death imagery is retained, but the sexual passion normally suggested by erotic metaphor is superseded by the concern of a mother, exactly the effect gained in medieval poems dedicated to Mary. This is not to argue that traditional singers had some special awareness of medieval poetic conventions, but rather that both medieval and more recent folk tradition show the capacity to use powerfully suggestive patterns from the cultural past. In the absence of a widely understood and resilient metaphoric language functioning in the culture, such observations would have to be based merely on the appreciation of felicitous coincidence. But where longevity of usage and coherence of image are so pronounced, it would seem more simple and sensible to acknowledge the considerable poetic talent that ballad singers have transmitted and used through the years.

Even so, it is clear that this poetic ability is demonstrated in performance situations that change from one context to another according to the shared values of the group in which the song is used. Thus, it is not enough to point out that "The Wife of Usher's Well" contains elements that might suggest a Christian metaphor or incest, for the two possibilities seem too opposed to be fruitfully registered in the same song. We need more immediate contextual information from the actual performance events in order to be more certain about the assumed meaning of each particular version. Some metaphors seem opposed initially yet actually create ambiguities directly related to plot or theme, and in many cases these relationships can be seen clearly in the texts. Nonetheless, for much of the sense of what is going on in the sensibilities of folksong audiences, it is necessary to get as deep a contextual picture as possible.

It is important, for example, to know when we encounter one of the *aubade*-revenant songs that it is common for surviving spouses and other partners of long-term relationships in Northern Europe and America to report visits from deceased companions. Indeed, based on his surveys and the fieldwork of others, David Hufford estimates that between 40 and 45 percent of surviving spouses say that their dead partner's visit occurred at night when they were asleep and dreaming; the visitor departed when the dreamer became fully awake, and the survivor was left with a sense of having had a real experience.[29] Whether this experience constitutes a real encounter with a departed spirit, or a mere psychological phenomenon, or a nostalgic and hopeful dream, it is a common enough customary idea. This shared sense of validity and plausibility means that anecdotes, legends, personal experiences, and songs about ghosts can possess an aura of potential believability as they articulate through figurative speech the abstractions of life and love after, and in spite of, death. These considerations illustrate Susan Stewart's point that intertextuality is fueled by elements from "the common-sense world."[30] Religions and philosophies may prepare us intellectually, even spiritually, for the fact of death, but folksongs, legends, and personal anecdotes dramatize areas of anxiety and ambiguity that are not well covered by catechisms and formal thinkers. Context provides a useful and necessary framework for understanding the ways in which figurative language explores these important areas of human concern.

4

"üba d'Alm"
Regional Context and Cultural Nuance

Thus far, my discussion of folksong metaphor has been largely hypothetical, based on assumptions and inferences derived from amassing similar and parallel themes, motifs, and figures of speech in apparently consistent contexts. The recurrence of such motifs and figures in analogous situations has quite logically led such scholars as Flemming Anderson, James Reeves, and Roger deV. Renwick to conclude that there is more than a merely fortuitous patterning to folksong language—my point in this study. Similar considerations have led David Buchan to conclude that the nuance of dramatic actions in the ballad is not fortuitous either, and that it can therefore be discussed as having laws of operation—consistent tendencies that have meaning and import in and of themselves. In all such arguments, there is the sense that the text, either in print or on a tape recording, does not constitute the total field of meaning. The story, its figures of speech, its character line-up, or its semiotic locutions somehow trigger associations and previous knowledge in the minds of audiences that share cultural and performative contexts.

Accounts of actual singing events are rare enough in folksong studies; even then, they often indicate more about the ordering of songs within the occasion than they do about people and their values. The well-known description of a typical night of singing at the Wagon and Horses Public House in Lark Rise provided by Flora Thompson and referred to by several folksong scholars does provide a few hints.[1] One song offered during the evening was "The Old Maid's Song," sung by an older man whose own bachelor status was seen in the community as lending a particular "point" to the song. Yet analytical and interpretive comments by singers and audiences are rare in the vast literature of ballad and folksong study. In fact, in earlier works on vernacular songs, it was fashionable for well-educated collectors and editors to identify singers by the haziest and most impersonal of terms ("an aged nurse once resident of the north," for example). How much less likely were the same scholars to ask for critical insight from their sources? Although now we have become accustomed to seeing the documentation of time, place, and persons present, conversation—such as that provided by Alan Jabbour and Carl Fleischhauer on their recording *The Hammons Family: A Study of a West Virginia Family's Traditions*—is rare between songs.[2]

Where possible in this book, I have tried to refer to singing events I have witnessed in which the attitudes, actions, or comments of singers and their audiences provided something more than a hypothetical reason for considering the topic of folksong metaphor as valid. Witnessing the North Carolina couple singing "The Riddle Song" allowed me to see an element of meaning that I had not suspected previously. Being able to ask Bob Beers or Walt Bolton about songs they considered figuratively meaningful—and to be there when they sang those songs to friends who supplied the apparently appropriate responses—provided empirical evidence for this study that most essays and books, including my own, lack. Such moments are ephemeral and rare and do not allow for complicated examination of the ongoing contextual systems in which the songs normally operate, even though they do confirm the premise that some folksong meanings are not made manifest in the text.

I wanted to see what vernacular songs and everyday musical expression meant over time to the same group of people, and so I arranged to spend a year studying an extended singing family in their own milieu.[3] I had become acquainted with the family when my Austrian friend, Hannes Erlbacher, married into a family in which literally every member sings traditional songs year-round. The family made me welcome on their dairy farm near Salzburg on several occasions and treated me to hours of singing from dawn until midnight. Later, when I asked whether I could record them over a year, they willingly agreed to participate in the project.

My attempt in this chapter is to describe their lives, their uses of singing, and their comments about meaning. The basis of my research was friendly and personal, for I was not allowed to observe the family's events objectively. I was treated as a part of the family, expected to sing my own family's songs from time to time, encouraged to sing their songs along with them, and put in the position of participating in all events during which singing normally took place. Although the interactive complexity of the singing is difficult to describe, it is possible to see the richly overlapping ways in which meaning and connotation are in constant use among people who are closely associated in culture and expression and share the contexts of everyday life intensely.

The Hermann Koessner family now lives in the small mountain village of Goldegg-Weng, not far from Bischofshofen, Land Salzburg, Austria. When I first met them in the 1960s, Hermann was chief herdsman for a large diary farm near Salzburg city and was still using yodels and cow calls to wake his children in the morning and call the family to supper. The Koessners also signaled their whereabouts in the fields and entertained themselves after supper over liberal doses of *Obstler* (locally distilled fruit schnapps). Although the parents have since retired to the mountains, yodeling and singing remain their daily passion. Yodeling is performed at virtually every family gathering (marriages, baptisms, parties, outings, visits to the hospital), and grandchildren start making yodeling noises before they learn to speak.

Family members not only sing and yodel at such family-oriented times, but several of them have also become active in more formalized and re-hearsed musical presentations with larger groups, such as the Salzburger Adventsingen, which draws thousands of spectators annually. I was con-vinced that a close scrutiny of the family's singing would provide insights into the functional aspects of folksinging and the relationship between the vernacular and formal levels of music usage in a single culture.

Yodeling—especially in three- and four-part harmony—is far from easy; it carries the potential of sounding absolutely terrible. Because my work in folklore has focused on the performance aspect, I was interested in finding out why the family continued to perform such difficult music among themselves as well as for others. When do they do it, and why? Is this kind of singing a mere survival, something they do because they think their culture is threatened and they need to prop it up? Perhaps it is something more organic to the way they express themselves or the values central to their way of life. Furthermore, what does singing and yodeling *mean* for them? Yodels offer a particularly challenging view of the idea of meaning in song, for usually the texts have very few or no words. Nonetheless, people get tears in their eyes when they sing or hear certain yodels, and others elicit a sudden burst of laughter and delight.

Yodel texts and tunes in common traditional circulation have been collected, notated, described, and discussed in articles and books from the late 1800s to the present (with a heavy representation from the 1930s). But I have found no extensive studies of the yodel as expressive behav-ior, no discussions of yodeling semiotics, and no theories about yodeling as a reflection of worldview; nothing is available on implication, conno-tation, metaphor, symbol, nuance, cultural maintenance, or traditional performance.[4] Because my interests are in actual performances within living traditional contexts where such topics have meaning, people actually sing-ing yodels to each other under everyday circumstances comprised the most important area of my research. Yet several German colleagues warned that I would be disappointed if I tried to find "authentic" yodeling anywhere; it had disappeared with the olden times I was told.

Yodeling is very much alive in southern Germany, Austria, and Switzerland, however, although the type found most easily and heard most often is a commercial variety encountered on records (often over the radio) or in local taverns and restaurants. Traditional yodels of alpine farmers seem to have faded in favor of high-powered popular yodeling, songs by regional church choirs (often recorded in old cathedrals with impressive echoes), or drinking songs by groups of local enthusiasts dressed in lederhosen and matching blue-and-white checkered shirts.

American researchers might see an analogy to the many popular songs in the United States that ostensibly come from rural—especially western—backgrounds and are performed professionally by sophisticated singers with electronic helps and also by tavern singers dressed in cowboy shirts, jeans, feathered hats, and boots not designed for the barnyard. In both cases, on the surface, songs in which content and style embody something culturally valuable and old-fashioned have been made into hits. In both cases, rural clothing seems to bear some relation to professional performance. Both kinds of music are culturally chauvinistic and appeal to the most basic and conservative tastes in their respective cultures, which is probably why they continue to thrive despite the unreality of their sounds and the occasional mediocrity of their words. Folklorists often ignore both kinds because the continued success of such popular music is a sign of what people buy and not a direct indication of shared traditional expressions that people shape.

As we now recognize through the help of D. K. Wilgus and others, however, vernacular-based popular music also retains and develops distinct traditions of its own. Moreover, many of the earliest country-western singers in the United States were formerly traditional singers in their own families and came from areas where traditional singing was an expressive custom of long standing. Thus, they brought some traditional elements to their professional singing. The dissemination of popular commercial country singing over the radio also had considerable impact on traditional singers back home—roughly analogous to the interaction of the broadside ballads and oral ballads of England in an earlier century. And in all these areas, some traditional singers still sing traditional songs, so it is clear that popular music has not killed off the folk music entirely.[5]

Just as popular country-western music in the United States cannot be entirely separated from the traditional aspects of its background, modern pop yodeling in Germany and Austria cannot be fairly separated from the ongoing oral traditions with which it retains continuing and strong ties.

Indeed, proportionately more people in Germany and Austria are consciously engaged in performing and maintaining the nonprofessional oral tradition in yodeling than are involved in maintaining the analogous country singing tradition in the United States. Yodeling has shifted contexts considerably but has gained rather than lost ground.

Many of the yodelers I heard were also active in church and regional choirs and choruses, several have also sung with well-known trios and quartets on records, and many are avid participants in the *Heimatpflege* movement, so it seems likely that there are continual chances for interpenetration, mutual enrichment, and maintenance of some traditional tastes between and among the several kinds of yodeling heard today.[6] Rather than defining or classifying the various kinds of yodeling merely by the distinction of amateur-professional, noncommercial-commercial, old-modern (all of which disguise an implied judgment of good-bad or authentic-fake), my description of the kinds of yodeling I was able to observe is arranged primarily by aspects of performance (occasion, context, size of audience, and usage). These contextual and situational details help us understand that the figurative language of the songs, although not used to the same degree by all singers, has a currency throughout the culture and is not limited to the ken of farmers, the secret language of singers, or the codes of semioticists.

The basic yodel, the model on which the other kinds seem to be grounded, is the alpine yell in which a singer moves in and out of falsetto, using a loud volume and a sharp attack that makes the resultant tone audible at considerable distances. At one time, these yodels were used as signals and as ways of calling cows on mountain meadows. The style and the setting have become heavily admired and idealized as symbolic of something in the national and regional character: the self-sufficient dairy farmer caring for his herds in the pure mountain air (much the way the American farm scene has become symbolic of ideals shared more than of everyday reality). To use phrases often heard in the yodels themselves and seen on the record jackets of many yodeling groups, this kind of yodel might be termed *auf da Alm* (on the meadow) or *üba d'Alm* (across the meadow).

The outdoor yodel can still be heard in alpine areas. Although it is used less and less to call cattle, it has remained in use among foresters, hikers, and herders as a means of expressing and pleasing themselves and also as a way of signaling their whereabouts. The aspect of personal entertainment, perhaps always a strong ingredient in yodeling, has been retained. Today, while walking through the forests of Austria with farm people, one will suddenly be halted and treated to a solo or duet yodel on a spot where the farmer has previously discovered a good echo. People on torchlight hikes at holidays like Christmas or New Year's yodel to themselves and to others across the valley. In *"Alm* yodeling," the principal audience is one-self, possibly a few companions, cows, and—if the wind is right—probably others in the local community below, who will not only recognize the yodel itself but will also be able to identify the yodeler.

Yodeling, because it is done outdoors in all kinds of weather and temperature and at all elevations, is open to considerable variation in tone and quality. It is done so spontaneously that in several months of carrying a battery-powered tape recorder in a backpack, only once was I able to get it out and operating in time to catch an impromptu tune on tape, in spite of the fact that my companions knew I was trying to record the yodels and had promised to help. So sudden is the inclination to yodel *üba d'Alm* that electronic considerations are always secondary.

The phrase *da Alm* (pronounced *d'oym*), the local term for mountain meadows on which cattle are grazed during the summer, is productive of a great number of cultural, regional, and occupational reverberations. It is perhaps because of the combined cultural assumptions in the phrase that it and the brief yodels in which it is heard have survived so well and come to mean so much. Mountain meadows have been the scenes for most prevalent kinds of freedom and privacy for the young teenagers who traditionally accompany the herds into the mountains during summer months. Free from immediate family supervision, the young men and women, usually referred to respectively as *Buam* and *Dianei* (*Buben* and *Dirndl* in "standard" Bavarian German) who herded in the mountains had mostly to keep the cows from straying and milk them twice a day. Horse-drawn sleds (now tractors) were sent up for the accumulated milk, but generally the young people were relatively free to do what they liked, and many whiled away the summer visiting each other.

Being *auf da Alm* for rural Austrian youths was something akin to being "out" or down by the greenwood side for English farm youths in the past. Many elderly Austrian couples in mountain communities recall that they met each other *auf da Alm,* and a number of stories and legends are told to illustrate the joys and disappointments of young life in the mountains. Thus, this particular kind of yodel not only awakens personal and family memories about youth, romance, marriage, pregnancy, and the like, but it also expresses a field of metaphorical reference in these topical areas that all who have heard the songs, stories, and figures of speech as part of the fabric of everyday life can share.

Closely related to *Alm* yodeling in content and style (but much easier to record) are the yodels done at home around the kitchen table in the evening. Of course, not all mountain families do it, but the Koessner family sings whenever the occasion permits. The family—with or without guests—faces each other around the table and sings yodels of two- , three- , and four-part harmony. This requires more control and regularity than the *Alm* yodeling because of the demands of maintaining harmony while breaking in and out of falsetto tones. The table situation allows for eye contact and musical correction, but the audience is mainly the family itself, and the reason for yodeling is the expression of their own pleasure.

Many yodels are sung on social occasions outside the home (in taverns while on a trip, or at picnics, for example) or when a family occasion such as a baptism or wedding provides a more formal opportunity. The more relaxed audiences of taverns and picnics allow for the singing of single-voiced *Alm* yodels, especially cow calls, whereas the more restrained setting of the church demands a more restricted repertoire and a more conscious rehearsal. At this level, audiences outside the immediate family begin to exert not-so-subtle influences on content and style. Nonetheless, these influences are not false ones nor are they new considerations. People have been singing in taverns and churches for many generations, and it would be a wonder had the tavern and picnic setting not encouraged humorous, sexual, farm-oriented songs and yodels, and had the church setting not encouraged something more sober and careful. Together, context and performance create the "meaning" of any particular yodel because some tunes may be heard in all of these situations, whereas others are chosen for performance (or nonperformance) because of contextual exigencies.

A still more conscious application of these elements, a greater stress on rehearsal, and a more self-conscious study of music is found in the singing and yodeling associated with the *Heimatpflege* movement. Local groups make a concerted effort to maintain selected older customs, to wear local costume on special occasions, and to perpetuate traditional music. The movement is much more than a fad and often includes consciously maintaining or building a barn or house in older local style, taking up various stringed instruments associated with older music (such as the zither and the *Hackbrett*), and wearing *Tracht* (local costume) on all possible occasions. Nonetheless, the effort is selective rather than wholly traditional, and the clothing and singing are more associated with church and festival than with the barnyard. The music is carefully rehearsed, carefully presented, carefully and tastefully costumed. Yet it is solidly based on the accepted tastes, conventions, and meanings of local tradition, and local people comprise most of its audience. Many of them sing at home around their own tables and thus know the tunes, harmonies, conventions, and proper contexts for the songs.

Heimatpflege groups, almost all of them associated with real cultural or dialectal districts, put on occasional evenings of music for larger audiences and also arrange for small groups—like trios—to sing at weddings.

Some restaurant owners arrange their own *Heimat-Abend* during the Advent season and invite local singing groups. In most of these cases, whether the occasion is a church service, an Advent observance, a special occasion such as *Koppler Hoagascht* (a program put on annually by those interested in *Heimatpflege* in the small village of Koppl), or an evening of singing open only to the singers themselves put on by the owner of one of Salzburg's oldest restaurants, the singing and yodeling, although rehearsed, reflects and expresses local singers' values. The audience is made up of other knowledgeable insiders who are in attendance for that very reason. The topics are not as sober as in church yodeling, but the musical styles tend toward refinement or elevation. There is a tendency toward beautiful, dignified, and regular singing, less of an inclination toward the piercing tones or improvisation or spontaneity of the *Alm* yodels. Certain elements already in the tradition are selected for foregrounding and special development.

The next step away from *Alm* tradition is toward the commercial and media presentation of yodeling. In some cases the performers are the same, but they are presented on commercial recordings, over the radio, or on live programs such as the Salzburger Adventsingen, which has become almost an obligatory institution—and a beautiful one—of the Bavarian and Austrian Christmas season. Here, of course, the audience is made up chiefly of outsiders to the yodeling tradition, and here some of the greatest changes in yodeling style take place in order to provide a merchantable record or a live act. On the serious side of yodeling, what might now be called the classical, large and beautiful choruses sing, not yodel, what were once yodel tunes. All the tones are modulated and controlled, and the attempt is to provide acceptably old-sounding music made palatable to modern tastes in classical music.

On the more popular side of the tradition, traveling musical shows, as well as shows for tourists, highlight or spotlight a yodeler or two who specializes in yodeling acrobatics, sacrificing tone, context, and meaning for speed and vocal dexterity. In local taverns and restaurants one also finds yodeling acts or sing-along groups that the management has hired to provide an ostensibly rural atmosphere. Here the tendency is toward slapstick, rural foolishness, or unabashed kitsch, all of which seem attractive to some patrons, not all of whom are tourists, which indicates that the projected image has some local meaning.

Past the *Heimatpflege* level, the yodel, like all other cultural phenomena, survives as a form of popular culture and depends more on the tastes of outsider audiences than on the expressive attitudes of traditional performers. But all of these phenomena are meaningful and require consideration. In the classical yodeling of the *Heimatpflege* enthusiasts there is a conscious foregrounding of certain features of style and content that are genuine aspects of traditional yodeling, whose very performance is a dramatic metaphor of being in home territory. Special focus on these aspects of style amounts to cultural and musical hyperbole. Why is it done? What do people feel they gain from it? In a modern world, why don't the people simply drop yodeling altogether?

In the more popular forms found in tourist hotels, taverns and performances for organized tours, there is a foregrounding of another dimension of style and content that approximates the attitude known in the United States as "redneck" or "hillbilly" insofar as rural stereotypes are presented as self-selected positive markers of down-home conservatism. Thus, there is a hyperbolic stress on certain meaningful features. But meaningful to whom, and why? Why does this style remain successful, popular, lucrative?

These important and complex questions relate so much to local politics, local conceptions, national views, and history that they should be more properly taken up by German or Austrian social historians. Here, I hope to show where one family of yodelers fits into the schema and indicate how intensive fieldwork can provide the groundwork for understanding more about family traditions, learning of traditional songs, and the meaning of traditional nuances within a small group of insiders.

Because I wanted to find out how the Koessner family felt about yodeling, it was necessary to record them singing and conversing among themselves in their own daily contexts. To increase the possibility that I might record comments that expressed values shared with each other rather than addressed to me or the recorder, I decided to use two tape recorders, both of them visible. An unobtrusive cassette recorder was left running throughout to catch all conversation, and another, a reel-to-reel with a good microphone loaned to me by the Folklore Department at the University of Freiburg, was used to record only songs and yodels so I would have high-quality sound-texts.

During the various occasions when I recorded the family, I also joined in the conversation, as did others at the table, and often asked leading questions about the meaning of a title, the source of a particular yodel, the interpretation of a figure of speech, or even about why it was they yodeled. Some statements on the tapes are thus openly addressed to me in answer to particular queries, but the most interesting parts concern impromptu conversations and interactions: the family's excited comments to each other between yodels, their joking, their friendly arguments over who should begin, and their earnest disagreements over the background or meaning of a title. From these elements it is possible to infer a philosophy and esthetics of vernacular song performance that allows us to see beyond popular fads and into real and serious local conceptions.

During a series of visits over a ten-month period, I recorded the Koessners several times, singing in their home in Goldegg-Weng, out in the mountains, and in their daughters' homes in Salzburg. From their comments and from my own observations, I can attest to the fact that many families sing at home as they do, but I have no figures on exactly how many do so or on whether the Koessners' singing is typical of the sort going on in other homes. Thus my field research is representative primarily of the Koessner family itself, yet they are part of a much larger family system and thus no anomaly.

Hermann and Elisabeth Koessner are both in their seventies. Hermann's family is originally from the area, and Elisabeth's family is from the Flachau area in the nearby Ennstal. Elisabeth's grandfather had twenty-eight children by three wives, and virtually the whole family grew up yodeling. Many of the best yodelers who perform today on records (the Pongauer Viergesang, for example) come from this area and are connected in some way with the family. Hermann grew up learning an extensive body of local songs. Many, termed *Gelegenheitslieder,* are fairly lengthy (ten to twenty-five stanzas) topical songs, while others are more compact lyrics.[7] Although Hermann also yodeled in his youth, most of the yodels now done by the Koessners are from the large Weiss family repertoire brought by Elisabeth.

Their daughters, Anneliese and Hermi, and their son, Rudi, grew up singing and yodeling at home with their parents. After marriage, all three moved to Salzburg and continued to yodel at home with their own families, and their children began to yodel (or at least tried to do so) long before they spoke in connected sentences. All three Koessner children sang not only at home but also with choirs and singing groups that have been part of the *Heimatpflege* movement. All three have performed with the Salzburger Adventsingen program (as a child, Rudi had a role as one of the shepherd boys). All three still sing with various groups when their personal schedules and family lives permit. Anneliese and Hermi, along with Christl Klappacher of nearby Niederalm, sang together at churches and concerts as the Salzburger Dreigesang, and their songs are found on a number of commercial recordings of Advent music and local folk music. Rudi and his family have moved to an *Alm* above Goldegg-weng, where he and his parents occasionally signal to each other with yodels. Their favorite form of yodeling remains the home-style singing around the kitchen table.

The family custom of the larger Wiess family, however, is not limited in any way to the kitchen table. They sing at nearly every gathering, whatever the occasion. Family reunions are, of course, a favorite context, but anytime two or more of the family gather, a yodel will result. When two elderly sisters in the family visited their older brother in a hospital, his first words were, "If I hadn't just had an operation I would explode into a yodel!" When they began yodeling for him, they were asked to leave. For this family, yodeling is a continual way of expressing membership and identification, for the yodels and songs themselves refer to local scenes and people. As the family has slowly spread out across the countryside, opportunities to sing together regularly have been fewer and fewer, so when reunions do take place, the singing is intense and lasts for longer periods.

Not all yodels sung by the Koessners have titles, and even those that do are identified usually by their first musical phrase, sung by the person who is suggesting a particular yodel. For example, Anneliese says, "Let's try 'der Obdacher.'" Her father replies, "Which one?" "You know," she responds (and sings the first line). "Oh that one!" Hermann says, "That's really beautiful; you start off, right?" Nonetheless, titles are an important aspect of the meaning in yodeling and are discussed at great length, often because they feature local or dialectal terms and pronunciations and refer to particular geographical spots, which may or may not retain the same name on maps. References to geographical places are indicated in such titles as "Der Puchberger" (the family's favorite), "Der Rinnegger," "Der alt' Moarbacher," "Der Zauchenseer," "Der Gosauer," and "Der Wolfganseer," but meaning becomes more complicated with "Der Walchauer," because it names the precise place where Elisabeth is from and therefore produces special family nostalgia.

Other titles such as "Der Rehbockler" (The buck), "Der Obdacher" (The steep slope), "Der Kohlmoassa" (The great titmouse), and "Der Stegngrindei" (The roughened trail) are descriptive of local animals and terrain, whereas such titles as "Der Dahoam Z'schad Is" (Because it's too sad at home) and "Der Langenwanger" (Long cheeks) suggest human emotions. Some yodels are associated with particular people who made them up or sang them as distinctive identifying signals, as reflected in such titles as "Heinrich Seine" (Henry's). Still others are known by their practical function, such as the cow call (referred to generically as a *Lockruf,* a summoning call) Elisabeth learned from her brother while herding in the mountains years ago: "Der Kuahschroa" (*Kuh-Schrei,* or "cow yell").

One song, which the family sings at virtually every reunion, is "Flachau." The Koessners' personal response to the song is nostalgic in remembrance of their home place, but the verses use double-entendre to express local pride in terms of fertility and protection of local women. On one occasion, when I asked about the meaning of the term *Stegngrindei,* Hermann and Elisabeth provided two separate and differing explanations, both delivered simultaneously and having to do with a path or retaining wall used in mountain pastures. The zeal with which the explanations were offered testified to the liveliness and importance of the subject and suggests a fascinating area of research in dialectology, folk history, and place-name legend.

Most yodels do not have texts in the normal sense of the term, which makes the perception and discussion of metaphor somewhat problematic but not impossible. Yodel "words" are vocables that allow for ready movement in and out of falsetto. Syllables with dark vowel sounds (*o:*) and (*u:*) usually match musical tones in a lower range, while syllables with (*i:*) and (*ü:*) sounds are almost always in falsetto. Of course, when a group of people sing together in harmony, they often sing the same syllable although only one or two are in falsetto, so the rule varies according to the demands of the song. In any case, when an identifiable word does suddenly appear in a yodel, it immediately seems foregrounded because of the automatic contrast to the surrounding vocables. One yodel heard in Koppl, for example, was sung by a group of four local men and had only one word, actually two words in one syllable, which appeared as the last note of the yodel: *schneit's* (it's snowing). Another yodel, "Der Kuckuck" (The cuckoo) sung by the Koessners, has *kukukukuku* as the last five syllables of the yodel, all sung on one note. In "Der Kuahschroa," words appear only toward the end, where the cow's name is called:

> Hei Rickl,
> hei Rickl,
> hei Rickl,
> hei Rickl,
> Feuch!

Some yodels end with the phrases *üba d'Alm*—in this dialect, (*al*) is like (*o:f*)—or *wohlauf da Alm,* which not only repeats the idealized setting almost all yodels evoke in their singers' minds but also provides a conventionalized formula for ending together, especially in a three-part yodel where the syllabification does not match. Rather than taking these conventional formulas as clichés, it is more productive to study how they rhetorically foreground ideas that are important to yodelers.

The text of "Flachau," for example, is powerful for the Koessner family because the song provides tones, harmonies, and words that have been shared throughout the family. The words allow for still more articulate metaphorical expression of shared values concerning the area, its agricultural richness, and the lively attitudes of its inhabitants, especially in defense of their most valued treasures: grass and women.

> Und in Flachauertal, da geht's kreuzlustig zua:
> hat da pfarra nia g'heirat', is a no a Bua.

CHORUS (yodeled):
  Djo-e iti-ju-i-a,
  Diriti-ju-i-o, etc.

Und in Flachauertal, bei der ersten Stiegl,
und da geht a scho an, da frisch' Buama-Zügl.

CHORUS

Und in Flachauertal wochst a greana Wosn,
und do derf holt koa fremder Bua eini Grosn.

CHORUS

When the family is away from home visiting, especially under jolly circumstances, they are likely to add another verse:

Und a frische Moas Bier hot'n Foam an weissen,
und heut gehn ma nit Hoam bis uns aussischmeissn.

(And in Flachau valley there are great times:
the pastor [priest] has never married, he's still just a young man.

And in Flachau valley, by the first stile,
A parade of energetic young men is already beginning.

And in Flachau valley grows a green meadow,
and there a young stranger is not allowed to get a single blade of grass.

And a fresh mug of beer has a white foam,
and we're not going home today til they throw us out.)

The first three verses are the central part of the song, the fourth appearing only as a friendly signal of enjoyment while drinking with friends. The song suggests, but does not describe, illicit sex. The implication is that the priest would be married if he were not a young man, someone (the priest?) is trying to get past the barriers and curbs placed on the behavior of lusty (*frisch*) young men, and the declaration that nonlocal herdsmen are not allowed access to the local grazing lands. Because of the connotations of the first two verses and what I took to be the familiar sexual innuendo of the third, I asked the Koessners whether they thought verse three was really concerned with protection of Flachau grass. Their response, laced with heavy laughter, was a simultaneous burst from four people:

Hermann: Certainly, certainly!
Elisabeth: Of course that's it!
Hannes: Well, it means that the young men from other communities will not be tolerated if they. . . .
Anneliese: He understands it already my dear; there's no need to say it.
Hannes: . . . try to graze among the local girls. How do you call them in English? (Speaking in English) "cow-ladies," perhaps?

Everyone in chorus, laughing in English: Cow-ladies! cow-ladies! That's it!
No one may have our cow-ladies!

In addition to discussions about the meaning and background of titles
and texts, the Koessners' conversations range widely over a number of
areas of interest to folklorists. There are references to customs and food-
lore; many examples of words and phrases used before, during, and after
drinking schnapps; proverbs and proverbial expressions (e.g., "Du hast
leicht lachen—Du hast kein Schmalz kaufen"),[8] along with discussion and
arguments over their meanings; and incidental but extremely important
comments on yodeling and yodel esthetics.

For example, one hears faintly, after one yodel that had gone slightly
off-key, the single word *furchtbar!* (terrible) followed by a solemn silence.
At the end of other songs there is a flurry of several people talking at once,
each pointing out a note that another had missed. After making several
false starts on a yodel that Anneliese and Elisabeth appeared to know better
than Hermann, the three went on into the yodel and the two women began
to laugh and had to stop. Hermann finished the entire yodel alone and
then yelled—without taking a breath—"And after all that, *I* was the only
one who could hold out!" After starting a yodel, Hermann noticed that
Elisabeth, Anneliese, and Hermi were almost strangling on the high notes.
Pausing, he asked innocently, "Ist's hoch?" (Is it high?). The others, almost
choking, responded "Ja, bissel hoch" (Yes, a little high).

The ability to sing loud and long is something to brag about within the
family, although it is not the feature most stressed in singing for formal
occasions outside the home. At home, both the songs and the banter tend
to stress personal commitment, the ability to sing loud, and the humor of
the entire situation. For example, a yodel, led by Hermann, had just been
sung at maximum volume and high pitch, and the singers' faces were red
with exertion. Directly at the conclusion of the song came the following:

Hermann: Sharp! That was a good one!
Toelken: You sang so high, my glass broke!
Hermann: Hear that? His glass is. . . .
Anneliese: But Dad, you got off-key!
Hermann: No, I did *not* get off-key. It wasn't off key. Boy, it was *not* off!
Anneliese (screaming): Ach!
Elisabeth (laughing): The main thing is for it to be loud.
Hermann (with mock seriousness): Yes, it *was* loud all right.

Such light-hearted interchange to cover embarrassment over singing off-
key is nicely juxtaposed to brief, quiet comments heard at the end of several yodels—"a nice yodel, not long," as well as explanations about variations in ways of singing the same yodel ("I'll tell you one thing, in a yodel,

the text is not always exact"). Such comments give proper testimony to the existence of a range of esthetic and functional expectations among yodelers that go beyond the level of joking. When I inquired further and asked pointed questions about the meaning of yodeling itself, I found more evidence of an active awareness and an articulation of values. The following conversation ensued in response to my question, "Why do you yodel, really? What is yodeling for you?"

> Hermann: Well, now, these yodels were originally used for practical purposes, and afterward, afterward, as an expression. . . .
> Anneliese: . . . and it's a family tradition, something that's in everyone!
> Elisabeth: An inheritance, isn't it? From the forefathers. You get to take it with you!
> Hermann: . . . and pass it onward.
> Elisabeth: See, when you feel joy, then you sing.
> Anneliese: We say, a yodel is an expression of joy that can't be captured in words.

The comments came one on top of the other, with family members breaking in on each other in their excitement over the topic. Later, after a pause, Hermann is heard quietly saying, "Well, somehow we've prepared our voices to yodel. It's improvised family singing." And his son-in-law Hannes adds, "But beautiful!"

Other observations, such as "O, der is wahr schön" (Oh, that one is really beautiful), as well as unspoken but easily observed nonverbal behavior (facial expressions of relief, satisfaction, and open joy while a yodel is being sung), are further indications of a shared esthetic system that is more to be perceived in actual performance than to be found in philosophical statements. It is of central importance to recognize that there is a shared esthetic system, however, because precisely in this area can performances at home be compared and contrasted to the beautified performances on commercial recordings; it is the difference between inside and outside esthetic systems operating upon performers and not a matter to be defined in terms of kitsch or any other extraneous evaluations. Of course, it is within this intensely shared system that metaphors, connotations, and nuances are naturally meaningful. Because this system is most fully engaged and functional in the performative context and its principles are almost never articulated except in passionate explanations to outsiders, it is evident that an understanding of natural contextual factors is important to perceiving and appreciating music and its language.

Clearly, if the Koessners are in any way typical of singing families, shared metaphorical possibilities are only a small part of the whole range of signification in folksong, for many important signals or meanings are held together and expressed by significant syllabic arrangements and tones without employing metaphorical words. The whole network functions connotatively in a complex of interdependent—intertextual, in the broadest sense—cultural meanings. If we change our focus to a whole village, a district, or a country, the data become more diffuse, although it is likely that singers who share the same general cultural area will be aware of each others' frame of reference. In terms of yodel-singing in Austria, for example, particular details are most evident within a family like the Koessners, but it is also likely that yodelers in other families, in other villages, in other valleys, and in other provinces share much of the same attitude and value system.

Indeed, this shared repertoire becomes evident when yodelers and singers from different areas come together. They know many of the same yodels, even though the words or yodeled syllables differ somewhat and the styles may diverge. Some areas, for example, the Steiermark, allow for a brief series of descending falsetto notes to be appended to any yodel as an end-marker, whereas the Koessners use this device only at the end of cow calls (and they pretend nausea when they hear anyone do it otherwise). What the singers share more intensely than notes is a cultural background in which yodels are serious forms of expression. One aspect of this background has been the experience or the reminiscence of life in the mountain meadows, a way of life now limited to a very few people indeed.

The following yodel is found all over Austria, probably because it exploits some understood meanings of the *Alm* experience. It is less metaphorical than connotative or suggestive, for its meaning is chiefly triggered by accumulated human experience, interpreted culturally. The version given here is a hybrid, for it was sung by Hermi and Anneliese Koessner, who learned it from their mother's family repertoire, and Christl Klappacher from nearby Niederalm, who learned it in her family. The words are not exactly the same, but the meaning is consistent. The yodel is divided into three discrete segments. Verse 1 is to be understood as sung by a young man; verse 2 is a young woman's response; and part 3 is a position-marker yodel with no words, the kind that farm people sing when they are working in the woods or fields and want now and then to let others know of their location. The understood scene is in autumn, when the herds (usually decorated with evergreens, flowers, bells, and tinsel) are brought back down to the villages, and young people return to their families. For those who have formed romantic liaisons or close friendships, it can be a time of sadness. As farm families are reunited with their children and cattle, the youngsters are deprived of each other's company.

Pfiat di Gott, schiane Alma,
Pfiat di Gott, du schians Gläut, tra la la;
    djo-e-i-ti-ri
    djo-e-i-ti-ri
    djo-i-di-ri.
Pfiat di Gott, du schians Dianei—
Zu dia hat's mi gfreut, tra la la;
    djo-e-i-ti-ri
    djo-e-i-ti-ri
    djo-i-di-ri-huljo,
    dri-huljo drai-hu-la-ro
    drai-hu-la-ro dri-huljo,
    dri-ri-ri-rai-hularo,
    frisch auf da Alm.

Pfiat di Gott, schiana Jaga,
Und du bist iatz dahi, tra la la;
    djo-e-i-ti-ri
    djo-e-i-ti-ri
    djo-i-di-ri.
Meine Augn steahn in Wassa,
Load is ma um di, tra la la;
    djo-e-i-ti-ri
    djo-e-i-ti-ri
    djo-i-di-ri huljo,
    dri-huljo drai-hu-la-ro
    drai-hu-la-ro-dri-huljo,
    dri-ri-ri-rai-hularo,
    frisch auf da Alm.

(Position call without words, yodeled in three-part harmony, to say, "I'm here.")

(Farewell, beautiful mountain pastures,
farewell, you beautiful sounds, tra la la;
farewell you beautiful young woman,
coming to you has delighted me.

Farewell, handsome hunter,
And you're now gone far away, tra la la;
my eyes are full of water,
I am suffering because of you.)

(Position yodel: "I'm here.")

First, the boy bids farewell to the meadows and the sounds (mostly cowbells) associated with the summer life on the *Alm,* using a term normally employed when talking to people. "Pfiat di Gott," dialect for "Behüte Dich Gott" (God protect you), signals that he is actually saying good-bye to the young woman in the third line. He has visited her during the summer months, and the meetings have brought him joy. The phrase "frisch auf da Alm," a common yodel formula, suggests that the meetings have not been primarily for intellectual reasons: *frisch* means "vigorous," "lusty," or "lively."

The young woman's response begins directly with her farewell to him, undisguised by nostalgic references to the scenery. Although his comment that she has brought him joy shows *his* central concerns, her comment that he is now *dahi* (away), that he is in another valley and thus not likely to be encountered, reveals *her* sense of abandonment. Why does she not share the positive recollection of a nice romantic summer? She describes herself as weeping and suffering because of him, and certainly the contrast might be a typical one: The man has had his fun, while the woman has fallen in love and experiences a sense of loss. For many singers, however, the distinct inference is that she is pregnant, even though there is no metaphor or figure of speech that might lead directly to that conclusion.

Most eloquent in the song is the wordless signal: I am here. No matter whether the song describes just a wounded heart or suggests something more complex for the girl, the heaviest meaning occurs in the part with no words; it communicates the idea that she is waiting for him and signaling to him, no matter what has happened.

Such an example transcends articulated metaphor and yields connotative understanding based on the scenes and frames of action as they reference personal, local experience. To be sure, there is the heavily suggestive meadow setting found in romantic songs across Europe, connotative possibilities like *frisch,* and the venery theme (hunter-lover) that has been popular in European tradition since before Chaucer's time. But the full impact of such a song—which regularly brings tears to the eyes of singers and audiences in mountain villages in Austria—cannot be appreciated through such academic observations. At this level, it is clear, the imagery is an articulation of the living culture, not of a specific lingua franca used in a text. One function of fieldwork should be to achieve some kind of contact with and understanding of this dimension of folksong meaning. Indeed, one wonders what we would know about any of the famous old ballads had we access to similar fields of cultural reference. What is needed is more work like the studies of the Stewart and Robertson families, which are excellent examples of the depth of understanding that can come from lengthy and full interaction with a group of singers.[9]

An example of how fully a culture can maintain a sense of meaning with few words occurs in the following brief yodel. When sung, it usually brings smiles, and sometimes open laughter, from singers and audiences. The question is, of course, what are they laughing at?

> Hops hol da re, huljo-i,
> Hol da re, huljo-i,
> Dü dü dü dü dü dü dü
> "Pass auf!" hat's g'sagt ("Watch out!" she said);
> Hops hol da re, huljo-i,
> Hol da re, huljo-i,
> Dü dü dü dü dü dü dü
> "Pass auf!" (Watch out!)

For several years I asked about the song but received only smiles and the impression that its meaning should be self-evident. More recently, as Anneliese was singing some of her favorite family songs to me, she said, "Oh, have I sung the old contraceptive song for you?" and I was able to put the song in its place. In the absence of contraceptives up in the mountain meadows, and lacking the inhibiting presence of family members, the traditional form of birth control was "watch out!" In this song, moreover, it is the unmarried (virginal?) girl who must remind the boy to watch out. The neuter gender in *hat's* refers to *das Mädchen* or *das Dirndl*. Does this mean that all singers of the song share this interpretation? Probably not, but it does indicate the extent to which shared attitudes can provide a sense of meaning for some singers. What is humorous about the song, given that people often laugh at topics that express anxiety, fear, or concern for values? This particular sort of contraception has not been notably successful, and, in looking back over the various groups I have heard singing the yodel, it is difficult to recall any in which the people present had not been affected directly by the reality of romance *auf da Alm.*

More fully articulated and richly metaphorical than the spare "Watch out!" is "The Mower's Song," which voices a steady sexual contentment in an agricultural mode:

> Wo is denn der Mahder
> der mei Wiesei mahd?
> wia wetzt er so selten!
> wia mahd er so schtad!
>
> Er sitzt sö in Schattn
> und raucht an Tabak,
> und weil a eahm so schmeckt
> ja drum is er so schtad.
>
> Hab gestern erst dangelt,
> und heut no nia gmahd;

i bins halt der Mahder
der gar so schtad mahd.

(Where is the mower
who will mow my meadow?
How seldom he whets!
How smoothly he mows!

He sits there in the shade
and smokes tobacco,
and because it tastes so good to him
that's why he's so smooth.

I hammered for the first time yesterday,
and I haven't mowed yet today.
I'm indeed the mower
who mows so smoothly.)[10]

The metaphor of mowing someone's meadow is a familiar one; in particular the terms *wetzen* and *dangeln* (standard German, *dengeln*) refer to
the readying of a sickle or scythe for action, the latter indicating the ham-
mering of the edge until it is even. Because *dengeln* can also mean to
castrate an animal, a sexual field of possibility is readily connected with
the word. Here the mowing instrument is kept in good shape by someone who knows how to use it well and smoothly, but another, more sin-
ister application for "knife" and "scythe" is discussed in chapter 6. The
reference to smoking tobacco appears as a metaphor in other German
songs of courtship and seduction. In a song called "The Gypsy Life Is Fun,"
a young man says:

"Young girl, do you want to smoke some tobacco?
You don't need to buy a pipe:
There hidden in my bag
Is a pipe and smoking-tobacco."

"The Mower's Song" can have at least two interpretations according to
singers in the Salzburg area. If the whole song is envisioned as sung by
one persona, there is humorous irony in the mower saying, in effect, "Who
is it who mows my meadow so well and so smoothly?" and then bragging
that he does it himself. But most people assume the first two verses are
"spoken" by an amorous woman, and the third is the patient, steady ad-
mission of the male suitor that he's not in any hurry. The Fuchsberger and
Koessner families remember being stunned when a very proper older
woman sang the song in the company of other Austrian singers at an
evening of *Heimatpflege* songs. "How could she have sung that song without knowing what it meant?" one of the men queried, and everyone smiled
and sang it for me again.

It would be difficult, if not impossible, to construct a list of terms and subjects that could consistently be expected to produce certain meanings in all vernacular texts. At the same time, it would also be difficult, even impossible, to ignore the rich possibilities presented by connotative language and culturally loaded scenes when talented singers articulate the central values of everyday life for their neighbors, family members, and friends.

5

"I sowed some seeds all in some grove"
Multiple Metaphors and Meaning

Although vernacular singers have not developed an analytical jargon for their poetic and musical concepts, their songs testify to a striking command of language nuance, generic coherence, dramatic impact, and cultural imagery. Naturally, as with all the arts, some practitioners are more talented than others, some more adept at memorization, others more at ease with recomposition, some perhaps more passionately involved than others. In any case, I do not consider the poetic ability demonstrated so widely in folksong to be either coincidental or exceptional, nor is it an example of *"gesunkenes"* (debased) talent. Rather, as the many studies of oral literature have shown, the ability to use metaphor is based on active language usage, and singers, by virtue of singing, are likely to have been very active. Indeed, if many had not had great poetic ability through the years, and if the many listeners had not understood, appreciated, and encouraged that ability, metaphor could not have survived as a central feature of folksong. If talent had not been widespread and had not been passed down through time, the examples we find would not be so coherent and consistent.

Birds and plants appear so regularly in folksong that they are often classified among the commonplaces. Yet their appearance is often closely associated with plot and meaning, instances so consistent that they argue for a closer look at the function of these elements as more complex and central than one would expect of cliché, commonplace, or everyday scenery. For example, in narrative ballads, birds most often occur in particularized thematic contexts, and one of the most common of these is sexuality-seduction; Renwick has written persuasively about the appearance of larks, cuckoos, and thrushes, for example.[1]

Even more widespread are two other ballad situations: birds are strongly associated with death and function as messengers that carry dramatically significant information. Considering the extensive folklore about birds in

England and America—for example, a bird is a death omen if it flies in a house or, in certain situations, if it flies overhead; birds carry the souls of departed persons or bring the souls to newly born babies; and birds bring information ("a little bird told me")—it would be wise not to overlook the strong possibility that the appearance of a bird in a ballad can suggest a rich constellation of ready associations that will direct how listeners understand the development of the plot. It is unlikely that singers would use an image so rich in associations if its implications ran counter to the plot, for such a usage would impede meaning and essentially undercut the song's internal logic and narrative coherence. Of course, there are instances of incoherent metaphors being used to create tension or undermine the apparent meaning of a plot, as is the case with "The Cambric Shirt" (chapter 6), but in the main, consistency of metaphor is the rule in ballads.

In the ballad "Young Hunting," a bird appears prominently in many versions, even the so-called fragmentary ones, which would lead to the suspicion that the bird, for many singers, has some central function in the ballad's meaning.[2] After she kills the protagonist, the murderer invites a bird to come to her:

> "Fly down, fly down, little parrot," she cried,
>   "and come perch upon my knee;
> Your cage it will be made of the fine, beaten gold
>   and the bars made of ivory."
>
> "I won't fly down, Lady Marget," he said,
>   "nor perch upon your knee;
> For I just seen you murder your own true love—
>   you'd kill a little bird like me."
>
> "Oh, how I wish I had me a new cedar bow,
>   and an arrow to fit my string;
> I'd shoot you right through that neat little breast
>   that looks so bright and green."
>
> "But you ain't got no new cedar bow,
>   nor an arrow to fit your string;
> So I'll perch right here on the topmost branch,
>   and bitterly I will sing."

The bird functions dramatically as a speaker for the dead man, threatening to bring the information to others; in some earlier versions it actually advises searchers on how to find the body and how to identify the murderer. As Lowry C. Wimberly points out, birds are well known in European folklore as carriers of the soul, and it may well be in this capacity that the bird—only sometimes rationalized into a parrot—appears here.

The bird is also dramatically parallel to the male character in several ways. The woman's phrasing to the bird—"'Fly down, fly down, little parrot,' she cried / 'And perch upon my knee'"—including its offer of plush accommodations, is almost exactly like her earlier invitation to her lover—"'Light down, light down, Lovin' Henry,' she cried / 'And stay all night with me.'" In this version the two sets of lines even rhyme. Admittedly, the device is not found enough in other versions to argue for it as characteristic of this ballad, but in many versions the two invitations are very close. Just as the man refuses to "light down," the bird declines to "fly down."

The bird image is suggestive enough to offer a rich field of meaning. The bird as messenger, as possible carrier of the soul, and as dramatic parallel to the male character clearly does at least triple duty. The simultaneous roles argue for a function far more complex than would be expected from a commonplace decoration (chapter 7).

Plants have similar usages. Like birds, they appear in a number of songs, but when combined with important human actions their function becomes more specifically dramatic. Plants are, of course, common in folk medicinal beliefs, and several ballads indicate that the use of some plants produces abortion. In "Tam Lin" (Child 39), Tam Lin erroneously accuses Janet of pulling a rose in order to abort her pregnancy with his child. As an earlier audience would have recognized immediately, however, the rose in English folklore was associated not with abortion but with female genitalia and active sexuality. The ballad drama of "Tam Lin" focuses not on abortion but on pregnant Janet's vigorous actions in recovering her lover from the fairy world, an assertion of life, not death, quite consistent with the traditional associations of the rose. Some irony is produced when the audience apprehends the heroine's actions before her lover does.

Pulling or plucking a flower, fruit, nut, or branch is almost always followed in English ballads by the appearance of an aggressive male. Often there is an attack, either violent or seductive, or else there is a scene with sexual interaction. Because flowers, nuts, fruits, and boughs appear abundantly in English folklore in association with sexuality and fertility, the connection is appropriate, but it is not entirely clear why aggressive behavior should be a part of the complex. In any case, the logic of the ballad's meaning comes not only from the metaphorical possibilities of the plant, but also from the particular way in which it relates to human action. Probably not all listeners will respond in the same way, but the metaphor does fit the action, deepen its potential meaning, and is there, culturally speaking, for those who perceive it. In many versions of "Tam Lin," Janet plucks a rose twice, and both times Tam Lin appears immediately and quite aggressively. In "Babylon" (Child 14), three sisters living in a bower go out picking flowers and immediately a "banished man" appears and starts killing them one by one. I do not believe that these elements appear so consistently by coincidence or because of a particular singer's ability to memorize a text. Nor do they become apparent only because a scholar is looking for them; were that the case, their appearance would not be so consistent.

Common in the Child ballads are the many plants (typically willows, lilies, roses, and briars) that grow on graves, apparently in the role of metamorphosed souls. As Wimberly comments, "One could not ask for better evidence of the primitive character of ballad tradition," and ascribes their use to implicit belief in the transmigration of souls, not to a sense of imagery.[3] Child calls the motif of plants growing on graves a "beautiful fancy" that illustrates the belief that "an earthly passion has not been extinguished by death."[4] But the motif functions poetically with considerably more coherence than one would normally expect of a mere fancy. Although it certainly may be a bit of pagan residue, its continued use suggests that singers—despite the ballad scholars—have considered it an important element of ballad nuance.

Among the many ballads in this category, eight in the Child collection concern two lovers who die and on whose graves plants grow, eventually meeting and twining together. In these ballads several plants are mentioned or described as growing on graves, but by far most versions favor the rose and briar, usually as in "Earl Brand" (Child 7B):

> Lord William was buried in St. Mary's kirk,
>   Lady Margret in Mary's quire;
> Out o' the Lady's grave grew a bonny red rose,
>   And out o' the knight's a briar.

In nearly every version using this motif a verse follows that describes the plants growing together into a true-lovers' knot. The rose almost invariably appears on the lady's grave, the briar on the man's. More specifically, in six ballads ("Earl Brand," "Lady Maisry," "Lord Thomas and Fair Annet," "Fair Margaret and Sweet William" "Lord Lovel," and "Lady Alice") a total of sixty-eight versions have the rose on the woman's grave, the briar on the man's, and end with the true-lovers' knot, while six versions of the same ballads reverse the sexes (usually retaining the knot). In the case of "Prince Robert" (Child 87), versions A and B use birk and briar and love knot, but no connection with gender is discernible. (It is likely that the connection was thought to be obvious.) On the other hand, in "Barbara Allen" twelve versions connect the rose with the woman, eleven of which end with the true-lovers' knot, while fifty-one relate the rose with the man and briar with the woman, most of them retaining the knot. Forty-eight of these fifty-one are American.

With the single exception of "Barbara Allen," then, whenever a distinction in gender is made, the preference is clearly for the identification of rose with woman, briar with man, and some background in English cultural slang and imagery might suggest why. The stiff, thorny briar, evoked in references to thorn and pricking from the time of Chaucer onward, is surely appropriate to the male image, at least as it is conceived in Northern Europe and America.[5] The rose, however, has had an even richer set of associations with the female gender, having been prominent in love divinations and in medication for female ailments since medieval times (chapter 2).[6]

Because the rose is a flower, it can suggest actions and descriptions that have used flowers as euphemisms or metaphors (for example, "flower of my body" for virginity and "deflower" for taking someone's virginity). Beyond that, the rose—whose blossom is small and hard before maturity, hence, no doubt, the term *rosebud* for a young girl or debutante—opens with maturity and becomes larger and softer as it blooms. In medieval times, the rose was used to refer both to the virginity of Mary and to the central object of male amorous pursuit, as is well illustrated by such works as *Romance of the Rose*. Partridge notes Shakespeare's use of the rose to refer to virginity in such passages as "He that sweetest rose will find, / Must find love's prick and Rosalind." Maria Leach lists the rose as a common pattern on virgins' tombstones and notes that in Wales white roses (presumably for innocence) were planted on the graves of virgins.[7]

With all this as available figurative background, the meaning of the line in Sharp's version of "Poor Nell" is evident: "'My virgin rose you stole away, O wed me Sir,' said she." Two versions of "The Irish Girl" have a similar point: "I wish my love was a red red rose and in some garden grew / With lilies I would garnish her, Sweet William, thyme and rue" and "I wish my love was a red ripe rose that in the garden grows / And I to be the gardener that's my love I would know."[8]

Thus the rose image has a long and stable history as a colorful vaginal reference, and it is not surprising that it appears in English folksong and balladry with a statistically heavy relationship to a female character. For this reason, the association of rose with a male character would be potentially confusing. Even so, closer examination of the ballad stories here concerned indicates that the departure from this preference in the case of "Barbara Allen" is probably not a matter of degeneration. All eight share one contextual trait: the frustration of what is known in the ballads as "true love." In each instance the couple is kept from physical union by death. One partner is killed or dies of sorrow, and the other soon follows, usually on the morrow, succumbing to a broken heart. Plants seem to appear in the conclusions of these ballads as complements to or metaphors that

resolve the theme of thwarted love. They not only suggest stasis and re-
pose at the end of an often furious series of actions—an important narrative function that Axel Olrik terms *das Gesetz des Abschlusses*—but they
also become stand-in characters, performing physically what the couple
presumably wanted to but could not and thus forming a suitable dramatic resolution to the tensions central to the story (especially that part of the
story Tristram P. Coffin would call the "emotional core").

Plants do not simply represent souls, for in frustrated true love neither
the audience nor the participants find much comfort in death only, even
in vegetable immortality. Rather, resolution lies in the couple's vicarious
reunion when plants form a love knot, a device traditionally considered a
sign of amorousness and sexual intercourse because of its appearance
when loosely tied. Because the plants actually take part in the dramatic
denouement, their function is thematic as well as symbolic. In some variants, their role is further extended to allow for still another level of meaning when someone (the girl's father, a parish priest, a clerk, a meddlesome
old woman, or a cold wind) cuts them down again, as in one version of
"Earl Brand":

> But bye and rade the Black Douglas,
> And wow but he was rough!
> For he pulld up the bonny brier,
> And flang't in St. Mary's Loch.

It is the male's plant that is considered at fault here, a sign of the sexual
overtones of the image.

The notable departure in "Barbara Allen" from the gender connections
seen in the previous ballads is significant. There seems to be no confusion about where the rose belongs. In the other ballads it is predominantly
on the girl's grave; in "Barbara Allen," it is predominantly on the man's,
and "Barbara Allen" is the only one of the eight ballads in which one of
the lovers is consciously at fault in the other's demise. Barbara has willfully rejected Sweet William's plea to return his love and has told him in
effect to go ahead and die. He does so promptly, and it seems reasonable
that ballad singers have capitalized on this aberration by providing for a
sense of justice at the end of the story, placing the inhospitable or aggressive briar on the grave of the guilty female and the rose on the grave of
her innocent male victim who died in the flower of his youth.[9]

Because most versions that connect the rose with Sweet William are
American, it is also possible that, in the American tradition, the specific
connections between plants and particular gender are deemphasized. Yet
American versions of the other ballads retain the gender connection, suggesting that the tradition is far from dead and that a consistency remains

in the employment of plants to denote gender in one instance and imply judgment in another. On this basis, it is likely that ballad singers have worked from a body of traditional images that may be used variously. A fair amount of conscious artistry is also likely, at least in the instances discussed here, rather than simple knee-jerk references to a stock of familiar stanzas. If it is indeed just a matter of borrowing, it is a selective and coherent process and demonstrably satisfying on poetic grounds to a traditional audience, which would share and understand the connotations—perhaps almost subliminally. The system of reference is consistently applied and based not on explicit description in the ballad text but on folk traditions about plants and their possible range of meanings.

Some ballad metaphors are so rich in divergent possibilities that they can be termed "multivalent." They are employed in scenes of such recognizably heightened or intensified human concern that when their traditional associations (e.g., the rose with both sex and death) are brought to bear, they have the capacity to excite a broad range of implied meanings not mentioned overtly in the text. M. J. C. Hodgart suggests that ballads are less like linear plot sequences and more like plays or film montages. They contain little explanation, little detail, and almost no data but have a great deal of pointed and heightened dialogue and visual image that is presented as if listeners already know (or can quickly perceive) the story's basic situation and dilemma.[10]

In such a highly suggestive narrative setting, the associations in traditional metaphors help establish a deeper recognition of cultural meaning for folksong audiences. Because these metaphors appear in different contexts (where, for example, a rose might suggest death on the one hand or sexuality on the other or alternatively and ironically both), the term *multivalent* calls attention to the multiple possibilities of meaning as well as the metaphor's capacity for ambiguity in its most positive poetic sense. Beyond that, the metaphor is not so much a part of a sequential structure as it is "excited" and contexted by that structure. Folksong metaphors are aspects of how singers engage meaning with performance. They are more elements of texture than of structure, and for that reason the term *textural formula* can be used to characterize them. In some instances, they can even take over the structural role in ballads that narrative sequencing usually fills.

Otto Holzapfel uses the term *epic formula* to indicate the phrases in ballads that go beyond denotative or simple descriptive functions and actually become parts of the dramatic meaning—foreshadowing and highlighting important actions and processes.[11] Although this is very close to the position I take in this book, I feel that the term *epic* in English implies a complex narrative sequencing. Instead, I want to call attention to the fact that metaphors function in a number of ways. Some may have to do with story structure and narrative style, but most have to do with a shared range of textural understanding among the members of a folksong audience in which the song is understood and used.

In some ballads, as I have indicated, metaphor is used as a powerful way to resolve complications of the linear plot; the physical twining together of rose and briar into a true-love's knot brings the lovers together in a physical union denied them in life, and the emotional dilemma is resolved. As in "Young Hunting," a metaphorical image at the close may also clarify or deepen the meaning of a parallel scene near the beginning. In some other ballads, however, the metaphor is so strongly presented that it takes the place of a plot sequence, losing neither the story's complication nor its resolution. For example, most versions of "Captain Wedderburn" develop a lengthy dialectic in the form of double-entendre riddles that Wedderburn must solve before he can realize his goal of bedding the lady. As the resolution of the riddles is slowly accomplished, so is the resolution to the ballad narrative. The woman's name is now Mrs. Wedderburn, and she sleeps next to the wall, a neat if overbearing image of subordination to the winner of the match.

"The Riddle Song," found widely in the United States as a variant (or forerunner) of "Captain Wedderburn," dramatizes exactly the same rhetorical situation and the same resolution without the complex narrative structure. Both the longer narrative versions and the shorter, "lyric" versions present essentially the same event, the same attitude, and the same resolution. Yet the shorter one carries the interactive situation only, and the audience must supply the meaning, aided by the metaphors, by the important resolution in the last line and (in some instances) by the way the song is performed. Many, of course, hear in the song only a naive courtship scene in which two lovers pose pretty riddles to each other. Because the result in any case is a baby, however, the song still retains the same meaning, even though some may perceive it antiseptically or less sensuously. The multivalence of the metaphors allows for the metaphoric dramatization (not necessarily a narration) of an important and recognizable human event, whether or not it is overtly phrased in a sequential narrative structure. The dramatic resolution of a riddle sequence is the resolution of the emotions, anxieties, and questions of courtship.[12]

Similarly, virtually every version of "The Lass of Roch Royal" (Child 76) expresses concern about who will provide clothing and support for a pregnant young lass and be the father of her potentially illegitimate child. Because even "fragments" of the ballad almost always feature this concern, and most American versions focus on it primarily, it likely is, or has become, the ballad's primary human issue. In the narrative sequence, the question of who will provide, protect, and marry is resolved when Lord Gregory's mother denies the lass's entry into Gregory's castle and sends her off into the storm. The answer, as sequentially dramatized and suggested by the more abbreviated versions, is the same: no one. Again, whether the ballad consists of twenty or thirty narrative verses (as is the case with the English-Scottish versions) or whether the song is sung as a two-verse lyric dialogue (as is most often the case in America), the same question is set up and resolved. Moreover, a new, expanded set of options for meaning emerges in the American versions, although they are phrased in almost identical terms to those of the equivalent verses in England. Rejecting the idea that she even needs a man at all, the woman's persona strikes a more optimistic and self-sufficient stance:

> Who's gonna shoe your pretty little foot?
> Who's gonna glove your hand?
> Who's gonna kiss your ruby red lips?
> And who's gonna be your man?
>
> > CHORUS: Who's gonna be your man?
> > Who's gonna be your man?
> > Who's gonna kiss your ruby red lips?
> > And who's gonna be your man?
>
> Papa's gonna shoe my pretty little foot;
> Mama's gonna glove my hand
> Sister's gonna kiss my ruby red lips,
> And I don't need no man.
>
> > I don't need no man;
> > I don't need no man;
> > Sister's gonna kiss my ruby red lips,
> > And I don't need no man.

The progression from shoe, to glove, to lips (all of which carry considerable metaphorical power in and of themselves) carries the audience's attention closer and closer to the real issue: Who will be the woman's romantic partner? That key question is then intensified by "his" repetition of the question in the first chorus (as "her" negative response is intensified by the second chorus). As is the case with question-answer jokes, the question-and-answer format itself provides a rhetorical frame of uncertainty, which is resolved by the provision of an answer that clearly responds to the emotional theme of the question in a culturally meaningful way. Dramatically, rhetorically, both narrative and lyric versions thus achieve the very same ends.

Beyond that, the shorter version allows for yet other possible understandings for this dramatic tableau. I have heard several singers comment on their understanding of the song. Some typical assumptions about it are that (1) the young man hopes to court her, but she refuses his attentions by saying that her family provides for her well enough; (2) her brother asks who will support her now that she is pregnant, and she assures him she will simply stay with her family and rely on their love and protection; (3) a young man is going away and asks his lover who will be her sweetheart while he is gone, to which she replies that she will be faithful to him and stay with her family; and (4) a man recalls with irony what a previous sweetheart had told him (that she would remain faithful during his absence, after which she had betrayed him).[13] The shorter American versions clearly lose the irony of Lord Gregory's mother turning the pregnant girl away from the door, yet they have developed additional possibilities for irony or humor. It is hardly a case of deterioration; the metaphor itself is so tightly structured that no further narrative detail is necessary.

So central is the organizing metaphor, the textural formula, to the establishment of meaning in folksongs that in some cases even poor broadsides are distilled into powerful dramatic events when a particularly moving metaphor takes over the meaning of the songs. Such a case is provided by "Two Babes in the Woods" (chapter 1), which seems to have been so popular among British broadsides from the sixteenth through the eighteenth centuries that it may well have provided the origin of the proverbial expression "innocent as babes in the woods." In its early broadside forms, "Two Babes in the Woods" is a sentimental, moralistic narrative of as many as forty verses. A husband and wife die, leaving a substantial sum of money to the man's brother for the support of the couple's two small children. The uncle eventually becomes greedy and, in order to have all of the money for himself, hires two murderers to get rid of the children. One murderer is soft-hearted, fights with the other and kills him, and then tells the children to wait for him in the woods while he goes to town for food. He never returns, and the innocent children starve to death. The ballad ends with a number of moralistic instructions to those in the audience who might ever be given the task of protecting children.

Recent oral versions, mercifully much shorter, have only three verses, and they focus entirely on the plight of the children. The oral distillation was begun in England and carried to America, where "Two Babes in the Woods" became one of the most widely sung lullabies on the western frontier. It is still current in the oral traditions of westerners who are older than sixty. Concern for undefended children in the wilderness has virtually forced out the extraneous family details and established itself as the primary theme of the song. Naturally, a song cannot accomplish such a thing by itself, so once again the ballad's singers' and audiences' sense of meaning have affect the song's ultimate articulation over time. The bal-

lad, probably composed by a single person, has been distilled and intensified into what subsequent singers wanted.

> One day, as I remember, a long time ago,
> Two sweet little babes, their names I don't know,
> Were stolen away one bright summer's day.
> And were left in the woods, or so people say.
>
> And when it was night, so sad was their plight:
> The stars came out, but the moon gave no light;
> They sat side by side and they bitterly cried;
> Two babes in the woods, they laid down and died.
>
> And when they were dead, the robin so red
> Brought strawberry leaves and over them spread,
> And sang them a song the whole night long,
> Two babes in the wood, two babes in the wood.[14]

Such processes of abbreviation led Coffin to suggest the term *emotional
core* for an idea that still persisted after long-term oral editing had cut away
unneeded verses, and I believe the concept is a good one.[15] My point,
however, is the extent to which a central, rich metaphor can bring forth
or suggest a cluster of important shared cultural values and apply them
meaningfully to a scene or event. The story, if indeed there is one, is not
articulated fully; it is implicit, and its intensive scene, saturated with culturally resonant metaphor, is foregrounded.

My concern is with the singing of the ballad in its live, cultural context
and not the text as it may later appear in print as a fossil. In this particular
case, it is clear that the ballad began in printed form and became dynamic in later oral tradition, so the shorter oral versions of the song provide a
better idea of what the song has meant to its many singers. It is difficult
to say whether the song achieved its tremendous popularity and geographical spread because sentimentality had become endemic in the Anglo-
American world or whether the song caught on due to the growing concern for the fates of children during the Romantic and Victorian periods
of liberal political activity in England.

A song's chances of survival are increased when it fits the mood of an
era. In the western United States, the song was almost universally sung as
a lullaby, and older people who grew up with it get tears in their eyes
when they hear it today. They recall how their parents feared that they
might wander off from familiar surroundings and into the plains, deserts,
or darkened forests that surrounded many lonely homesteads until very
recently. They recall family stories about children who did get lost—or
who had to be buried along the trail west—and who remained behind to

be mourned only by the "wolves and wild birds," as the traditional singer Clarissa Judkins of Eugene, Oregon, put it during the 1970s. In such a case, the "story" of the song exists almost entirely in the recollections of its singers, and those memories are direct outgrowths of family experience, legends, anecdotes, personal experiences and interpretations, and also what the person has heard from others who know and sing the same song. The tight dramatic metaphor of the song has the power to suggest a constellation of shared experiences and values interpreted in an intensely personal frame.

Still other employments of figurative language in ballads are more structurally oriented than the preceding examples. "Babylon" (Child 14), for instance, contains a sequence of actions that seems almost insane. Without ruling out the possibility of insane, vicious crimes in ballads, one wonders about the logic of a story in which three girls are attacked one by one and two are stabbed to death. Why do the others not run for help or escape? Why does only the last one think to ask the attacker's identity? Why does the first one not warn the attacker that her brother is in the neighborhood (as the third one later does)? Rather, the macabre event is drawn out like a compulsive ritual. Does the sequence, taken together with the figurative language, suggest something beyond blind, unmotivated murder? The ballad opens with the three girls out picking flowers, the common prelude to attack and seduction. A "banished man" comes up and asks each in turn: "'Will you be a robber's wife? / Or will you die by my penknife?'" Each of the first two girls answers him in his own terms and with his own logic: "'No, I'll not be no robber's wife, / So I must die by your penknife.'" After having had this dialogue with two girls and killing them, he turns to the third, who alters her answer only slightly and brings forth the climax of the ballad:

> "No, I'll not be no robber's wife,
> Nor I'll not die by your penknife.
> For I have a brother, brave and free:
> If you kill me, then he'll kill thee."[16]

The attacker then asks for the brother's name and occupation, and they discover together that he himself is the brother and has just killed two of his three sisters. He takes out his penknife again and kills himself. Although the ballad does not say so manifestly, the scene nonetheless ends with the audience imagining the one last sister surrounded by the bodies of her sisters and brother. Because virtually every version turns on whether the girls will "marry" the attacker (or give up their maidenheads), and because several versions use the familiar plucking of flowers motif, it is safe to assume that sex is just as central here as is murder. Indeed, in some of the Scandinavian analogues to the ballad, the attacker or attackers rape the girls before killing them.[17]

The threefold sequence can be seen as a way of intensifying a metaphorical or symbolic action by repetition: an essentially incestuous act, entering and violating sisters' bodies with a knife (knives and sheaths also appear in other ballads with sexual connotations). The structural metaphor enacts a scene that equates incest with death, suicide, and unspoken misery for the innocent survivors. Thus, the ballad is actually "about" incest as much as it is "about" murder. Just as the German song "Dat du min leevste bist" (chapter 3) dramatizes a sexual encounter in recognizable stages (negotiation-invitation, entrance, ejaculation, and withdrawal) without describing the sex act explicitly, so "Babylon" dramatizes incest metaphorically in an equally recognizable series without naming it: plucking flowers (inadvertent invitation), aggressive encounter featuring a choice between death and sex, male entry into female characters (stabbing), and revelation of relationship after the fact, suicide, survival of one potential victim. The dramatic equation would seem to equate incest with the destruction of family ties, as well as with self-destruction and the survivor traumatized and alone. The irony is powerful because a family presumably protects, nurtures, and includes its members, especially those deemed in need of protection. In this family, a male, who normally would protect the females, has already been separated and banished. Such considerations go beyond the mere plot of an apparently illogical series of actions. As with most good poetry, the plot does not explain or articulate its meaning; rather, it dramatizes it metaphorically, thus necessitating bringing as much to the experience as possible as long as it is not extraneous to the story.

Evidence like this suggests that narrative sequencing alone does not make ballads what they are. Obviously, all ballads have some sort of structure, but the narrative progression itself may constitute an optional dimension that can be employed and may be used more by some singers or in some areas than in others. Narrative sequencing can be used to focus attention, rationalize action, and localize theme, but it is not always the key to dramatic meaning. What seems more important in balladry is the dramatic evocation or recapitulation of a culturally meaningful human event in its emotional terms. Ballads exist through time not because their singers recall all the stanzas and sequential details (an idea that has led us to see shorter versions as incomplete, fragmentary, or eroded) or because singers have remembered the emotional core of a hypothetical text (which may be conducive to seeing the text as more important than the singer), but because singers and their audiences have continued to respond deeply to well-articulated, culturally shared metaphors and dramatizations of human stress, frustration, joy, and anxiety.

Shorter versions of "The Lass of Roch Royal," "Captain Wedderburn's Courtship," or any other ballad need not be seen as signs of deterioration and loss, then, but—at least provisionally—as hallmarks of intensification, distillation, and vernacular recognition of the smallest critical mass that can still evoke an audience's response through the employment of appropriate cultural nuance and metaphor. Ballads achieve their characteristic effect through masterful dramatic recreation of culturally meaningful situations or events. Because human concerns about love, betrayal, family violence, ethnic identity, sex, security, vulnerability, courtship, and death are powerful, we respond deeply when they are made palpable in a dramatic scene with cultural meaning. Because these areas of human concern are seldom unambiguous, and everyone responds to them differently, the poetic devices used are appropriately open to multiple interpretation. Metaphors have the capacity to animate and direct our responses to the situations described or suggested in a ballad. Indeed, ballads may have persisted not because they have successfully transmitted strings of narrative detail, but because—whether narrational or not—they have continued to dramatize powerful constellations of personal and cultural meaning. The multivalent metaphor has played a key role in this process.

6

"Riddles Wisely Expounded"
Poetic Ambiguity in the Riddle Songs

Having seen in the previous chapter how integral metaphors can be to
narrative meaning, we now move to a more complex consideration of the
ways in which suggestive metaphors can be used so skillfully that they
virtually replace the narrative plot with a dramatic scene, for such is the
case with riddle ballads and related songs. The riddles used in these songs
have to be carefully chosen and used, for were they to function in the
way of true riddles—if they playfully blocked the audience's recognition
of meaning—they would be counterproductive in establishing a story line
or presenting implied meaning coherently. On the other hand, deleting
them would make the songs virtually meaningless. The metaphors discussed in this chapter are articulated as if they were riddles, but—as in
the case of the metaphors discussed thus far—their function is to suggest
meaning rather than cloak it. Because their style is that of the riddle genre,
it is instructive to examine just how they work.

Riddling is contexted differently from one culture to another, of course,
but as Frank deCaro has pointed out (following Thomas A. Burns), riddling tends cross-culturally to take place at liminal moments, thresholds
where two modes of existence or custom intersect: courtship, initiation,
death rituals, moments of greeting and getting acquainted, and intercultural relations (e.g., Samson's riddle in Judges 14–15 dramatizes compet-
itive friction with the Philistines at the time of a betrothal).[1] In borderline
experiences like courtship, where two people (and two families) are about
to be united or in initiation or funeral rituals that celebrate the move from
one kind of existence to another, things have the appearance of being or
becoming more than the sum of their parts. There is an overlap—ambiguous, to be sure—between two previously unrelated entities. This unexpected intersection is the basis for riddling: Two ideas not normally considered related are brought into at least partial congruity through
metaphoric exercise. The metaphor causes the audience to consider and

appreciate a previously unrecognized connection or parallel, at least the first time a riddle is asked. Subsequent use of the same riddle seems clearly to be based on the pleasure of savoring and retaining that sense of congruity—unless one wants to argue that humans are so dull that they have to figure out the metaphor anew each time. It is more likely that solving a riddle the first time one is confronted with it requires some metaphorical thought; subsequent occasions are opportunities to demonstrate the ability to remember culturally important figures.

Normal spoken riddles use a particular rhetoric or style seldom recognized by those who use a semiotic or structural approach.[2] A question is asked or implied in which one object or action is described in terms of another. The dramatic interaction of a riddler (who knows something) and a riddlee (who is required to admit not knowing) is in itself an enactment of uncertainty. In this way, riddles use a rhetorical tactic very much like that of contemporary question-and-answer jokes (moron/elephant/dead baby/Polish pope/disabled veteran/shuttle disaster/dumb blonde) that play upon an immediate context of uncertainty, anxiety, or ambiguity by phrasing a question in ambiguous and anxiety-provoking style. Then, in order to make the exchange complete, someone must say, "I don't know."

But question-and-answer jokes are immediate and thus time-bound. Elephant jokes if told today would contain the same incongruities they did in the 1960s, but would not dramatize current cultural and social anxieties. Riddles, by contrast, are far less tied to immediate historical matrices for their content and are instead responsive to broader ongoing themes in the culture, especially those that mark liminal processes and events like maturation, marriage, and death. As Roger Abrahams insists, "One cannot hope to understand riddles within a specific culture until one learns about the imaginative domains of the group." Further, "Riddles rely on the basic metaphors of cultural existence, those conventional tropes recognized implicitly by the membership which bring together objects or ideas or movements in terms of these cultural recognized similarities." Abrahams aptly terms the apparent discontinuities in the phrasing of riddles a kind of "epistemological foreplay."[3]

Ambiguity or apparent discontinuity in riddle songs is contexted not only in the culture's "imaginative domains" but also in a textual context—in the story line, the rhetoric, or expressive load of a traditional song. Usually, characters in the song play the roles of riddler and riddlee, and the coherence (or "fit," in Lyndon Harries's term) is judged not by those characters, but by the song's audience. In these songs, moreover, unlike true riddles, there is a larger dramatic frame. As is the case with most traditional ballads, the audience is placed in the position of the voyeur who seems to have arrived right at the edge of the dramatic scene in time to observe the climactic moment. Not all riddle songs are ballads, of course, but the metaphorical and rhetorical functions remain quite similar.

In riddle ballads, the usual series of montage images in which the action is phrased or implied is supplanted by a series of riddles. The frame in which the sequence is presented allows a rationale for the questions and a sense of congruity when they are answered. For example, "King John and the Bishop" uses death as a penalty for the wrong answer in an attempt to impose a serious dramatic framework on a collection of otherwise ordinary riddles or conundrums, just as Chaucer's use of the frame-story technique lends richness and unity to a group of originally unconnected tales.[4] The result is a ballad in which the psychological dilemma of the bishop is the "emotional core," to use Tristram Coffin's term. As the dilemma is resolved, the characters gain stature. The type is parallel to the Oedipus riddle, in which the question and its answer are almost whimsical out of context but deadly serious in their frame of reference just as in the *Vafþrúðnismál* the riddles are not in themselves ominous but take on a dramatic tension from the ever-present penalty of beheading for the loser of the contest. Odin escapes only by resorting to a neck-riddle, the answer to which only he, the questioner, can know.[5]

In ballads such as "Captain Wedderburn's Courtship" (Child 46), on the other hand, the same sort of dramatic interplay between contestants is turned to humor by their opposite sex and by a threatened "penalty" of copulation or marriage. In this ballad, furthermore, many of the riddles are themselves highly suggestive of the ballad's theme—the attempt of a man to bed a woman ("neist the wa'"). To such questions as "What's higher than the tree?" and "What's deeper than the sea?" the captain replies, "Heaven" and "Hell." But in the Southern Appalachian area, *tree* is often used as either a metaphor or a euphemism for *penis,* as it is in the Scottish original of "John Anderson, My Jo":

> John Anderson, my jo, John,
> When first that ye began,
> Ye had as good a tail-tree
> As ony ither man;
> But now it's waxen wan, John,
> And wrinkles to and fro,
> And aft requires my helping hand,
> John Anderson, my jo.[6]

This connotation of the term is also very likely the key to another meaning of the Faroese riddle: "What tree grows with its roots up and its top hanging down?" *Given* answer: "An icicle."[7]

Among North Carolina loggers I heard the riddle "What's deeper than the sea?" bring the answer, "Vagina—it can't be fathomed." In Child's version A, verse 12, the lady asks for "winter fruit that in December grew" and for "a silk mantil that waft gaed never through." Both of these, phrased as conundrums and with certain simple but vivid differences in terminology, were current among rural men in Buncombe County, North Carolina, in the summer of 1953, and there seems to be no reason to believe they are anything but traditional. The answers were, respectively, "penis" or "baby" and "pubic hair" and are simply derived from the not very subtle suggestions of the figures of speech themselves. What *kind* of "fruit" can be said to "grow" at a time of year when normal fruits do not? What *kind* of silken mantle (French *manteau,* from Latin *mantellum,* a napkin for covering) can be described as not woven (see the discussion of weaving imagery in the epilogue)? Moreover, because *waft* was once a common substantive for a breath of air, there is the possibility of a pun parallel to the "well where water never flowed" discussed later in this chapter.

The fruit that grows in December is also connected with a number of older associations that do not depend on a pun. A child conceived in the erotic (according to folksong tradition) month of May will, of course, be obviously growing in December. The medlar pear, a fruit that matures in winter long after it is picked, was used by Chaucer in the Prologue to the Reeve's Tale (lines 3869–82) to represent the late erotism of what we would now call "dirty old men." And it is a pear tree in the erotic garden of Chaucer's Merchant's Tale in which the young squire Damyan copulates with young May—she being the frustrated bride in a "January-May" marriage. A well-known fifteenth-century lyric describes a young man's "newe garden," in the middle of which is a pear tree. The fairest maid in his town asks him to give her a graft from his tree, whereupon

> And I griffed her
> Right up in her honde (membrane):
> And by that day twenty wowkes (weeks)
> It was quik (alive) in her womb.[8]

Fruits are so abundantly used for their sexual references that they constitute another of the several topics so loaded that their function must be almost assumed rather than found puzzling.

While he gives metaphorical answers to the other questions, Captain Wedderburn responds to these by stating only that his father has such a fruit, and his mother such a mantle. His pointed side-stepping of the concretely suggestive answer in this otherwise clearly stated sequence of riddles indicates that the audience could be expected to recognize both his cute avoidance and the sexual allusions, although we cannot know which of the many possibilities might have entered each person's mind. The story line in "Captain Wedderburn's Courtship" is thus created by a constant metaphorical reference to body parts and passions. A tension is further set up by the disparity between the answer as given and the answer as vividly suggested but unstated.

In "Riddles Wisely Expounded" (Child 1), many of the preceding riddles are found, and most develop the same or similar implications, except in this instance the young maid does stop the advances of her antagonist by answering all his riddles. Her dilemma is the more severe because, depicted as a virgin trying to fight off the forces of evil (sex especially), she must not only give an acceptable answer to each riddle but, in those cases where there are two diametrically opposed possibilities, she must also give the pure and virginal one. Again, listeners find humorous tension between the obscenity inherent in the way the riddle is posed and the almost naive innocence of her answer. Although the characters in "Captain Wedderburn's Courtship" are not so naive, the situation is parallel, while the outcome is quite different.

In still another type of ballad, represented in Child by "Proud Lady Margaret" (47), the thematic combination of death and sex is presented by way of a series of riddles, very much on the order of neck-riddles. In the narrative context of the night visit, a young woman poses questions to her suitor. It emerges from their dialogue that she is both amorous and dangerous, and she attempts to trick him by calling his answers wrong. We are given to understand that previous suitors have lost their lives for giving the wrong answers (or at least answers she would not accept). Ironically, the only successful "suitor" is her dead brother, who knows the right answers. As we have already seen, the metaphorical overlapping of death and sex (often in combination with incest) is far from rare in ballads. The riddling in "Proud Lady Margaret," suggestive of several liminal areas (courtship, death, family relations, and contest for land, among others) deepens the possibilities for complexity of meaning without restricting the ballad to a particular interpretation.

Yet another type of ballad, unlike any of the preceding except for the use of riddles, poses a series of ambiguous tasks that are apparently left unanswered. Specific solutions to each riddle are neither articulated nor suggested, but the riddles are responded to with other riddles, as if in competition. Like the riddles in "Captain Wedderburn," these tasks are suggestive of key issues in the narrative, and on more than one level simultaneously. When there is such coherence—where one level actually enhances or amplifies another—there is good reason to suspect that the song has been developed and sung with some care. Indeed, the dual coherence in most riddle songs refutes the opinions of Gordon Hall Gerould and Lowry Charles Wimberly that ballads tend not to be metaphorical and figurative. It would lend support to James Reeves's notion that folksong uses "a fund of imagery which belongs not to the mind of a single poet but to the hidden emotional life of all who speak and know English."[9] Yet evidence should now be abundant enough that this emotional life, and the metaphors through which it reaches expression, are not all hidden.

"The Riddle Song" ("I gave my love a cherry that had no stone"), a descendant of "Captain Wedderburn," gained a widespread audience in the United States when Burl Ives, and later Harry Belafonte, popularized it on stage and in recordings during the 1950s and 1960s. Perhaps many Americans, no longer participants in the cultural contexts in which these riddles fully resonated but caught by a set of customs that inhibited the expression of sexual matters in public places, simply registered the song as quaint and homey, made up of a few cute riddles suggestive of rural origin. But anyone who recalled the use of "cherry" to mean virginity must have had at least some suspicions about its connection with an egg, a ring, and a baby. Knowing the courting customs of the rural Old World (chapter 3) and of the American frontier (to say nothing of the realities of modern urbia), who would want to insist that the sequence—cherry, egg, ring, and baby—is entirely fortuitous?

The suspicion that the sequence refers to impregnation is strengthened by a variant answer listed by Cecil Sharp. In place of the usual "a baby when it's sleepin' has no cryin'," Sharp notes that a Mr. Thomas's version went, "When the baby's in the belly, there's no cry within."[10] It was probably not coincidental that when I first heard "The Riddle Song" sung by friends near Grassy Branch, North Carolina, a girl sang the first and third lines of verse 1 in alternation with a boy who sang the second and fourth lines. In the second verse, the boy began with "How can there be a cherry without a stone?"; in the third verse the girl began again with her innocent answer, "A cherry when it's bloomin'"; and the last line, which they sang together in appropriate harmony, was, "And a baby when it's makin', there's no cryin'."

That some other versions occasionally use "a story without an end" for the seamless ring does not in the least alter the fact that some traditional singers have maintained a solid coherence of sexual ambiguities in the song. Not knowing of these matters might have led some later singers to assume the song was made of near-nonsense clichés that beg for parodic answers: A maraschino cherry has no stone; a chicken salad sandwich has no bone; ringbinder notebooks have (alternatively, a shaggy-dog story has) no end; and a baby grand piano (or a baby when it's whistling) has no cryin'. But well-attested English language figurative usage indicates that it is not stretching matters to believe that still other sexual images were functioning for many singers and audiences who developed "The Riddle Song."[11] It is, of course, impossible to say whether all these possibilities must have been present in the minds of all the folk singers who passed along their versions of the riddles. On the other hand, given the common understanding of the terms in colloquial language and given the neat coherence often observable in riddle sequences, it is impossible to deny that folk beliefs, colloquial metaphors, and ambiguous figures of speech have been used to construct humorously dramatic episodes dependent on double meanings for their impact. Moreover, the dramatic coherence of the riddles in this song allows for the shorter version to "mean" virtually the same thing as the longer versions.

Double entendre in riddles is neither a new idea nor a recent discovery by scholars. It has been observed for many years, but few have dealt with it critically in print. Archer Taylor comments, "A trick characteristic of riddling at all times has been the description of an erotic scene with the intent of confusing the hearer by an entirely innocent answer."[12] But, in deference to the delicate sensitivities of other scholars (and, one presumes, squeamish publishers), Taylor reproduces only the answers for most of the riddles numbered 1739–49, "Erotic Scenes." Perhaps this scholarly unwillingness to discuss the erotic element in figurative speech has inclined us to overlook or deny its use in folksong, but the evidence is quite clear that interest in figurative language—particularly erotic imagery—has a long and rich history. A few specimens from the Old English *Exeter Book* (from the eleventh century or earlier) illustrate the antiquity and the range of erotic riddling double entendre. There are at least a dozen such riddles in Old English.

> Riddle 37: I saw the creature. Behind it was its belly, hugely distended. It was served by an attendant, a man of great strength, who had accomplished much when what filled it flew out through its eye. It never dies when it must give what is inside it to the other, but this is restored again in its bosom, its breath revived. It creates a son and is its own father. Answer: a bellows.

> Riddle 44: A strange thing hangs by a man's thigh under its master's clothes. It is pierced in front, is stiff and hard, has a good fixed place. When the man lifts his own garment up above his knee, he wishes to visit with the head of this hanging instrument the familiar hole which it, when of equal length, has often filled before. Answer: a key (alternative possibility, a knife).

> Riddle 54: There came a young man, where he knew her to be standing in a corner. The lusty bachelor went up to her from a distance, lifted up his own garment with his hands, and thrust something stiff under her girdle where she stood, wrought his will; both of them shook. The thane hurried; his good servant was sometimes useful; nevertheless, though strong, he always became tired, and weary of the work, sooner than she. There began

to grow under her girdle what good men often love in their hearts and buy with money. Answer: a churn.

Riddle 62: I am hard and sharp, resolute in my going forth, active in my journey onwards, faithful to my lord. I go under a belly and I clear for myself a straight path. The man is in haste, the hero who pushes me on from behind with the help of his dress. Sometimes he draws me out hot from the hole, sometimes again takes me somewhere into a narrow place; the man from the south presses me on vigorously. Say what I am called. Answer: a poker.[13]

Although modern riddles tend to run much shorter than these examples, the double approach is still the same. Sometimes the underlying "off-color" theme is seen in the ambiguity of the phrasing of a single riddle:

> It goes in dry and comes out wet,
> It tickles your stomach and makes you sweat.
> Answer: a washboard.[14]

or:

> The old woman pidded it and padded it;
> The old man took of his britches and jumped at it.
> Answer: a feather bed.[15]

Probably the good Reverend Walter Gregor, in *Notes on the Folk-Lore of the North-East of Scotland,* reproduced the following riddle because he did not understand it:

> It's lang an it's roon,
> An it's as black's coal,
> Wi' a lang and a plump hole?
> Answer: a bottle.[16]

Prose riddles in the form of orally circulating jokes often capitalize on the suggestive context of an ambiguous sequence, such as in the story of the psychiatrist who asked all his patients but three questions: (1) "What does a dog do in your front yard that you don't want to step in?" (2) "What does a man do standing up, a woman sitting down, and a dog on three legs?" and (3) "What is a four-letter word ending in 'k' that means 'intercourse'"? His expected answers were (1) digs holes, (2) shakes hands, and (3) talk. "But you'd be surprised at the crazy answers I get."

The fact that the possible levels of interpretation are not always as blatant as this in riddle ballads does not rule out their use and detection by a group of people familiar with the metaphors and frame of reference. Witness the young girl who in great embarrassment gave the following riddle to Vance Randolph and Mary Celestia Parler, remarking as she did so that it was "not very nice":

> Riddledy riddledy, riddledy, rye,
> Old lady only got one eye;
> Runs in and out of every gap,
> Leaves her tail in every trap.
>   Answer: a needle.[17]

Obviously, her own knowledge of the "other" answer impeded her will-ingness to pose the riddle out loud for the collectors. Without an expla-nation, one can only wonder just what part of the image was the sugges-tive key to the other level; perhaps because of the ambiguous way in which the eye can be described, the crux lies in the second line.[18] In the medi-eval riddles of the cleric Claret, for example, appear the following:

> XX. Hair climbs upon hair as soon as it is dark.—At night your eyelashes keep out the light.

> XXXVII. My riddle consists of living baths, their entrances covered with hair: one washes within, two strike without.—The tongue inside the mouth, and the eyes in their two recesses.

> XXXIX. What I speak of seeks to keep the master's measure in the mistress' hole.—The mistress' ring is a perfect fit on the master's finger.

> XLIV. With one I penetrate, and two hang down behind.—A needle has a single point, and two threads hang from the end [the Latin phrase is *pendet in ano*].

> LVII. Father's thing stands out, something it cannot do in mother's hole.—It is the ring on his finger, at variance wherever he goes.

> LXXXII. A vessel have I that is round like a pear, moist in the middle, sur-rounded by hair; and often it happens that water flows there.—It is only my eye, and I frequently cry.

> CXVIII. The better he bangs me, the sweeter it is.—The thresher and his corn.

> CXX. It is hairy round about, it is pretty in the middle, but at the bottom it wears a little thorn.—The answer is a rose.[19]

I will not argue that these double entendres from another time and coun-try can provide an explicit illustration for why the young girl from Arkan-sas was embarrassed, nor would I push the application of some of these references (*rose, threshing,* and *ring*) to specific images being discussed in this chapter beyond noting that such figurative uses are not rare in Europe, and therefore this direction of inquiry is not misguided. The gen-eral perspective gained from *Clareti Enigmata* is found in a point Peachy makes in his notes for Riddle XX. He observes that the aim of such rid-dles is to evoke "a salacious image in the listener's mind and then to re-lease his inhibition in a burst of laughter by giving an innocent answer."[20]

Certainly, there are many modern examples of this mode, including the question used when initiating someone into the fictitious Turtle Club: "What's hard and round and sticks out of a man's pajamas so far you can hang his hat on it?" "His head." But when suggestive riddles are incorporated into the framework of a drama—such as in "Captain Wedderburn," for example— the function goes beyond a quick release of inhibition and entails the application of a constellation of metaphorical images to a coherent plot. Instead of being "released," the audience is caught because the available possibilities for meaning in the plot are limited, focused, and deepened.

The ballad "The Cambric Shirt," an Ozark variant of "The Elfin Knight" (Child 2), stands as an example of this focusing. A line-by-line examination of the traditional allusions, although hampered to some extent by our lack of full knowledge of the actual qualities of metaphorical expression among all the ballad singers who have sung the song, may suggest the depth and complexity of the riddle ballad form. The following discussion is based on the listeners' willingness to play, to believe that the impossible-sounding items and situations mentioned in the ballad are metaphoric riddles with answers that can be fruitfully sought, recognized, and appreciated because of our acquaintance with our own folklore, including the vernacular resources of our language.

I choose "The Cambric Shirt" as an example because it has not been adequately discussed as a riddle ballad, although both Child and Wimberly called attention to the riddlecraft exhibited in it. It not only illustrates the fourth kind of riddle ballad mentioned earlier, but it also sheds light on the use of riddles in larger contexts generally. In addition, it leads to some insights on the function of metaphor in the construction of folksong meaning. This particular version of the ballad is presented over other possible candidates as a point of reference because it was collected in this century from a prolific singer (Allie Long Parker, of Hogscald Hollow, Arkansas) who had been visited by a number of collectors. The rendition was recorded by Joan O'Bryant, who met Mrs. Parker through Max Hunter and Vance Randolph and visited her often enough to have engaged her in conversation about many of her songs. The alternative lines provided for verses 6 and 7 were explained to O'Bryant as dependent on immediate context. The first option in each case was what Mrs. Parker usually sang, especially in mixed company; she used the second options occasionally when her audience was made up entirely of adult women.

Because one reason for discussing this particular text is its richness of metaphor, an objection might be raised that the example does not really exemplify the range of variants for this ballad. This is a fair consideration, but the version at hand is nonetheless a handy example of the ways in which these metaphors can be combined, and many parallels to its metaphors can be found in numerous other versions. The text demonstrates beautifully that a field of metaphorical possibility exists that some singers use more extensively than others, under varying circumstances modifying their usage of these possibilities according to contextual considerations.

The Cambric Shirt

1. "As you go up to yonders town,
    Rosemary and thyme,
    Go give my love and best respects to that young lady,
    And tell her she'll be a true lover of mine.

2. "Tell her to make me a cambric shirt,
    Rosemary and thyme,
    Without any seam or needleswork,
    And she shall be a true lover of mine.

3. "Tell her to wash it in yonders well,
    Rosemary and thyme,
    Where water never flowed, nor rain never fell,
    And she shall be a true lover of mine.

4. "Tell her to hang it on yonders thorn,
    Rosemary and thyme,
    That never was budded since Adam was born,
    And she shall be a true lover of mine."

5. "As you go up to yonders town,
    Rosemary and thyme,
    Go give my love and best respects to that young man,
    And tell him he'll be a true lover of mine.

6a. "Tell him to buy me five acres of land,
    Rosemary and thyme,
    Between the salt sea and the lay sea sand,
    And he shall be a true lover of mine.

(6b. "Tell him to find my acre of land,
    Rosemary and thyme
    That lies all fallow by the yon sea strand,
    And he shall be a true lover of mine.)

7a. "Tell him to plow it with a muley cow's horn,
    Rosemary and thyme,
    And seed it all over with one grain of corn,
    And he shall be a true lover of mine.

(7b. "Tell him to plow it with his ram's horn,
    Rosemary and thyme,
    And seed it all over with one grain of corn,
    And he shall be a true lover of mine.)

8. "Tell him to reap it with a sickle of leather,
    Rosemary and thyme,
    And gather it in on a pea-fowl's feather,
    And he shall be a true lover of mine.

9. "Tell him to thrash it on yonders wall,
    Rosemary and thyme,
    And for his life let one grain fall,
    And he shall be a true lover of mine.

10. "Tell him to take it to yonders mill,
    Rosemary and thyme,
    And every grain must one barrel fill,
    And he shall be a true lover of mine.

11. "Tell him when he has done this work,
    Rosemary and thyme,
    To come to me for his cambric shirt,
    And he shall be a true lover of mine."

"The Cambric Shirt" carries two levels of meaning: the narrative and the figurative. The narrative thread is quite simply restated: The young man sets forth three humorously impossible tasks for the young woman to perform before she can qualify as his true love. In apparent rejection of his suggestion, she indicates her lack of interest (or her assertion of independence) with sarcastic humor by setting him even more impossible tasks before he can be worthy of her efforts. The canceling of impossible tasks by setting one's opponent a series of equally or more impossible chores is well known in the folklore of Europe.[21] But a closer look at this particular manifestation of the motif reveals that in the light of well-known beliefs, customs, and figures of speech the tasks themselves are coherently ambiguous. They appear on the narrative level to be impossible, even nonsensical. Yet on the figurative level—viewed as riddles—they not only have meaning, but their meanings are also linked to each other. This suggests other, richer possibilities for interpretation and perception of meaning than the manifest content of the narrative level can provide.

Because the herbs mentioned constantly in the refrain—where through redundancy one is not allowed to forget them—are traditional funerary plants in Britain (as are parsley and sage, found in the refrains of other variants),[22] and because "Yonders Town" (like "Marble Town" and "Tarry Town") is used as a euphemism for the graveyard in many parts of the southern United States, there is a distinct possibility that the cambric (linen) shirt is a figurative reference to a shroud, especially because a shroud traditionally has no seam. In North Carolina, among men working in the woods, I have heard phrases like "Watch out! They'll have you in a shirt with no sleeves!" used to mean that someone was in danger of getting himself killed. A shirt ("sark") is used as a shroud in Child's version E of "Lord Thomas and Fair Annet" (73), in his version F of "Glenlogie" (238), as well as in "The Gay Goshawk" (96a), although in the latter case the shirt is half of needlework. In version D of "Geordie" (209), the protagonist, awaiting his death, sends a messenger to his lady:

> You may tell her to sew me a gude side shirt,
> She'll no need to sew me mony;
> Tell her to bring me a gude side shirt,
> It will be the last of any.

In the Swedish and Faroese versions of "Babylon" (Child 14) there is a distinct connection between a shirt, death, and the loss of virginity.[23] Parallels are seen in a riddle given by Gregor that describes a coffin in terms of a coat, and in one of the songs provided by Reeves from Cecil Sharp's manuscript, "The Tailor by His Trade" (probably from a broadside), which has the lines: "And now she's dead and her tongue lies still / She must wear the wooden breeches."[24] There is enough such cultural evidence to suggest that one possible field of reference for "The Cambric Shirt" is death and burial, and the next two riddle tasks bear this out. But to force this interpretation on the song when there is also evidence of other possibilities would be myopic, and doing so would blind us to interesting complications. Rosemary, sage, and thyme are equally prominent in British and American folklore for their roles in courtship and fertility. For divining and influencing lovers, for example,

> On St. Agnes' Day, take a sprig of rosemary, and another of thyme, and sprinkle them thrice with water: in the evening put one in each shoe, placing a shoe on each side of the bed, and say the following lines when you retire to rest, and your future husband will appear—
>
> > "St. Agnes that's to lovers kind,
> > Come, ease the trouble of my mind."[25]

Here the customary powers of the herbs are placed in a constellation that includes shoes (well known in connection with sexuality and weddings), water, and a ritual-of-threes. Probably the nature of the young woman's "trouble" can be inferred from the anatomical position symbolized by a shoe on each side of the bed. Maria Leach notes that rosemary was used in both funeral and wedding ceremonies and that brides in Germany wore it to guard against pregnancy.[26] In Sharp's manuscript version of "Rosemary Lane," a young girl in a place of that name is easily seduced by a sailor. Thyme is listed as an aphrodisiac by Wedeck, along with parsley, sage, savory, and camomile.[27] In a Middle English translation of an earlier Latin herbal, sage is recognized as a purgative for the menses and as an abortifacient; moreover, it will "destroie the icche of the cunte and of a mannes yerde if it be ofte wassh ther-with."[28]

The shirt or sark also has associations with lovers. In two versions of "Clerk Colvill" (Child 42), the mermaid is washing a silken sark, apparently as a means of allurement. Child mentions a Gaelic poem in which a seamless white robe is used as a test for an unchaste wife; it will not cover a person guilty of infidelity.[29] A woman of local fame and commodious anatomy was described to me by an Asheville, North Carolina, logger as "just like wearin' a great big wool shirt." In versions B and C of "Jellon Grame" (Child 90), a young girl is told to bring her lover a shirt when she comes to the woods. She replies that she has made (or brought) him three every month (she, of course, is revealed to be pregnant in subsequent verses). The antiquity of the image is seen as well in the references to shirt (*cyrtel, hraegl*) mentioned previously in Anglo-Saxon riddles (numbers 44, 54, and especially 61). The possibilities of metaphorical connection in this category suggest that there may be two distinct answers to the riddle of a linen shirt with no seam. One would be a shroud, and the other would be that part of the female anatomy referred to in "Captain Wedderburn's Courtship" as the "silk mantil that waft gaed never through." Although the two answers might seem to be in opposition when read superficially, they are coherently related to the recurrent double theme of death and fertility discussed in the previous chapters.

It is striking to note that although "The Cambric Shirt" has come to us in numerous versions from widely separated places in the English-speaking world, its imagery has remained coherent. The rest of its verses maintain the sense of impossibility on the narrative level and two ironically contrastive themes on the figurative level. For example, the "well where water never flowed" "nor rain never fell" would be, on the first figurative level, the grave. The *Oxford English Dictionary* lists an archaic use of *well* to mean any pit dug in the ground. Parallel terms are also found in other ballads, such as in "The Three Ravens" (Child 26), in which a knight is buried in "the earthen lake," a usage that may derive from the Latin Vulgate *lacus,* "a pit or den"—itself susceptible of ambiguous interpretation. The *Oxford English Dictionary* notes that *lake* has been used to mean a grave; for example, in the alliterative poem *Erkenwald* (sometimes attributed to the author of *Sir Gawain and the Green Knight* about the mid-1300s) a grave is called the "depe lake" (line 302). A Bavarian-Austrian folksong uses the same image:

> Und wannst mi nit magst,
> Bua, sagst mia na g'wiss;
> Dann spring i in 'n Brunne
> wo koa wassa drinn is.

(And if you don't like me,
Boy, tell me directly;
Then I'll jump into the well
That has no water in it.)[30]

Partridge gives "to take an earth bath" as a slang term for "to die," and the Middle English *Debate of the Body and the Soul* develops a parallel image in reference to the grave. Although such terms seem to verge on the Anglo-Saxon idea of *kenning* (a metaphorical substitute for a common noun, such as *hran-rode*, "whale-road," for ocean),[31] they may actually function in part as euphemisms for death and dying in the same spirit as "Marble Town." In a larger way, due to the richness with which they are brought together and savored in this song, they also function as metaphors that add other, more important emotional and cultural dimensions to the otherwise dismal aspects of death.

On the second figurative level, the anatomical referent of *well* (womb or vagina) should be obvious enough. There seems to be a parallel usage in some versions of "Lord Thomas and Fair Annet" when the heroine, replying to the Brown Girl's query of where she got the cloth or the water to make her complexion so light and clear, says that she got it from her mother's womb (Child, versions A, E, and G), "Aneath yon bouer o bane" in version B, and from a well in her father's yard (G and H).[32] The well image in folklore also juxtaposes death and love in beliefs concerning marriage divination. Hand lists the common tradition that if someone looks down an old well on the first of May and uses a mirror to throw the beams of the sun on the water, that person will see the face of his or her future spouse; those who are to die unwed will see a coffin.[33]

The next enigma is the thorn that never was budded since Adam was born. On the narrative—"impossible"—level, this is a reference to an unnatural thorn bush, but the word *thorn* itself may have a variety of nuances. Although the etymology of the word is not totally clear, it seems to have been derived from a root that designated something hard. *World Dictionary* prefers to derive it from **ster* (to be stiff, to be rigid), whereas Skeat traces it to the Aryan *Tar* (to bore, to pierce), "so the sense is 'piercer.'"[34] Because the figurative answers in verses 1 and 2 seem to be "shroud" and "grave," perhaps the thorn on which the cambric shirt is hung suggests the "body" or "corpse." Again, it is possible that recognition of the figure depends on the listener's ability to detect a kenninglike appellation. The Old English *gar-beam*, literally, "spear-tree," comes to mind as a fortuitous parallel kenning for man or warrior. On the second (sexual) figurative level, "thorn"—and "horn" in other variants—can mean, archaically, any hard protuberance on the human body, and thus the anatomical referent is again clear.[35]

The holy well with a thorn bush growing beside it is a well-known scene in British folklore, and modern beliefs suggest that such wells were used to cure diseases and promote fertility in women. The cure often involved (and still does in some areas of Scotland) dipping a linen (cambric) rag in the well, stroking it on the affected part of the body, then hanging the cloth on the nearby thorn bush.[36] *The Brown Collection* mentions a belief in North Carolina that if a person washes a handkerchief and leaves it on a sagebush to dry, the next morning the initials of his or her future mate will be found on it. Vance Randolph cites an Ozark belief that the hawthorn indicates a bad omen if touched while budded; apparently there is some connection between this action and "sexual misadventures—rapes and unfortunate pregnancies and disastrous abortions."[37] Is the suggestion that touching an unbudded hawthorn might presage normal sexual contacts? Certainly the first three enigmas of "The Cambric Shirt" are worded to make listeners think of a rich fabric of traditional associations, most of them concerned with death and sex.

"The Cambric Shirt" has thus far set one problem on the narrative level, has implied a rather ominous but coherent subject (death) in the riddles given, and has allowed for the comprehension of still another theme (sex) by the use of nuance and ambiguity. The referents on the first figurative level—shroud, grave, and corpse—fit together as coherently as do the anatomical referents on the second and neither level seems thus far to have any overt connection to the "impossible" tasks suggesting invitation and refusal that form the basis for the narrative level.

The woman's response follows a pattern similar to that of the man's approach. On the narrative level, she implies that she is not interested because she sets more and equally "impossible" tasks for him than he had for her. Seen as riddles, they can be "answered" right out of Frazer's *Golden Bough,* although I do not suggest that the ballad therefore comes from the grain fields of primitive Northern Europe. The use of a single seed or grain head, the extreme care taken with sheaves and corn dollies, and the plowing of a ritual row are all motifs familiar to folklorists. Even though (despite the claims of Frazer and Robert Graves) we do not know a lot about what these images really mean, they have nonetheless come into this century in the form of customs, traditions, and figures of speech. Like all elements of cultural worldview, they present not a set of precise references (x equals y) or denotations, but rather a field of related and familiar figurative possibilities.

Reaping with a sickle of leather recalls the flail with which grain was "beheaded" and with which the last sheaf was often threatened during older harvest rites. A custom in the north of Scotland at the turn of the century called for the reaper of the last sheaf to be beaten with flails, and Harry Wenden has suggested that the leather thongs found in the graves of the Danish "peat-bog men" (such as Tollund Man), because they are the same length as flail cords, may have been used for analogous ritual killings.[38] In most of these harvest ceremonies, of course, the linked ideas are death and sacrifice as forerunners of fertility.

The sexual connotations of reaping and mowing are well known, but perhaps a verse from broadsheet tradition will set them in perspective:

> With courage bold undaunted she took him to the ground,
> With his taring scythe in hand to mow the meadow down;
> He moved from nine to breakfast time, so far beyond his skill,
> He was forced to yield and quit the field, for the grass was growing still.[39]

That the sickle should be made of leather makes the riddle both more vivid and susceptible to solution. It is reminiscent of the cowboy image of "swinging the rawhide" (chapter 2). In the broadside "Mutton and Leather," "leather" is used in the sense of "penis," while in the song "As I Came O'er the Cairney Mount" the connection is reversed: "The Highland laddie drew his dirk / And sheath'd it in my wanton leather."[40] The latter is reminiscent of a version of "The Elfin Knight" recorded in Sussex, England, by Peter Kennedy in which the man "reaped it with the blade of his knife" and later "winn'd it on the tail of his shirt."[41] Indeed, in German folksongs, even the sound of a sickle is enough to set the stage for seduction or sexual play:

> Es dunkelt schon in der Heide,
> nach Hause lasst uns gehen.
> Wir haben das Korn geschnitten,
> mit unserm scharfen Schwert.
>
> Ich horte die Sichel rauschen,
> sie rauscht wohl durch das Korn.
> Ich horte mein Feinslieb klagen,
> sie hatte ihr Lieb verlor'n.
>
> (It's already getting dark on the heath,
>   let's go home.
> We've mowed the grain
>   with our sharp sword.
>
> I heard the sickle rustling,
> It's rustling through the grain.
> I heard my girlfriend complaining
> that she had lost her lover.)[42]

The lovers then weave a wreath of roses and clover. The references to cutting and mowing discussed in previous chapters are strong parallels, but the cutting imagery need not always be agricultural. In a fifteenth-century lyric titled "Too Much Sex," a lecher's "chamber swords" are described as having been dulled by their labor, and his "warderer" (truncheon), which had once been strong and vital, is no longer interested in lechery. The Latin word *gladius,* from which we get the word *gladiator,* denoted a sword but connoted the erect penis. Some gladiators, for example Lucius Marcellus, were so famous for being able to lift weights with their penises that they became popular among the women of Rome. In the words of E. W. Heine, "Ein Gladiator ist also nicht nur ein 'Schwer-Schwert-Träger,' sondern auch ein 'Schwer-Schwanz-Athlet'" (A gladiator is thus not only a heavy-sword-carrier [as *gladius* would denote], but as well a heavyweight-penis-athlete.) (*Schwanz* means *tail* in normal usage, *penis* in the vernacular.)[43] See also Partridge's entries in *Shakespeare's Bawdy* under *sword, knife, lance, pike,* and *weapon.* Of course, the figure of the sickle or the scythe in the hands of the Grim Reaper is found all across Europe as a sign of death. Again, both possibilities are in one image.

The impossibility of every grain filling one barrel is plausible if it is seen as a reference to liquid made from the grain (or sperm in a womb). In *Silva Gadelica,* for example, there appears a similar allusion when King Dermot asks his magicians to prophesy the manner in which he will die. One tells him he will drown and that before he dies he will drink ale "brewed of one grain of corn."[44]

Overall, the girl in "The Cambric Shirt" has selected for her riddles tasks that use the traditional references to fecundity, planting, and harvest, and they seem to reinforce the surface (narrative) competition between the two young people by taking advantage of the natural contrast between images of death (which he suggests) and images of life (which she suggests). The distinction between life and death, however, need not be a sharply delineated opposition; the boy's death references are shot through with undertones of sex. But it is significant that the girl's images of plowing, planting, reaping, and milling are all far more salaciously ambiguous than even her suitor's. Their possible interpretations are even more easily recognizable for erotic import.

In Child's version A, the young girl even initiates the advances of the knight by wishing "that horn were in my kist, / Yea, and the knight in my armes two." At once the knight appears by her bed. Both the vocabulary of her wish and her environment are important. It is no puzzle to decide what she means by "aiker of good ley-land, / Which lyeth low by yon sea-strand"; one is reminded of the old proverb, "One acre of possession is worth a whole land of promise." It then comes as no surprise to hear her tell the knight, "For thou must eare it with thy horn, / So thou must sow it with thy corn."[45] To plow or ear another man's land and put a sickle in another man's corn have traditionally meant to commit adultery. "To plow" is still in common usage among men as a crude way of denoting "to copulate with," and its currency as easily understood metaphor is attested to by Shakespeare, among others. In *All's Well That Ends Well* (I:3) is the passage, "He that ears (plows) my land spares my team and gives me leave to inn the crop. If I be his cuckold, he's my drudge."[46] As in "I Sowed Some Seeds" when "I sowed some seed, all in some grove / All in some grove, there grows no green," the girl subsequently becomes pregnant.[47]

The reaping and milling terms in nearly all versions of the ballad are common also in many erotic folksongs and broadsides; the metaphor usually presents a girl who goes to the farmer to see his threshing machine or one who goes to the miller to have her grain ground and then comes home later swearing "she'd been ground by a score or more, but never been ground so well before."[48] Some of the ramifications of the ancient tradition that connects women with milling were explored more than a century ago by a German scholar:

> In symbolic language, *mill* means the feminine member (*mullos,* from which *mulier*), and the man is the miller, and thus the satirist Petronius uses the term *molere mulierem* for cohabitation. . . . Samson, robbed of his strength by his lover, has to grind in the mill . . . on which passage the Talmud comments: under "milling" is always to be understood the sin of cohabitation. For that reason, on the feast of the vestal virgins in Rome all the mills were stopped. . . . It is now clear that every man is a miller and every woman a mill, from which we can understand that every marriage (*Vermählung*) is a milling or flouring (*Vermehlung*).[49]

Chaucer used the ambiguities of milling in relation to human actions in several places. In the Reeve's Tale it comes out vividly in the shifting contexts of millers, real and figurative, robbing each other during the grinding. Two students have brought the grain from their college to a miller to have it ground, and the miller contrives to steal a large share of it during the milling process; the students in turn manage to bed both the miller's daughter and his wife, quite consciously—as Chaucer describes it—as a direct compensation. One student says to the other:

> Som esement has lawe yshapen us,
> For, John, ther is a lawe that says thus:
> That gif a man in a point be agreved,
> That in another he sal be releved.
> Oure corn is stoln, sothly, it is na nay,
> And we han had an il fit al this day;

And syn I sal have neen amendement
Agayn my los, I will have esement.
(lines 4180–86)

The "easement" they get, of course, is sexual; in fact, both of them make
love all night "til that the thridde cok bigan to synge" and they tire and
get ready to leave. Because the daughter reveals to them the hiding place
where they can recover the stolen wheat (which has been baked into a
cake), they feel fully compensated. The miller's loss, both economic and
sexual, is described metaphorically: "Thus is the proude millere wel ybete,
/ And hath ylost the gryndynge of the whete" (lines 4313–14). The Wife
of Bath, talking in her Prologue about her adulterous activities with younger
men, says proverbially, "Whoso that first to mille comth, first grynt" (line
389). And a southern German song warns young men of the energetic
propensities of young women who work or live at a mill:

> Bua, wannst aufs Fensterl gäihst,
> gäih auf kåiñ Mühl!
> d' Mühlmadla håm's Hoppan gwohnt,
> håltens nia still.
>
> (Boy, when you go "windowing" ["courting," see chapter 3]
> Don't go to any mill!
> The mill maidens are used to jumping around,
> They never hold it still.)[50]

The possibility that the girl's references to threshing and milling may also
be suggestive of body parts is strengthened by the verse in Child: "Ye maun
thresh't atween your lufes (palms), / And ye maun sack't atween your thies"
(1:14).

In Child's version A, the knight leaves in haste as soon as he sees that
he is about to get more than he had bargained for and the girl concludes,
in what may be either disappointment or triumph, "My maidenhead I'll
then keep still, / Let the elphin knight do what he will." The Ozark version, "The Cambric Shirt," leaves off the denouement and simply ends with
what appears to be the girl's taunt. From a strictly structural point of view,
the American version lacks both the elfin knight opening and the ending
in Child's version A, and some would thus likely view it as "deteriorated."
From a textural point of view, however, this version has added a new
dimension. Instead of carrying the story out to a stated conclusion, "The
Cambric Shirt" focuses attention on the drama of reflective ambiguities
because each level has connotations of its own and thus the listener per-
ceives that the girl is heard to say no (in her impossible tasks) but may be
understood to mean yes (in her metaphors). If the young man succeeds

in doing the tasks she outlines for him properly, he will have had his "cambric shirt" in the process.

Ambiguity, rather than denotative resolution, is what characterizes "The Cambric Shirt," but it allows for a coherent understanding of the song's meaning—or better, its possible range of meanings—rather than confusion or a feeling of nonsense. Moreover, just as a precise resolution is left up to the metaphorical capacities of the audience, so the music for this particular version leaves the audience in doubt, for each verse and chorus ends not on a tonic chord but on the dominant. Because this is not true for every version, it cannot be listed as a constant element in the song's ongoing constellation of ambiguity, but it can certainly indicate that somewhere along the line of transmission some singers have seen fit to intensify the suggestiveness of the song by manipulating the tune.

William Empson has said that "the machinations of ambiguity are among the very roots of poetry."[51] "The Cambric Shirt" uses multilevel ambiguous riddles to achieve complex dramatic and humorous poetic effects through the skilled manipulation of culturally shared ambiguities. Although other folksong references to connotative traditions are not usually phrased as riddles, they nonetheless present the critical audience with metaphorical puzzles like those encountered in this song. It is my goal to amplify awareness of the possible fields of reference in which cultural connotations may function with poetic coherence.

"The Cambric Shirt," as well as several songs discussed in earlier chapters, employs seemingly opposed images of sexuality and death. As Flemming Anderson has noted, love and death appear to be the most common ballad and folksong topics, perhaps for the same reason that they are prominent in literature: They encompass the most common and enduring concerns and emotions in the culture. Each is common as an everyday process, yet each is difficult to articulate, especially with regard to associated emotions and values. Because of our cultural attitudes toward these subjects, they inspire complex anxiety and uncertainty, feelings well mirrored in the ambiguity of metaphorical language, where nuance and suggestion are more powerful than certainty and definition. Even so, the juxtaposition of sex and death still makes for striking ironies, and some of the reasons may lie in the accumulated religious and agricultural imagery of Northern European culture. For example, many of the church's commentators of the fourteenth century propounded the notion that demons would appear to men in the form of the female succubus, whose wish it was to collect semen and then, in the form of a male incubus, inject it into women. Incubi and succubi were thought by many to be spirits of the dead, or at least the forms of dead persons used by demons to copulate with the dead and with the living, a mixture of spiritual death and living sex that would have had a dramatic effect on people's attitude toward sexuality.[52]

Moreover, most extant folksongs and ballads seem to have enjoyed their most lively social currency from the 1600s to the early 1900s—times of uncertainty and anxiety. The processes of industrialization, whose metaphors appear in a great number of vernacular songs, shifted people's sense of time, reality, and purpose, and humans were compared with machines (not always with flattering results). For the bulk of European populations, which were chiefly agrarian until the mid-1800s, there were the annual cycles of planting and harvest, hot and cold weather, dry and wet seasons, indoor work and outdoor work, and tool sequencing, all of which had to do with survival but none of which could be depended upon to overlap predictably. The period of time between the consumption of last year's harvest and the availability of the new harvest might be negligible one year but substantial the next, for example. One could be starving in the midst of growing food—dying surrounded by fertility—or faced with rat infestations because of a surplus. It was also, until fairly recently, common for people to die young. Not only was infant mortality a commonly experienced dimension of existence, but a greater number of people also died during their reproductive years. Small wonder then that the ambiguities of life and death are articulated so abundantly in metaphors that allow for a multiplicity of response.[53] Life and death are favorite topics; what folksongs and ballads do is to phrase and focus these topics in terms of community concern and cultural value. The riddles of life and death, and not a narrative string of adventures, are what take center stage in the poetic dramas we call riddle ballads.

7

"My golden cup is down the strand"
Wellsprings and Channels of Folksong Nuance

The seemingly impossible tasks given each other by two apparently opposed potential lovers in "The Cambric Shirt" can be understood as com-
petitive riddles suggestive of death and sexuality. In particular, the reference to a "well where water never flowed nor rain never fell," "cistern,
where water never stood or ran," "spring-well, where ne'er wind blew nor
rain yet fell," or "yonder strand, where wood never grew and water ne'er
ran" fits other riddles in the song suggestive of death and burial and can
be taken to be a metaphor for the grave. Parallel to other sexual references in the ballad, the same metaphor or riddle also connotes womb or
vagina.

This complex chain of double-level riddles shows not only a facility for
ambiguity on the part of singers and their audiences but also helps us
understand something that the content of the ballad does not make clear:
If the man superficially takes the woman's riddles to represent impossible actions, he will understand that he is being denied, but if he understands them on the sexual level, he will indeed get his cambric shirt, that
is, the woman herself, who, being without "seam or needlework," can be
metaphorically "put on."

In the parallel song, "Captain Wedderburn's Courtship," the man does
answer the woman's riddles and at the end "beds her next the wall." The
outcome of "The Cambric Shirt" is ambiguous, but it is the woman who
poses more—and more provocative—tasks; if the man achieves his sexual goal, it will be on her terms. The meaning of such ballads resides in
their metaphors more than in their narrative structure. Moreover, the same
kind of imagery appears coherently and consistently enough in other
ballads and songs that a frame of reference larger than that of the immediate song can be assumed as being brought into play by many—although
by no means all—singers. It is also clear that this larger frame is referenced
by figures of speech that are analogous but not always exactly alike in

phrasing, glossary, or meter; thus, terms like *formula, commonplace,* and *code* do not seem adequate to capture the essence of the range, richness, and evocativeness of this system of reference.

Coping with similar issues in the presumed oral poetry of Homer, Michael Nagler notes many instances in Greek epic in which phrases containing the same semantic import are not metrically equivalent and thus do not operate like the formulas posited by Milman Parry and Albert Lord. Nagler therefore moves from a formulaic model to something more reflective of the range of expressive possibilities in the minds of the singers. Using the terminology of Gestalt studies, he deals with recurrent oral phrases as formula "families" in which a particular allomorph is chosen by a singer for its capacity to express a gestalt-based cluster of associated characteristics.[1] Although the argument is refreshing for its insistence on the dynamics of performance, it is problematic, for not only is "a gestalt" difficult to verify clearly, but the theory also rests on theoretical possibilities that presumably were in the minds of past singers rather than on readily perceivable, semantically discussable elements of language that exist widely in the language and culture of contemporary singers.

Otto Holzapfel's term *epic formula* is not entirely satisfactory either, for he defines it as any "stylized action or iconographical gesture which is the result of stylistic concentration," a tidy and succinct description that does not deal with the cultural field of meaning.[2] In 1967, I suggested the term *textural formula* to suggest recurrent figurative phrases whose chief effect was on the texture of the folksong rather than on its structure or meter, and I have used the term accordingly in preceding chapters.[3] In this book, beyond text and texture, I focus on the currency of figures of speech in the shared traditions of the folksong community, as well as on the consistency in usage of those figures in live performance contexts. The works of James Reeves and Roger Renwick, although based primarily on the study of printed texts and using terms like *lingua franca* and *code,* which I have questioned, at least have the advantage of dealing with evidence that recurs in the many texts of folksong tradition rather than exists hypothetically in the minds of unknown singers.

Flemming Andersen uses the term *supra-narrative function* to try to account for the phenomenon in something closer to linguistic terms that take the text and its network of meaning into consideration. For understanding phrases that appear consistently in more than one ballad and have variations in terminology but not meaning, he suggests applying a tripartite model in which the basic narrative idea is parallel to the concept of deep structure, the formulaic lines and stanzas parallel to surface structure, and the supra-narrative elements suggestive of an associative level on which there can be various "actualizations of the basic idea." In order to persist, of course, such actualizations must be understandable and consistent, and Andersen assumes the singers' knowledge of the connotative aspects of these "functions."[4]

He notes that some gestures and actions are virtually always followed by certain details of plot. Thus, the action of sewing or of combing hair, usually followed by a romantic encounter, can be understood as a meaningful, recognizable expression of a lady's secret longing for a lover (secret, probably, in the sense of unverbalized) as well as a figurative prologue to romantic action. Using Nagler's notion of "formula families," Andersen sees the "playing-at-the-ball" scene as a prelude to sexual relationships, which deepens the irony of "Sir Hugh" and suggests romantic jealousy or homosexual incest rather than petulance as grounds for the murder in "The Twa Brothers."[5] He presents the phrase, "He's taken her by the milk/lily-white hand" as a ballad harbinger of rape or seduction, and there are other logically related aspects or nuances: A father may *give* the hand of his daughter, a woman may *offer* her hand, or a man may *ask* for her hand. Andersen suggests that the pulling of a flower is almost always a prelude to sexual assault and relates the action to magic, probably in view of the immediate appearance of the aggressive male, as in "Tam Lin," although, as I have noted in previous chapters, it is just as likely that the flower is a figurative reference to the female genitalia. Andersen also sees sexual overtones in such standard scenes as "x came to y's gate," "he mounted her on a steed," and even "when bells were rung," all based on their overwhelming appearance in sexual or at least romantic contexts.[6]

This is not a matter of reading meaning into the ballads, but rather illustrates Andersen's insistence on the more optimistic of two options. Either folksong commonplaces are related to their poetic contexts (and that is why they are so often used), or they are irrelevant and used because singers are too dull to invent suitable descriptive phrases. I agree with Andersen that the former alternative is more promising, for it leads to fuller understanding. But it does not necessarily explain how the metaphorical power of a given phrase, figure of speech, or "formula family" can animate a song or ballad as fully as I have shown in this book. In order to see the workings of the process more clearly, it is necessary to examine a particular cluster of metaphorical references and show how these figures unite with other consistent clusters to produce an apparently simple narrative or lyric that nonetheless carries a complex load of cultural meaning. For this purpose, I will focus on water imagery, which is widely encountered in fairly consistent contexts in ballads and folksongs and often combined with several of the other clusters or families of metaphorical ideas.

Actions that take place in connection with water provide a particularly rich area of connotative meaning. Some water metaphors indicate sexual dalliance, others death and disaster, and still others separation and isolation. Discussing a ballad reference to "Annan's Water," Nicolaisen observes, "The name of that river takes on the role of metaphor in this context . . . not only a metaphor for the painful physical separation of two lovers, but also of the human tragedy that befalls when one of the two attempts to reduce that separation in the face of adversity. . . . Beyond all this, it is a symbol for everything that divides, separates and disrupts, a poignant reminder that all is not well in this world and that so much that is broken and fractured still has to be healed."[7]

In "Babylon," "Lady Isabel and the Elf-Knight," "Young Hunting," and others, the riverside is the scene of another poignant reminder of disruption. It is the site of a sexual event (often seduction or rape) or the place where—in the case of Young Hunting—the murdered victim is dumped after an aborted tryst. On one level, it may well be that these scenes are depicted along river banks because they represent being "out" and "away" from the home and community, as Renwick has suggested. But water carries a more complex metaphorical usage, of which setting is only one of several important components. For example, in many versions of "Lord Thomas and Fair Annet" (Child 73) an interchange occurs between the Brown Girl and Fair Elinor on the difference in their skin color. The Brown Girl demands (in version A), "And whair gat ye that rose-water / That does mak ye sae white?" Elinor answers:

> O I did get the rose-water
> Whair ye wull neir get nane,
> For I did get that very rose-water
> Into my mither's wame.

Leaving aside the equally interesting rose image, which has had a long history of vaginal reference, consider how some of the other versions published by Child handle this same interchange. In version B:

> "O whare gat ye the water, Annie,
> That washed your face sae white?"
>
> "O I gat een the water," quo she,
> "Whare ye will ne'er get nane;
>
> It's I gat een the water," quo she
> "Aneath yon marble stane."

When asked again where she got the cloth that dried her face so clean, she replies that she got it "aneath yon bouer o bane (bone)."

In version C, the question is, "Where did you get that water-cherry that washes you so white?" And the answer is, "That water thou'll never see; for thou's sunburnt from thy mother's womb, and thou'll never be like me."

In version E, Annie answers, "I got it in my mother's womb, where you'll never get the like; for you've been washed in Dunny's well, and dried on Dunny's dike, and all the water of the sea will never wash you white." At this, Willie takes a rose and places it in Annie's lap. She gives it back and tells him to "take up and wear your rose." Willie and the Brown Girl go to bed and are awakened later by Annie, standing at the foot of the bed saying, "Enjoy your brown, brown bride, and I'll enjoy my winding sheet; enjoy your brown, brown bride and I'll enjoy *my* black, black box that has neither key nor lock." This example uses the same sexual connotations as in "The Cambric Shirt" placed in direct connection with death metaphor (vagina-shroud, vagina-coffin).

In version F, Annie says that she got the water "beneath yon marble stone"; in G, "I got it in my father's garden beneath a marble stone," and then in the next verse—as if to make sure the metaphor is registered—"I got it in my mother's womb, where you'll never get the like." In version H, she says, "I got it in my father's garden below yon hollan dike" and contrasts this with the Brown Girl's birth: "You've been burnt in your mother's womb, and you never will be white." According to other fragments, "I got that roseberry water where she (the Brown Girl) could never get none, for I got it in my mother's womb, where in her mother's womb there was none"; "There is a well in my father's land, a place you'll never see"; and "There is a well in my father's yard that is both clear and spring, and if you were to live til the day you die that *doon* you never shall see." Is *doon* here an echo of Dunny's well in version E, or does it mean *down,* as in grassy slope or downy plumage, akin to the "grass" that Reeves discusses?[8] The word *well* is not used in each version, but the aggregate "family" demonstrates a consistency of image and sense of meaning in which the well metaphor is one of several alternate but appropriate figures for the womb.

In the Scots song "The Wee Staggie," sung by Norman Kennedy (who provided me with his text), the metaphor is developed more consciously:

> There wis an auld wife at the heid o' yon hill
>   The green leaves sae green-o;
> If she hisna gaen awa then she bides there still
>   An' ye ken pretty weel what I mean-o.
>
> She kept a pint o' the braw gweed ale
>   The green leaves sae green-o;
> An a bonnie young lassie for tae cairry it ben
>   An' ye ken pretty weel what I mean-o.

A sailor lad he passed by ae day
    The green leaves sae green-o;
He called for a pint o' the braw gweed ale
    An ye ken pretty weel what I mean-o.

He called for a pint an he called for anither
    The green leaves sae green-o;
An' the lassie an' the sailor they were bedded doon thegither
    An' ye ken pretty weel what I mean-o.

She drew her han' oot ower his wyme (belly)
    The green leaves sae green-o;
"Fits (what's) this I feel like a draig harra (drag-harrow) tine?"
    An' ye ken pretty weel what I mean-o.

"O that's my staggie (horse) that I ride on"
    The green leaves sae green-o;
"An' my wallet for haudin' my confidences in"
    An' ye ken pretty weel what I mean-o.

He drew his han' oot ower her wyme
    The green leaves sae green-o;
"Fit's this I feel like the birse (bristles) on a swine?"
    An' ye ken pretty weel what I mean-o.

"O that's my wall (well) that I draw fae (from)"
    The green leaves sae green-o;
"An' ye can water yer staggie in't"
    An' ye ken pretty weel what I mean-o.

"Fit if my staggie he should fa' in?"
    The green leaves sae green-o;
"He can aye grip a haud o' the girse (grass) roon the brim"
    An' ye ken pretty weel what I mean-o.

"Fit if my staggie hit should droon?"
    The green leaves sae green-o;
"He can hobble up an' doon till he comes oot again,"
    An' ye ken pretty weel what I mean-o.

No his staggie drank sae fair an' fine
    The green leaves sae green-o;
For the water in her wallie wis sweeter nor wine
    An' ye ken pretty weel what I mean-o.

For he put it in sae fair an' fat
    The green leaves sae green-o;
Bit he took it oot again like a half-droont rat
    An' ye ken pretty weel what I mean-o.[9]

David Buchan informs me that the handlers who brought breeding stallions from village to village in Scotland were believed to possess exceptionally powerful sexual capabilities, a field of reference that can be connected with the songs, jokes and phrases discussed in chapter 2 in which the horse image plays a prominent sexual role.[10]

Although not all folksong references to water and wells include an equine character, the horse appears so often in these contexts that it assumes a more pregnant meaning than a simple reference to common transportation. In "Lady Isabel and the Elf-Knight" (Child 4), a stranger on horseback entices a young woman away from her home and—usually by the sea or a river—reveals his intent to kill her rather than seduce or marry her. In version B, the scene is Wearie's Well, and the would-be murderer repeats three times that he has often watered his steed there. When he tries to kiss her, she throws him in and says, "Since seven kings' daughters you've drowned there, In the water of Wearie's Well, I'll make you a bridegroom to them all." In version D, she says, "Lie there you false Sir John, where you thought to lay me." In "Tam Lin" (Child 39), Janet meets Tam Lin by a well (where his steed has been standing), often after plucking a rose. She becomes pregnant by him and eventually rescues him from the fairies. Clark Colvill is seduced and enchanted by a mermaid at the Well of Stream, the Wells of Slane, or Clyde's Water; he eventually dies. The murdered boy in "Sir Hugh" (Child 155) is thrown into a well in ten of Child's versions; his death follows a seductive sequence in which he is offered an apple, a cherry, a ring, or other enticements to come into the "Jew's garden." In "Young Hunting" (Child 68), the protagonist refuses the amorous invitation of one sweetheart by explaining that his other girlfriend in Garlick's Wells, Brandie's Well, Clyde's Water, or Richard's Well is waiting for him or is a more desirable mate. When he leans down from his horse to kiss her goodbye, she stabs him and has him thrown in the deepest part of the river. The young lady in "Child Waters" (Child 63), who is already pregnant, is described wading through the water while her lover rides on horseback. She begins version C by saying, "The corn is turning ripe, Lord John / The nuts are growing fu (full)," certainly a fitting prelude to a story of pregnancy and disguise. When the young woman in "Young Benjie" (Child 86) refuses her lover entry and comes outside to him, he throws her in the river and she drowns. In "The Mother's Malison (Clyde's Water)" (Child 216), the young man goes to the girl's home to court; her mother, disguising her voice as that of her daughter, denies him entry. He is on horseback when he drowns on the way home. In "The Friar in the Well" (Child 276), a friar wants to have a young girl's maidenhead. She puts him off, asks for money, and hangs a cloth in front of her well while he goes to get the cash. Later, when she cries that her father is coming, the friar jumps behind the cloth and falls down the well. When he cries, "Alas, I am in the well," it is clear that his difficulty is real rather than metaphorical. When the girl says, "I'll make you pay for fouling my water," the effect is humorous relief, for it is only the culinary water—not her personal body fluids—that has been sullied. Child notes—with some naiveté—that wells inside houses are rare but does not speculate on the metaphorical possibilities.

All these scenes reflect meaningfully on each other but can be perceived only through the folkloristic method of broad textual comparison of the varied texts of one ballad as well as the texts of different ballads that have analogous scenes. Rather than being identical in phrasing each time, the related metaphors provide constellations that can intensify or focus the range of possibilities within a certain dramatic theme.

The well metaphor can either be used playfully or combined with other connotative dimensions that bring about ambiguity and irony of the deepest sort. In many folksongs, metaphors of sexuality and death are so delicately interposed that it would be fair to say that some ballads are not stories about an event itself, but are dramas of events in which narrative structure provides location for metaphorical images expressing the ironies and ambiguities of life's greatest puzzles. This can work only if the metaphors are employed consistently and coherently, but it does not require that all singers employ them all the time or in the same manner. For example, versions A and B of "The Wife of Usher's Well" (Child 79) feature a cluster of suggestive contexts and metaphors: The woman (especially in version A) is identified with a well; she brings about a night visit to herself by three men; she builds up the fire and prepares a bed for them; and their departure is brought about by dawn and the cock's crow. Ironically, these are all heavily connotative elements usually associated with the romance of the night visit, and some night visitors also turn out to be ghosts of departed lovers (chapter 3).[11] In "The Wife of Usher's Well," because the three night visitors are the woman's dead sons, there is an intense hint of incest. The use of connotative devices provides a powerful ambiguity in versions A and B totally lacking in other versions, which present a religiously oriented drama. The metaphors used, not the narrative structure of "the story," make the difference in meaning in different versions of the same ballad.

A similar tension between erotic and religious possibilities is encountered in "The Maid and the Palmer" (Child 21), another interaction that takes place at a well. An elderly palmer (someone who had been to the Holy Land) asks a maid by a well if she will give him a drink. She has no cup, she says. He tells her that if her lover were to come home from Rome she would find a cup soon enough, but she denies even having a lover. He calls her a liar and claims she has had nine children, all of them dead; she must do penance for seven years. In Scandinavian versions she is Mary

Magdalen and is approached by Jesus. The ballad easily calls up the ironies of erotic possibilities in a religious setting, as does the parallel story
of Jesus and the woman of Samaria at the well (John iv): Man speaks to
woman at well, setting up the implications of an proposition; she denies
having a husband and is called to account for having had five husbands
(adultery).

That water in "The Maid and the Palmer" suggests selfish vanity in
addition to sexuality is confirmed by the specific penances given the
woman in the many international variants of the ballad. In French versions,
for example, when she complains about a lack of water during her seven-year penitential stay in a cavern, she is sent back for another seven
years. When she finally says she wants no more water, she is sent directly
to Paradise. In a Catalan ballad, Magdalen, who is seen combing her hair
at the beginning, goes to church, intending to seduce the preacher. Instead, she repents and is sentenced to seven years on a mountain. Later,
she finds a spring and washes her hands in it, lamenting their disfigured
appearance; she then hears a voice telling her that she has sinned and
sending her back for another seven-year stint.[12]

In Child's version A of the ballad (from Bishop Percy's manuscript), the
maid goes to wash at the well, and the dew falls off her lily-white flesh
(surely a meaningful image, considering the relatively constant employment of dew to suggest virginity). She hangs her wash on a "hazel wand,"
which is parallel to the hanging of the cambric shirt on the thorn in Child
2 and suggests sexuality because of the folk associations of hazel. It is in
this provocative context that the old palmer appears and asks her for a
drink of water. Although the Percy version is clear enough in its implications, the interchange and its possibilities are even more obvious in a
version discussed by David Buchan in which the refrain is, not surprisingly, "The primrose o' the wood wants a name."[13] In it, an "eldren man"
asks the maid at the well for "a drink o' your cauld stream," to which she
replies, "My golden cup is down the strand; of my cold water ye sall drink
nane," obviously taking his request as metaphorical and rejecting what she
takes to be a sexual suggestion about her virginity. The old man pursues
the sexual dimension by accusing her of having borne and killed seven
children. Her penances (to be seven years a cock, seven years a stone,
seven years pregnant, and seven years a bell) are all images related to
sexuality, and thus the whole song demonstrates once more the poetic
richness of ironically juxtaposed inferences of sexuality and penance, youth
and age, female and male, life and death—all clustered around water,
whose uses can range from the secular to the sacred. Modalities of disguise and deception—the common medieval theme of appearance and
reality—also deepen the complex, interactive ironies: A palmer, or Jesus,

at first appears as a "dirty old man," while a sinful woman at first appears virtuous. In the case of this ballad, water is the suggestive medium through which the factors are all brought into mutual play, because it can imply physical sexuality on one hand and spiritual redemption on the other.

Considering the tremendous range of meanings associated with water— from destruction to fertility, from danger to nurture, from separation to purification—it is no wonder that water images have played a major role in poetic expression. Ballad appearances of water and well images in close association with certain animals (horses, cats, and birds) that also carry traditional implications, as well as the ironic interlacing of death and sexual metaphors in ambiguous situations, provide even richer constellations of meaning that are stunning in their philosophical and poetic import.

Two ballads somewhat differently combine the suggestive prominence of horses and the folklore of birds that appear as messengers, harbingers of death, or sexual or romantic provocateurs. "Lady Isabel and the Elf-Knight" and "Young Hunting" demonstrate the poetic range of complex metaphorical clusters in ballad usage.

Both ballads start out as romantic engagements; in both narratives, water, horses, and birds are key elements; in both, a heavy dose of sexual implication underlies the early part of the action. She invites him into her home to stay overnight in "Young Hunting," while in "Lady Isabel" he asks her to take off her clothes. If we allow for the strong parallel between Child's version B text and the horse and well of "Wee Staggie," moreover, the sexual suggestion in "Lady Isabel" is even stronger. Many versions of both ballads end with reference to a bird—often a parrot—who seems capable of spreading word of the action or raising an alarm. In "Young Hunting," the bird is bribed unsuccessfully with the promise of a golden cage and ivory key; in "Lady Isabel," the same bribe works, and the bird is silenced.

Moreover, vertical imagery is used to underscore the dominator-dominated theme in both ballads. In "Young Hunting," the man is first depicted as towering above the woman on horseback, and he has to lean *down* to kiss her; later, she throws him *down* into a deep pool after knifing him and then commands the bird to "fly *down*" and perch on her knee. By putting her lover "down" she turns the direction of the story, getting the upper hand over him even though in some versions she nonetheless must pay for it by being burned as a murderer. In "Lady Isabel," the man demands that the woman get down from her horse and prepare to die. Using a subterfuge, she throws him down into the sea, then mounts up on her horse and rides home, having, like the young woman in "Young Hunting," gained the upper hand.

Both ballads seem thus to dramatize on the vernacular level a reversal of the standard assumptions about male power over females by concluding with the woman in the "up" position—the woman-on-top topos so popular in Europe from the seventeenth century onward.[14] Both women win out by throwing the male into the water, a dramatic enough image in itself, considering the many ballads and folksongs in which female protagonists are heaved into the water to their deaths. The image is even more ironic if one accepts the Jungian possibilities of the water as related to and expressive of women's power. And yet, despite all these apparent similarities, the moral outcome—the empathetic "feel"—of the two ballads is quite different. What is it in their metaphors, their suggestive systems, or their cultural contexts that might account for our totally disparate evaluations of female protagonists who gain the upper hand by apparently similar means? After all, although they both kill a man, one is punished as a coldhearted murderer while the other one gets away with the deed, much to the audience's relief and satisfaction.

For the sake of convenience, I will provide a text of each ballad; both were collected from oral tradition in the United States, both from prolific ballad singers. Neither text can be taken as more authentic or typical than others, but both are complete and are good variants of their type. I collected "The Outlandish Lad" ("Lady Isabel") in 1956 from George Jensen of Logan, Utah; his grandmother had brought it from England and across the plains as a Mormon pioneer, and it was one of many such ballads she had sung for her family. The ballad thus provides a relatively live example of British folksong in American oral tradition. Jensen believed that his grandmother's interest in maintaining this particular song, and the reason for its enduring popularity among family members, stemmed from the fact that she had been wooed away from her English family by Mormon missionaries and had gone on to flourish in life in spite of all the real and imagined dangers along the way. Jensen's version is very much like Child's E text.

> There come an outlandish lad from the northland,
>   A-wooing unto me,
> Saying "If you will follow me to the northland
>   Then I will marry thee.
>
> "Go bring me some of your father's best gold,
>   And some of your mother's best fee,
> And two of your father's best nags from the stable
>   Where there stand thirty and three."
>
> She brought him some of her father's best gold,
>   And some of her mother's best fee,
> And two of her father's best nags in the stable
>   Where there stood thirty and three.

She mounted onto the milk-white steed,
 And he on the dapple-grey;
They rode til they came to the salt, salt sea,
 Six hours before it was day.

"Mount off, mount off your milk-white steed,
 Mount off, mount off," cried he;
"For six kings' daughters I've drownded here,
 Now the seventh one you shall be.

"And I pray you take off your fine silken gown,
 Take off that gown," cried he;
"For it is too rich, too rare and too fine
 To rot in the salt, salt sea."

"Well if I must take off my fine silken gown,
 I pray turn your back unto me,
For I think you are too great a rogue
 A naked woman to see."

He turned his back all on to her,
 Then she began for to weep;
She grabbed him around his middle so small,
 And threw him down into the deep.

He tossed up high and he floated low,
 Until he came up to the side,
Saying "Pull me out, my pretty fair maid,
 And I will make you my bride."

"Lie there, lie there, you false-hearted man,
 Lie there, lie there," cried she,
"For six kings' daughters you've drownded here,
 Now the seventh one's drownded thee."

She mounted on her milk-white steed
 And led the dapple-grey;
She rode til she came to her father's own house
 Three hours before it was day.

"Don't prittle, don't prattle, my pretty Polly,
 Don't tell no tales on me,
And your cage will be lined with a glittering gold
 And locked with an ivory key."

Note that the story opens with an amorous ("wooing") invitation from a foreigner to a young woman who is enticed away from her home with the promise of marriage. In typical ballad style, we do not learn until later that she is a princess. Her suitor demands and gets horses and money, or does "fee" mean cattle (*Vieh* in German, *feoh* in Anglo-Saxon)—a reference to the old custom of aggressive cattle raiding? They ride to the sea, where he prepares to kill her, asking her first to disrobe. She tricks him and kills him instead. She returns home and appeals to her parrot not to tattle on her.

In this version, the parrot scene is abbreviated, which would have suggested forgetting or "devolution" to earlier folklorists.[15] Although that possibility cannot be dismissed totally (many American versions end with an equally spare reference to the parrot), the fact remains that the scene figures in virtually all versions as an ending—perhaps even a resolution—and thus arguably has a function and a meaning. Moreover, because versions from the same geographical region contain both simple and complex articulations of the parrot interchange, it is possible that the scene itself suggests a meaning that does not require that all possible component details be mentioned in order to be understood or work as an effective conclusion. For example, Lester Hubbard gives two texts of "Lady Isabel" collected from two other Mormon pioneer families. Both, like the Jensen version, are closest to Child's E text, but both have a longer parrot scene in which the king, awakened by the conversation between his returning daughter and her parrot, is told by the parrot that the noise was caused by cats attacking the cage and that the princess has come to the rescue.[16] Vance Randolph provides three full versions of the ballad; one has the simple promise of a golden cage, another has the complex interaction with the king and the reference to predatory cats, while a third (text A) uses the interaction found more regularly in "Young Hunting," which is used here for comparison.[17]

The following text of "Young Hunting," the other ballad that concludes with a parrot, was collected in the 1950s by Joan O'Bryant, a folklorist at Wichita State University, from Allie Long Parker (who also sang "The Cambric Shirt") of Hogscald Hollow, Arkansas. O'Bryant conveyed a tape of the ballad to me but did not provide details about the particular family or personal functions the song may have had for Mrs. Parker, who called it "Lovin' Henry."

> "Light down, light down, Lovin' Henry," she cried,
>   "And stay all night with me;
> There's a chair for you and a chair for me,
>   And a candle a-burnin' free."

> "I can't light down, Lady Marget," he cried,
>   "Nor stay all night with thee
> For my lonely little girl in the Arkansas land
>   Will wait long for me comin' home."

Then he leaned down over the horn of his saddle,
 And he kissed her, one, two and three;
She took a sharp knife all out from her side,
 And she wounded him wide and deep.

"Ride on, ride on, Lovin' Henry," she cried,
 "And ride on beneath the sun;
And your lonely little girl in the Arkansas land
 Will wait long for you comin' home."

"But I can't ride on, Lady Marget," he cried,
 "Nor ride on beneath the sun;
For can't you see my own heart's blood
 A tricklin' down doth run?"

Some taken him by the lily-white hand,
 And some taken him by the feet;
And they throwen him into the dark riverside
 Which run so still and deep.

"Lie there, lie there, Lovin' Henry," she cried
 "Til the meat rots off of your bones;
And your lonely little girl in the Arkansas land
 Will wait long for you comin' home.

"Fly down, fly down, little parrot," she said,
 "And come perch upon my knee;
Your cage it will be made of the fine beaten gold,
 And the bars made of ivory."

"I won't fly down, Lady Marget," he cried,
 "Nor perch upon your knee,
For I just seen you murder your own true love;
 You'd kill a little bird like me."

"Oh, how I wish I had me a new cedar bow,
 And an arrow to fit my string;
I'd shoot you right through that neat little breast
 That looks so bright and green."

"But you ain't got no new cedar bow,
 Nor an arrow to fit your string;
So I'll perch right here on the topmost branch
 And bitterly I will sing."

It is now possible to make a few basic observations that go beyond the generalization that both stories feature women killing men and trying to bribe a talkative parrot. Clearly, both ballads begin with an amorous invitation, but the invitation in "The Outlandish Lad" comes from a stranger who wants to woo the young woman away from her home; in "Lovin' Henry," the invitation is made by the woman, who wants to woo someone she knows (her lover) into staying with her. The difference is in the male stranger's invitation *out* versus the female friend's invitation *in*. The Outlandish Lad takes money and horses, while Lovin' Henry (who already has a horse) gives a kiss. The Outlandish Lad leaves the scene with the young woman; Lovin' Henry stays. They both are killed, one by drowning, the other being thrown into the water after being stabbed. The young woman in "Outlandish Lad" leaves the body in the water at the scene of the murder and goes home, whereas Lady Marget leaves home to throw the body into the water. The princess in "The Outlandish Lad" is successful (usually) in persuading her parrot not to tell that she has been out; Lady Marget tries unsuccessfully to silence her parrot, and word of the murder "is out." Thus, although the two stories are alike in some regards, they contain more direct contrasts than similarities.

Moreover, the scenes on which each spends most attention in terms of focus and detail differ. The lengthiest scene in "The Outlandish Lad" is the four-verse segment at the seashore in which the seducer prepares to drown his lady and instead has the tables turned on him, followed by the two-verse description of his predicament in the water. In "Lovin' Henry," the lengthiest scene is the five-verse account of the murder itself, including being thrown in the water, all tied together rhetorically by the triple reference to the "lonely little girl in the Arkansas land" who will have to wait a long time (the implications of "long" becoming more ironically extreme with each repetition). Perhaps it is this apparent savoring of the murder that lends "Young Hunting" a different sense of morality than "Lady Isabel," for in other versions of "Young Hunting" the passionate murder and subsequent concealment of the body under water find even lengthier articulation, whereas in "Lady Isabel"—especially in the versions with complex parrot scenes—there is a clear sense of virtuous and clever escape from a murderous dilemma rather than an angrily jealous commitment to one. It is important to notice how the figurative language in the many versions of both ballads "says" essentially the same thing in plot and structure.

Holger Nygard provides the most extensive international comparative study of "Lady Isabel"; in it he notes that the use of water as the means of death is found primarily in Lowland tradition and in the French and English versions of the ballad (there are also strong parallels in German versions).[18] Nygard does not go into the possible cultural details that might account for this preference, but in light of our discussion of water imagery it is likely that culturally based metaphor is among the reasons. There is no way to ignore the fact that in some versions, notably those from

Scotland, the young woman actually seems to anticipate if not invite the amorous advance of the foreign stranger. In Child's A version, the fair Lady Isabel sits sewing in her bower (a standard preparation for romance). It is in the month of May; she hears an elf-knight blowing his horn and wishes she had the horn and the elf-knight "to sleep in my bosom." In Child's B text—in which the would-be abductor claims several times to have watered his steed at Wearie's Well—the first verse equates a bird coming out of a bush to dine on water with the heart throbs of the king's daughter. In virtually all versions except the Scottish A and B texts, marriage or courtship is mentioned; in the exceptions it is a clear case of forcible abduction with magical overtones. In version C, the abductor refers to the water in which the woman is to drown as her "bridal bed"; in version D, she asks him not to let it be said that he killed a maid on her wedding day and twice uses the pun "Lie there where you thought to lay me."

If anything, the metaphorical connections among water, horse, and bird are made more vivid in the German versions of "Lady Isabel." The water location is often described in connection with the linden tree (which has associations with water, childbirth, early marriages of young women, battle and slaughters, and fate) or the hazel bush (associated with erotic customs, aphrodisiacs, fertility, and mate divination).[19] In many German versions, moreover, the spring is described as running over with blood: "Wir müssen zu selbigem Bronnen / Wo Wasser und Blut heraus ronnen" (We have to go to the same spring where water and blood are flowing out). The attendant bird is usually a dove (or three doves) that takes the side of the maiden and tries to warn her of her coming fate.

In "Lady Isabel," the amorous or romantic possibilities of the opening scene move ironically to the ominous threat of death in the central scene. With the clever reversal, the once-threatened naive young woman—now presumably much wiser—gets to go home and reenter family life undiscovered by her father, the king. Only the parrot poses an impediment to her reintegration without loss of honor and reputation. Thus the final scene is not just a convenient ending but a key element in the resolution of the whole story. Nygard called the parrot episode—unique to the English-language variants of the "Heer Halewijn" type—unheroic, but in metaphorical terms it is a microcosm of the ballad's action, phrased once more in a symbolic vignette and deserving of a closer look.[20]

In Child's texts C and D, the parrot speaks to the returning maid and demands to know what she has done with the false man she ran off with earlier. In versions E and F (as well as in others) the parrot is more concerned with the safety of his mistress. In nearly every case, the king hears the noise and demands to know the cause of the disturbance (it is usually still before dawn). At this dangerous point the girl bribes the parrot with kind words and promise of a golden cage, and in the text of version C the parrot replies to the king:

> "There came a cat to my cage door,
>   It almost a worried me,
> And I was calling on May Colven
>   To take the cat from me."

In version D, it is "the cat she came to my cage-door"; in version E, "For the cats have got into the window so high, / And I'm afraid they will have me"; and in version F,

> "The cat's at my cage, master,
>   And sorely frightened me,
> And I call'd down my Polly
>   To take the cat away."

It seems clear that the reason for the tenacity and commonality of the scene lies in the way it dramatizes the predatory manner in which the girl is almost caught and killed. Although Partridge cites a seventeenth-century use of *bird* to mean prisoner, he traces "bird" as a reference to a girl or girlfriend only back to the nineteenth century, but Chaucer uses it in the Miller's Tale, so the possible identification of the speaking bird with the young woman of the story (phrased as a parrot because of the necessity to talk) could be cultural as well as structural. But the parallel is clear in any case: The clever words of the parrot raise the image of a sensuous predator making an attempt on an imprisoned bird, just as the Outlandish Lad had made an aggressively romantic attempt on the sheltered life of the princess. Both the girl and the parrot avoid disaster by a clever use of language. Thus the parrot interlude, even when it is referred to only partly, as in George Jensen's version, recaps and comments on the play of action in the story. Because the maid starts out naive, experiences betrayal and yet saves herself, then returns more mature to the family fold without even bruising her honor, the story seems heroic, or at least upbeat and productive of relief. This is a far cry from the effects of "Lovin' Henry"/"Young Hunting."

In most versions of "Young Hunting," although not explicitly in the text cited here, the protagonist is described as going hunting with a sword and a hunting horn by his side. Although a sword is not of much practical use in hunting, the total image is much more overtly aggressive than is the description of the suitor in "The Outlandish Knight." In several versions given by Child, the young man is not described as having sword and horn until he is being thrown or has ridden into the water, but it is plain that he has them.

Ironically, instead of the man's sword being used (really or figuratively) in the ensuing action, it is the woman's "little penknife" that enters his
body. She kills him not to save her own life but to express her anger and
jealousy; then, apparently to escape detection, she gets rid of the body in
a deep pool of water, although the intensity of her actions and the biting
sarcasm of her comments indicate that throwing him in the water, although
partly practical, is part and parcel of her emotional outburst. The motive
for killing, although understandable, is less defensible morally than is the
princess's motive in "Lady Isabel." Appropriately enough, the parrot episode reflects this difference in the form of a dramatic vignette. The bird
seems to function as a messenger or at least a representative for the murdered man (chapter 5), but the suggestion that strong narrative parallels
exist between the parrot and the murdered protagonist is overwhelming,
and, as in the case of "Lady Isabel," the parrot scene may provide a vignette of the ballad's raison d'être.

In the interaction between Lady Marget and the parrot, the command
to "Fly down and perch upon my knee" echoes "Light down and stay all
night with me." If such a similarity extends through the whole verse, an
equation might be implied: Lighting down and staying all night in Lady
Marget's home is functionally and dramatically the same as lighting down
to perch on her knee and be put in a golden cage. Perhaps Lovin' Henry
is responding to this suggestion of subordination when he refuses to get
off his horse. Lady Marget's aggressiveness is taken a step further when
she stabs him and later dumps his body in the water. Her appeal to the
parrot may thus seem to be a parallel to the scene in "Lady Isabel" where
avoiding detection is at stake, but it cuts in a different dramatic direction
because it can be read in both ways. Lovin' Henry, had he stayed, would
have risked being subjected to some kind of attractive or amorous entrap-
ment; the parrot, if he flies down, might be in the same danger as was
Lovin' Henry, a suspicion borne out in the next verse, where she says she
would kill him if she only had her bow and arrow. This suggests that had
Lovin' Henry stayed, he might have been killed anyway. If so, her invitation, like the abductor's in "Lady Isabel," is as potentially deadly as it is
sexual. It is probably impossible to tell which ballad "borrowed" the parrot scene from the other (Nygard believed that "Lady Isabel" borrowed
from "Young Hunting"), but it is clear that although their functions might
be similar on one level, a more complicated use is directly related to the
sense of the narrative in each case.[21] Each has become metaphorically and
dramatically situated in its ballad as a mode of comment, interpretation,
and resolution for the feel of the story.

Moreover, as in the case of "Lady Isabel," the accompanying imagery
in the many other versions of the ballad provides a rich array of sugges-

tiveness for the ballad's inner context, for the overwhelming majority feature in connection with the protagonist such items as a hunting sword and hunting horn (to say nothing of his name, Young Hunting, in some versions), boots, spurs, and horse—more than enough to suggest the mixed field of venery, which includes possibilities of sexuality and pursuit of wild game to the death. In connection with Lady Marget there are equally suggestive items, the burning candles, red charcoal fires, torches, her bower, her feelings (when she hears his bridle in version C, "It did her bodie gude"), and the well, river, or lake. In a nice irony (among several in this poetically loaded ballad), the candles that burn brightly on the water over the hidden corpse of the protagonist are juxtaposed with those at the beginning of the story, which might have been extinguished ("blowing the candles out") had he accepted the seductive invitation to stay all night.

Both ballads use many of the same commonplaces, images, and themes: water, horse, parrot-cage, love-death; yet the different ways in which these units of suggestive meaning are organized indicate a close, detailed, and complex—therefore not fortuitous—relationship between image and narrative meaning. The differences between the two ballads are subtle yet important. In "Lady Isabel," the man is active, the woman acted upon (until she saves herself); in "Young Hunting," both are active and engaged in one or another kind of hunting. In "Lady Isabel," she is naive and is seduced away from home; in "Young Hunting," she is sexually experienced (apparently), aggressive, and tries to seduce him into her home. In "Lady Isabel," the parrot is already in the home as a pet, even a friend or ally; in "Young Hunting," the parrot is outside in the wild, not yet in a cage, and sits "on the topmost branch" as an antagonist. The parrot in "Lady Isabel" provides a parallel to *her* because it, too, is almost a victim of predation; the parrot in "Young Hunting" is a dramatic parallel to *him* as well as a metaphorical parallel to her sexuality, which has become uncaged and cannot be recaptured. Parrots are not common to the wilds of either England or the United States; if they are out free, it is probably because they escaped from a cage. Moreover, if the unviolated golden cage in "Lady Isabel" can be seen as preservation of chastity, then the bird out of its cage in "Young Hunting" underscores Lady Marget's promiscuity. To look at the complex metaphors in these two ballads as mere commonplaces would be to overlook—as I believe several generations of ballad scholars have done—the intricate and delicate ways in which figurative language provides for metaphorical parallels, intensification of plot, identification of moral themes, and depth of culture-based responses for the ballad and folksong audience.

Water in the form of lakes, rivers, and seas is only one of several prominent components of an extensive constellation referring to the possibilities, ironies, and fears about death and sex. Along with such other components as animals (which may also have a range of further implications), tools and implements, and directional movements, these figurative references, far from being a secret or arcane system of meaning, are much like the grammar of language itself. We know how to use it and respond to it, although we often lack the conscious awareness of specific rules that might explain particular usages. We need not use all components (just as we need not use every part of speech in every sentence) in order to make perfect sense.

This suggestive language is not founded on the kind of sequential grammar suggested by Vladimir Propp's structural system, in which the functions of the dramatis personae usually occur in a predictable sequence even though they all need not be present.[22] Rather, this metaphorical system, drawing as it seems to do from the rich resources of culturally shared beliefs, assumptions, and values, is more supple and complex. It allows for a cluster of mutually reflective figurative expressions to be brought to bear on otherwise ambiguous human actions in a narrative or a lyric. Doing so gives those actions cultural meaning and moral import; we cheer the young murderess in "Lady Isabel" but not the one in "Young Hunting" even though they both kill a man. For scholars, moreover, the expressions provide unique insight into cultural values that are seldom articulated in any other way. They give a sense of meaning, cultural analysis, social critique, and vernacular commentary on human actions that are perceived and interpreted through the lens or screen of cultural logic not personal opinion. And, as I noted in chapter 2, such logic is often more intensely resonant for some groups than others, especially when the main characters appear in gender-heavy roles as victim or aggressor. Polly Stewart's provisos should be standard considerations in our readiness to understand the multiple possibilities of these ballads.[23]

David Buchan has spent years clarifying narrative coherence in ballads and has also addressed the metaphoric element, pointing out that the "oral poet is often concerned more with connotative effect than strict denotative meaning." He suggests that "through generations of use traditional language accrues a contextual force . . . and acquires connotative reverberations."[24] The examples that I have discussed demonstrate a *metaphorical* coherence that grows out of the shared semantic fields of singers and audiences. These figurative possibilities are foregrounded and intensified in the distilled, compact narrative sequences of ballads; in this way, metaphorical coherence grounded in culturally recognized images (rather than privately invented conceits, for example) works together with narrative coherence to re-create and intensify dramatic experience.

Epilogue: "The Golden Skein" and "The Bury New Loom":

The Weaving of Folksong Metaphor

This book began with Bob Beers's fiddle song, and in this concluding chapter I will discuss another of his songs, "The Golden Skein," which came from his "Grandpa Sullivan." Its quasi-literary language indicates a relatively recent, perhaps Victorian or broadside origin, yet for Bob Beers it was a song he heard sung on numerous occasions within his grandfather's family. Without the usual corroborative evidence supplied by variation, can we take Beers's word that the song is traditional? Most of the songs and ballads discussed in this book have variants whose aggregate evidence provides strong indicators of traditionality in theme and meaning. But in the case of family songs, "heart" songs, and broadsides, it is often the unique or duplicated (rather than dynamically varied) texts that must carry the weight of scrutiny. Because "The Golden Skein" does actually exist as a song and uses the metaphors of rural sexuality, a better question is whether we can afford to ignore it only because it is unique. Beyond that, as Kenneth Goldstein, a ballad scholar, remarked when I asked about the song's possible traditionality: "Look—either we believe our informants or we don't; I think we should believe them." And so do I. Besides, the song has a very close relative that uses an analogous metaphor: "The Little Ball of Yarn."

"The Golden Skein" is a wonderfully delicate example of the themes and figurative usages discussed in this book; in fact, the sexual references are so completely integrated into the imagery and the resolution of the song that it would be pointless to suggest that they are peripheral. Whatever the song's origins, it is a fine example of the ongoing capacity for effective employment of traditional metaphors based on human experience and interpreted by cultural attitude.

"The Golden Skein"

(as sung by Bob Beers)

Oh, it was in the month of May
When rams[a] and heifers sport and play,
And tiny birds do sing a charm,
I met a fair young maid.

The sun shone on her golden hair,
Her cheeks were bright and rosy fair,
And when she spoke so quietly
'Twas like a morn in spring.

"Oh would you mind," I said to her,
"If I should walk along with you?
Perhaps to help you bind your hair,
Or weave the golden skein."

"Oh no, kind sir, that cannot be,
For you're a stranger unto me;
My mistress bids me do not bide,
Or waste an idle day.

"It's best you go and search out those
With riches fine, and frilly clothes,
Where ladies fair do plait and bind,
Or weave the golden skein."

But, oh, the day was fair and warm,
And there was pleasure in her form;
To idle was my moment's ease,
The rest was her heart's desire.

So I gently took her by the hand
To wander softly o'er the land,
To pluck a rose, to bind her hair,
To tread the flowered stream.

And on her breast I wove a chain
Of daisies, round and back again,
And in a bower of leaves[b] entwined,
We wove the golden skein.[1]

(When women were present: a."lambs"; b. "lace.")

Sung to an almost nonrhythmic, slowly phrased tune, the song is a veritable display of suggestive references. In verse 1, the month of May, the sporting of active animals and the singing of young birds (compare Chaucer's "and smale foweles maken melodye / that slepen al the night with open eye / so priketh hem nature in hir corages") constitute the context for a meeting of a man with a young maid. In verse 2, the important detail of her golden hair establishes her physical attractiveness in folk stereotypical terms and sets up a pictorial understanding of the song's central metaphor in the loaded context of a morning in spring. Verse 3 uses a traditional triple sequence for the first articulation of the lover's invitation (walk along with you, bind your hair, weave the golden skein); her demure deflection of his advances takes two verses and echoes the metaphor only at the end of verse 5, where she suggests other ladies might be more ready than she. Verse 6 implies that they both are responding to the feelings of the moment, the meaning of "the rest" being clear to us only because of the preceding metaphors. Verses 7 and 8, saturated with such familiar figures as taking her by the hand, leading her into the fields, plucking a rose, binding her hair, treading a flowered stream, weaving a chain of daisies on her breast, and entwining with her in a bower of leaves, lead inexorably to the sexual resolution of "weaving" "the golden skein." It would be difficult—if not impossible—to argue that this is merely a pretty song of innocent love in a bucolic setting.

The same set of concerns, and even some of the same wording, can be seen operating in a less delicate manner and with a different metaphor in "The Little Ball of Yarn," discussed at length by Legman. The A version replaces lambs or rams and heifers with mules, but other details (which are italicized) are remarkably similar:

> *It was in the month of May* an' the jacks begin to bray,
> An' the jinnies begin to hover 'round the barn,
> An' *I met a* little *maid* an' unto her I said,
> Let me wind up your little ball of yarn, yarn, yarn,
> Let me wind up your little ball of yarn.
>
> *Oh, no sir*ee, said she, *you're a stranger unto me,*
> Perhaps you may have some other *charm,*
> But you'd better go to *those who have money an' fine clothes,*
> An' wind up their little ball of yarn, yarn, yarn,
> An' wind up their little ball of yarn.
>
> Well, I took her 'round the waist an' I gently laid her down,
> Not thinkin' I was doin' any harm,
> While the blackbird an' that thrush were a banging in the brush,
> I wound up her little ball of yarn, yarn, yarn,
> I wound up her little ball of yarn.[2]

The phrases in italics show how close (in some cases identical) the wording of the two songs is, and other versions show that this is no simple coincidence. In Randolph's version C there is the same rhetoric, same scenery, and more of the same phrasing.

> *It was in the* merry *month of May,*
> *When* the *lambs* did skip and *play,*
> That *I met a fair maid*
> And to her I did say,
> May I wind up your little ball of yarn?
>
> *Oh no,* said she, with her finger on my knee,
> And perhaps you have another *charm,*
> *You would have to look at those*
> *Who have money and fine clothes*
> For to wind up their little ball of yarn.

Version D has the line "You're a stranger unto me" as well. The scene of dalliance takes place in May in all the versions, and the metaphorical invitation is first rejected with the suggestion that ladies of higher station might be more eligible; then the consummation occurs somewhere in the bushes. In "The Little Ball of Yarn" the action is more boisterous, the animals are more lively and openly sexual (in one Ozark version: "Says the blackbird to the robin / Keep your little butt a-bobbin' / While I wind up your little ball of yarn"), and the sexuality is more athletic than tender but dramatically it is the same action as in "The Golden Skein." Legman traces the "Yarn" song to Burns's *The Merry Muses of Caledonia* (1800) and relates it to a similar one in which birds—especially a "yellow yorlin'" (a yellowhammer or finch) function as the metaphor or metonym for the young woman's blonde pubic hair. Because of the several examples of nearly identical phrasing and plot, it is possible that "The Golden Skein" and "The Little Ball of Yarn" are variants of the same song, and yet their central images—as their titles indicate—are quite different. It is, of course, possible that the ball of yarn figure is a rollicking permutation of a more sedate metaphor just as it is possible that the golden skein image is an attempt to make an earlier bawdy song more delicate (or euphemistic) or both may be descendants of an earlier cluster of songs with which the Burns texts are also related.

Goldstein has shown that Bob Beers's grandfather, George Sullivan, also sang a version of "The Little Ball of Yarn" that contained several phrases identical to those in "The Golden Skein." Rather than seeing them as alternative versions of the same song, however, Sullivan recognized them as variations on the same "ballad tale" (Goldstein's term) and employed them differently according to context. The overtly sexual "Little Ball" was sung solely in male company, while "Golden Skein" could be delivered in mixed company because of its romantic ambiguities.[3] The important point is that the metaphoric images are not the same (winding up a ball of yarn is quite different from taking yarn off a skein for weaving—doing and undoing, as it were), yet they both mean the same thing physically in the shared associations of the people who use them. The images are obviously not formulas—at least not in the usual understanding of that term—but are connected by our understanding of their usage within a familiar cultural context. The range of possibilities within the realm of spinning and weaving is even more extensive than these few texts indicate.[4]

Just as suggestive in its use of weaving metaphor is a broadside presented by A. L. Lloyd in *Folk Song in England*. "The Bury New Loom" was published and distributed by two prolific broadside printers in England's Northwest during the late eighteenth and early nineteenth centuries. Expressive of the times when itinerant weavers moved from town to town helping women weave while their husbands worked in the fields, the text is full of esoteric terms for tools, equipment, and processes of the weavers' trade. Nonetheless, their placement is so full of sexual implication (common in occupational songs) that a clear and active image of energetic copulation emerges, even for listeners who register little of the jargon beyond the common knowledge that a shuttle or shuttlecock goes back and forth between V-shaped open sheds of cloth:

> As I walked between Bolton and Bury,
>   'twas on a moon-shiny night.
> I met with a buxom young weaver
>   whose company gave me delight.
> She says: Young fellow, come tell me
>   if your level and rule are in tune.
> Come, give me an answer correct,
>   can you get up and square my new loom?
>
> I said: My dear lassie, believe me,
>   I am a good joiner by trade,
> And many a good loom and shuttle
>   before in my time I have made.
> Your short lams and jacks and long lams
>   I quickly can put them in tune.
> My rule is now in good order
>   to get up and square a new loom.
>
> She took me and showed me her loom,
>   the down on her warp did appear.
> The lam jacks and healds put in motion,
>   I levelled her loom to a hair.
> My shuttle ran well in her lathe,
>   my tread it worked up and down,
> My level stood close to her breast-bone,
>   the time I was squaring her loom.

> The cord of my lam jacks and treadles
> at length they began to give way.
> The bobbin I had in my shuttle,
> the weft in it no longer would stay.
> Her lathe it went bang to and fro,
> my main treadle it still kept in tune.
> My pickers went nicketty-nack
> all the time I was reiving her loom.
>
> My shuttle it still kept in motion,
> her lams she worked well up and down.
> The weight in her rods they did tremble;
> she said she would weave a new gown.
> My strength now began for to fail me.
> I said: It's now right to a hair.
> She turned up her eyes and said: Tommy,
> my loom you have got pretty square.
>
> But when her foreloom post she let go,
> it flew out of order again.
> She cried: Bring your rule and your level
> and help me to square it again.
> I said: My dear lassie, I'm sorry,
> at Bolton I must be by noon,
> But when that I come back this way,
> I will square up your jerry hand-loom.[5]

Of course, it helps somewhat to know that "lams" are foot treadles, that "jacks" raise a harness on the loom, that "pickers" help to push the shuttle back and forth, and that the "lathe" is a wooden beam on the loom which forces up the weft. "Squaring up," which Partridge lists as "justifying or setting in order," may very well have a particular weaving application relating to the necessity to keep yarns and sheds straight for proper weaving to occur, but Partridge also notes that "to square up" can also mean to pay a debt or settle an account. In any case, the burden of imagery in the old broadside clearly leans more toward clever sexuality than it does toward a technical account of the machinery of the weaving process. Even so, the sexual "meaning" emerges from the clever use of figurative language as well as from careful placement of the actions and not from direct description such as in openly "bawdy" songs like "The Big Red Wheel":

> Around and around went the big red wheel,
> In and out went the prick of steel;
> "Oh tarry a while," the maiden cried,
> For at least I think she was satisfied.

Bawdy songs achieve their affect in large part by the clever use of "naughty" language or verses that feature open puns like

> My husband's a mason, a mason, a mason,
> A very fine mason is he.
> All day he lays bricks, lays bricks, lays bricks,
> And at night he comes home and lays me.

Some of them use implied similes, for example, "I took down my pants and crawled in between, / And I started to sew on her sewing machine."[6] To say that bawdy songs are more overt in their application of figurative language and wordplay is not to suggest that other songs use covert imagery; rather, the traditional songs have come through performance contexts that have included persons of all ages and both genders. As a result, their imagery has tended to be more evocative and subtle than the open, rollicking, intentionally off-color songs of sailors, soldiers, university students, and rugby players.

"The Bury New Loom" comes close to the bawdy songs in its concentration on the sexual scene rather than its subordination of sexuality to other larger problematic issues like betrayal, but its figures are more metaphorical than explicit. In its use of mechanical metaphors, moreover, the song comes from an ancient ancestry that includes Chaucer (a good example is his description of milling machinery in the sexual episode of the Reeve's Tale) and the Anglo-Saxon riddle of key-and-lock (chapter 6), as well as more recent songs like "The Thrashing Machine," in which a young farm worker invites his girlfriend into the barn to see how the parts of his thresher work. The heartiness of the song is indicated by this Irish fragment:

> Her name it were Nellie, her age were sixteen,
> And she worked passing fair at the trashing machine.
>   Whoop! shilaylie, fiddle-aye-aylie,
>   Whoop! shilaylie hi ho.[7]

The esoteric occupational slang of weavers is probably closer to a code than anything that has been discussed thus far, but that code does not substantially impede an understanding of the metaphor in "The Bury New Loom." As long as we know what a skein is, "The Golden Skein" presents a network of rural imagery which—although perhaps nostalgic in its impact—is more "available" to most people from their experiences, memories, and family traditions. The use of nature metaphors in dramatic situations anthropomorphizes the elements of nature, making them symbols for meaningful themes in human experience. Nature is humanized, and human emotion is universalized. And—as the argument of this book goes—when particular nature images have been encountered in so many similar contexts over the years that their implications have become relatively consistent, the possibilities for deep and complex responses are greatly enhanced. But the same can be said of the mechanical metaphors of "The Bury New Loom": They anthropomorphize the machinery with which people make their living and use the characteristic movements and functions of that machinery to lend meaning and perhaps humor to human actions. Machinery is humanized, and human emotion is first universalized within the occupational culture and then within the larger culture of which it is a part.

Yet as poetically successful as the two songs may be for the cultures in which they are performed or encountered in printed form, neither would be considered "Great Poetry" or in any way "classic" by literary academicians, especially those Calvinists who prostrate themselves before the canons of elect works. Nonetheless, the songs have continued to exist, in the case of "The Golden Skein" by being sung avidly in at least one family through the years and in the case of "The Bury New Loom" by being printed as a broadside and presumably recited, sung, or at least actively read through the years (or else there would have been no demand for further reprinting and thus few exemplars of the text would be available). Clearly, the honest survival of a good, effective song does not require the approval of a formally educated audience, for it constitutes in and of itself, as Edward Ives puts it, "a moment of great integrity."[8]

In discussion of literature, the question of meaning, especially of intended meaning, has always been problematic, and yet generations of literary critics and commentators armed with historical perspectives, psychoanalytical systems, anthropological theories, or semiotic/performative/deconstructionist models, have persisted in adding to our capacity for understanding more fully what happens to an audience when a literary event takes place. In the areas of folklore and vernacular studies, where even the hypothetical intent of a particular author is usually out of the picture altogether, until recently there has been reluctance to develop a critical theory of poetic creativity. Yet newer scholars have successfully advanced the notion that vernacular and folk expressions must have some coherence, meaning, and effectiveness or else they could hardly continue to exist.

In addition to the more recent folksong and ballad scholars mentioned in this book, one thinks of Charles Joyner's *Down by the Riverside* (1984),[9] which has amplified and made more intelligible the many strands of understood meaning and the rich codes of performance in black vernacular expression. Roger Abrahams, by taking a form of street recitation seriously, brings contemporaneous black oral literature into focus in *Deep Down in the Jungle* (1964), as does Bruce Jackson in *Get Your Ass in the Water and Swim Like Me* (1974). Bruno Nettl's *Blackfoot Musical Thought* (1989) explores the range of cultural meanings in the extensive musical record of the Blackfoot tribe and discovers that Blackfoot musical taxonomy provides an alternative way of organizing meaning altogether, another way of classifying the universe. The social historians William M. Reddy, Laura Mason, and Robert Darnton have used popular media as well as folksongs and tales to show how social codes were maintained and expressed in the formative years leading up to the French Revolution.[10]

In his study of early Japanese literature, the social historian and literary critic Umebara Takeshi has suggested that many of the poems of the *Manyōshū* (Japan's earliest collection of literature from the eighth through the tenth centuries, which includes lengthy quoting of poems from still earlier times), once considered to have been expressions on love and nature, are better understood as encoded political critiques, references to unjust legal decisions, records of unfair or secret executions, locations of secret graves, and commentaries on illicit affairs and court intrigues. Working from recurrent nuances in style, consistency of images, constellations of metaphors, patterns of indirection, and well-socialized cultural assumptions, Takeshi has argued persuasively for the fullness with which ambiguity, metaphoric suggestion, and cultural phrasing can transmit important aspects of Japanese social history not articulated openly in any other way. His theories are still controversial, but they are coming into broader acceptance. Although he has not completely settled the question of intended meaning in the poems of the *Manyōshū,* he has created an irreversible shift in the way that classic is viewed.[11]

Although many of these studies have helped reveal some of the codes through which secret, publicly offensive, politically sensitive, or privileged information has been disseminated, others, including *Deep Down in the Jungle,* have also focused on the more common culturally recognizable styles of performance as elements of meaning. It is in that more open direction that I have tried to move with folksong metaphor. In doing so, I have tried to foreground the arguably provocative effects of performed wordplay and cultural reference upon live members of a culture who share many of the same assumptions. Although this argument does not assume that all members of a culture or social group will respond in the same ways to figurative language, it does posit that some generally shared coherence must be in the poetic vernacular or else so many songs would not contain the same sets of metaphoric references. The approach also relieves us of worrying about what the originator of a song might have intended by placing attention on how it seems to have functioned in the sensibilities of those among whom it has circulated. This does not allow the supposition that we have established "what folksongs mean" or what singers of folksongs mean when they sing a song. But I hope to have demonstrated some of the real possibilities of expression and understanding that seem to underlie this rich poetic and musical medium. Important to this approach is the realization that, for the most part, the poetic expressions are subtle and sometimes delightfully ambiguous but not indirect, secret, or misleading.

In "The Baffled Knight" and in a few medieval lyrics, a young woman narrowly escapes rape or seduction by slipping through the door of her father's house or castle and shutting it in the face of her pursuer.[12] She says, through the door, "Now you are a man without, and I am a maid within." It is certainly possible that her taunt refers only to her escape and that it means plainly, "You are a male person outside the walls, and I am a young unmarried female who is inside the walls." But because the pursuit was clearly sexually motivated and she follows the taunt with the old proverb, "He who will not when he may, can not when he will," we are equally free—even encouraged—to suppose that for many singers and audiences the lines were also understood as clever wordplay: "Now you are a man without (sex), and I am a maiden within (a virgin)." The folksong phrasing articulates this idea efficiently and poetically, and the double entendre allows for more to be said in the same phrase; both meanings are registered simultaneously and are appropriate to the sense of the song.

Similarly, the old German folksong "Zeit zum Rosenbrechen" (Time to break roses, or Time for rose-breaking, number 46 in Röhrich and Brednich) could be understood simply on the basis of its description of a young woman asking a young man for advice on when to pick roses, a quaint reminder of olden times when people shared their gardening customs through music. Yet knowing that "dew" often appears in folksongs where virginity is central and that roses and rose petals almost always have to do with romance and women's sexuality (even today in Germany one does not bring red roses to a married woman unless he wants to contend with an angry husband), and noting from shared cultural experience that people seldom pick flowers in the middle of the night, the key verse certainly registers more than a horticultural suggestion:

> One must break the little rose
>   just before midnight;
> Then all the petals
>   are laden with cool dew;
> That's the time for breaking little roses.

Until the recent development (I won't say acceptance) of postmodern and deconstructionist criticism literary scholars in general have not been willing to take into consideration such a great mass of detail not directly derivative of or expressly related to an immediate text, but students of oral tradition have been at this matter for some years. Homeric epics mean little as text unless we know a lot about the relationship between epic formulas and nuances of meaning in antique Greek culture; *Beowulf* is a barren gathering of hero anecdotes unless we know something about the meaning and use of the kenning, the *gylp,* and the humorous possibilities of litotes among the Anglo-Saxons. Especially in the case of traditional expressions—which exist, after all, precisely because they continue to pass through and among the living members of a closely associated group of human beings—we expect cultural knowledge to be at least as important as close textual inspection in our attempts to achieve an informed view of folk poetics.

Following Albert Lord's concept of the "tension of essences," David Buchan has called attention to the way in which certain related (I would say culturally related) elements in folksong, especially aspects of narrative, "automatically cohere."[13] I have tried in this book to focus on coherent metaphors that exercise the richest effects—especially those constellations of figures that foreground love and death. In so doing, I hope to have shown that at the various levels on which these metaphors function, this coherence is automatic, primarily because it reflects common assumptions and associations that singers and their audiences share. Moreover, the focus on love and death is neither arbitrary nor coincidental. Renwick has pointed out that the most popular topic in English folksong (I would say in the folksongs of Northern Europe generally) is the love relationship, and he admits that the figurative references to love are more typically metaphoric than symbolic or arbitrary. Of course, metaphors foregrounding love are heavily sexual in nature, for this allows for—perhaps insists upon—a deeper level of intensity, emotion, and hazard than can be had from a mere stroll among the posies.

Flemming Andersen notes, moreover, that "the main divide between the formula families is between those associated with Love and those associated with Death" and that typical stanzas made up of "formula lines"— those for which he claims a "supra-narrative function"—are the ones also associated with love or death.[14] Indeed, as we have seen, many of folksong metaphors place both subjects into a simultaneous relationship, which surely argues either for poetic blundering or for a rather complex and dramatic application of the "tension of essences" concept.

Sex and death perhaps do not automatically cohere, but they have enjoyed a long association in Northern European sensibilities. The medieval topos of the Dance of Death, so eloquently phrased in poetry, illustration, sculpture, and proverb (and brilliantly expressed in modern times by Horst Janssen, the German artist), is one vivacious example: The living person is seen dancing, singing, eating, and flirting with skeletons. From early times in Northern European grain fields, through the fifteenth-century *Ackermann aus Böhmen,* through Shakespeare's *A Winter's Tale* in which King John addresses Death as if she were a lover, through the seventeenth-century poets who referred to the sexual climax as "the little death," to Thomas Rowlandson's *English Dance of Death* (1816), to the poetic and artistic parodists of the Nazi era, to modern horror and war films, the direct juxtaposition and interaction of erotic and deadly elements has proven to be a tension of essences with considerable power.[15]

In a similar way, using apparently opposed images, medieval poets often expressed the intensity of their sexual love for a human woman by comparing it to their passionate reverence for and commitment to the Virgin Mary. At the same time, they articulated their spiritual dedication to Mary through analogy to sexual passion, as in the poem describing Christ's romantic approach to Mary's dewy bower (chapter 3). Obviously, some metaphorical topics are not considered to be as exclusively opposed as those qualities might objectively be registered. The interplay of sex and death themes works like a powerful oxymoron, each term mitigating and qualifying the other in extremely effective ways.

But the options are open, not obligatory. As I noted, in some versions of "The Cambric Shirt" (Child's "The Elphin Knight," number 2), there is a clear ambiguity in the metaphorical reference; death means no and sex means yes, the meaning of choice being based on the ability of the audience (and, by extension, the young man in the song) to register the coherence of the metaphors. But other versions do not make the same use of the available options; noncoherent metaphors can lead to nonsense and confusion rather than deeper insight, and some singers have apparently opted for that direction of reasoning. Thus, some versions of the ballad tend toward contrasting the patently impossible with the possible. For example, instead of being asked to plow the woman's fallow field with his ram's horn, the young man is told to plow sea sand with a muley cow's horn. Because one does not normally plow sand, and because a muley cow is by definition one without a horn, the task is impossible, not metaphorically sexual. Still other versions use a mixture, which admits for both ambiguity and impossibility. All options suggest that the range of choice is broad and rich, something that can be discovered only through textual comparison and by observation of singer and audience during normal performance situations.

Aside from its complexity, delicacy, emotional power, and narrative appropriateness, what can be said for the importance of traditional folksong and ballad metaphor? First, good poetic imagery of any sort, wheth-

er written or performed, is important because of its positive ambiguity—
its capacity to express an idea more fully and with greater complexity of
human feeling than can an objective statement. Moreover, metaphor and
image allow for the presentation of emotions and concepts that can reflect on one another profitably, a matter that could easily be confusing in
what passes for objective or expository prose. Beyond that, as Dell Hymes
has insisted, metaphor is "basic to rendering experience intelligible."[16]
Human experience, as Norwood Russell Hanson has pointed out, does
not cluster automatically into universally meaningful categories; rather, it
gets organized, processed, understood, and interpreted by the worldviews
that our culture and language supply.[17]

Ballad and folksong metaphors, deriving from culturally shared experiences, culturally interpreted responses, and ongoing cultural assumptions,
seem to have been developed chiefly to express the complexities and
ambiguities of human affairs: love, death, betrayal, reversals of fortune and
the like. Their function is to foreground or dramatize several reflective or
contrastive aspects of human concern at the same time, thereby creating
cameos or intense scenes redolent with the joys and ironies inherent in
the experiences and assumptions of everyday life. Because ballad stories
and folk lyric expressions are seldom exciting or inspiring in and of themselves, their power, like that of all good poetry and drama, resides in the
way the story or the lyric is articulated. Because a culture's nuances of
language and values inform the process of articulation, the resultant utterance is likely to be far more meaningful and effective than would be
the comparatively paltry vocabulary and repertoire of a single inventive
author, no matter how talented. Ballads and folksongs are like looms on
which skeins of culturally loaded color are woven into striking fabrics of
recognizable meaning, nuance, innuendo, and suggestiveness. The metaphors embodying these colors and designs touch off, enflame, dramatize,
and thus make palpable the greatest joys, ambiguities, and ironies of life.

Notes

Chapter 1: "All concealed in the flap of his pants"

1. Eliot, "The Music of Poetry," 58, quoted by G. Leach, *A Linguistic Guide*, 23.

2. G. Leech, *A Linguistic Guide*, 36.

3. Friedman, ed., *The Viking Book of Folk Ballads*, x.

4. Reeves, *Idiom of the People*, 1–57.

5. Lakoff and Johnson, *Metaphors We Live By*; de Saussure, *A Course in General Linguistics*; Gumpel, *Metaphor Reexamined* (1984).

6. Wilgus, *Anglo-American Folksong Scholarship*; Brunvand, *Study of American Folklore*, chs. 11, 12; Harris, ed., *The Ballad and Oral Literature*. Harris provides a full account of the works of Child, Kittredge, and Pound.

7. Bell, "'No Borders to the Ballad Maker's Art.'"

8. Sharp, *American-English Folk Songs* and *English Folk-Songs from the Southern Appalachians*; Wimberly, *Folklore in the English and Scottish Popular Ballads*; Friedman, *The Ballad Revival* and *The Viking Book of Folk Ballads*. For details on Gordon and his work, see Kodish, *Good Friends and Bad Enemies*, and Cohen, "Robert W. Gordon."

9. Nygard, *The Ballad of "Heer Halewijn"*; Richmond, "Rhyme, Reason and Recreation," in *Ballads and Ballad Research*, ed. Conroy; MacEdward Leach, *The Ballad Book*; Wilgus, *Anglo-American Folksong Scholarship*; Abrahams and Foss, *Anglo-American Folksong Style*.

10. Ives, *Twenty-one Folksongs from Prince Edward Island*; Creighton, *Songs and Ballads from Nova Scotia*; Fowke, *Lumbering Songs from the Northern Woods*.

11. Jones, "Commonplace and Memorization in the Oral Tradition"; Friedman, "Counterstatement"; Friedman, "The Oral-Formulaic Theory of Balladry," in *The Ballad Image*, ed. Porter.

12. The recent interpretive study of folksong can be seen developing in such works as del Giudice, "Erotic Metaphor in the Nigra Ballads"; Andersen, *Commonplace and Creativity*; Herrera-Sobek, *The Mexican Corrido*; Buchan's several articles on the "tale role" in ballads, among them "Tale Roles and Revenants"; Renwick's *English Folk Poetry*; and new work by such scholars as James Moreira of Memorial University (Newfoundland), whose essay, "'His Hawk, His Hound': Social Symbols and Ballad Metaphors," which he supplied to me, is a brilliant expo-

sition of the relation between metaphor and understood meaning in a select group of ballads.

13. Renwick's *English Folk Poetry* and Andersen's *Commonplace and Creativity* are the leading book-length studies on figurative language in folksong. Andersen neatly limits himself to Anglo-Scottish balladry, while Renwick ranges across the field of vernacular song and poetry with semiotic abandon and has taken heavy criticism for alleged subordination of the singers and their songs to academic jargon. See the pointed (if petulant) reviews by Russell, Richards, Pickering, and Palmer, in which the reviewers misunderstand—or reject—Renwick's placement of local written and oral texts under the same rubric as folk poetry (which, he conservatively insists, must achieve "oral transmission and variation, independently of its first begetter") and thereby lose Renwick's anthropological point about shared values and language in close communities. Also see Dugaw, "Anglo-American Folksong Reconsidered." Although as a folklorist I am also inclined toward texts that exhibit variation, language itself does not so neatly follow the presumed boundary between oral and written usage, as many of the written examples in this book will show, and as Wehse has illustrated so well in "The Erotic Metaphor in Humorous Narrative Songs" in *Folklore on Two Continents,* ed. Burlakoff and Lindahl.

14. For a brief description of Beers and his singing, see Goldstein, "Robert 'Fiddler' Beers and His Songs," in *Two Penny Ballads and Four Dollar Whiskey,* ed. Goldstein and Byington.

15. Legman, "'Unprintable' Folklore?" 266.

16. Pinto and Rodway, eds., *The Common Muse,* 273–75.

17. Ibid., 282–84.

18. Ibid., 284–85.

19. Ibid., 288–89.

20. Renwick, *English Folk Poetry,* 18–19.

21. Reeves, *Idiom of the People,* 85.

22. Ibid., 115.

23. Ibid., 104–5.

24. Collected by the author from T. J. Easterwood, Eugene, Ore., Oct. 15, 1968.

25. Reeves, *The Everlasting Circle,* 29.

26. Ives, *Joe Scott,* esp. 420–24.

27. Joseph Hickerson sings a modern song about a serious student of traditional songs who is unsuccessful in romance until he learns how to sing like Bob Dylan, hoarse voice and all. For the standard discussion and illustration of this process, see Laws, *American Balladry from British Broadsides,* esp. 59–62.

28. Cray, "'Barbara Allen,'" in *Folklore International,* ed. Wilgus; see also Dugaw, "Anglo-American Folksong Reconsidered."

29. For an extended analogy between folklore and biology, see Foster, "A Descriptive Nomenclature for the Study of Folklore."

30. For an effective characterization of the range of folksong from lyric to ballad, see Abrahams and Foss, *Anglo-American Folksong Style,* 37–60.

31. See Toelken, *The Dynamics of Folklore,* 382–83.

32. "Adam Bell" is number 116 and "A Gest of Robyn Hode" is number 117 in

Child, *English and Scottish Popular Ballads;* numbers of subsequent citations from this book are given in the text.

33. Lakoff and Johnson, *Metaphors We Live By,* 115.

34. Edmonson, *Lore,* 3.

35. Lakoff and Johnson, *Metaphors We Live By,* 19, 56.

36. Ives found this same prevalence of songs about love and death in the repertoire of one singer. See *Joe Scott,* 404–5. If, as Ives argues (431–33), such singers as Scott use a cluster of common metaphorical associations, it is clear that whether we look at widespread textual variation or at particularized songs by single "makers," we will still notice how a high-context audience can articulate and respond to such commonalities as love and death, arguably the principal concerns in European-American cultures generally. Bakhtin, in discussing the grotesque, carries the idea further, asserting that the forces of life and death are always closely related: "the grave is related to the earth's life-giving womb. Birth-death, death-birth, such are the components of life itself." See *Rabelais and His World,* trans. Iswoldsky, 50–51.

37. For examples, see Cray, ed., *The Erotic Muse;* and Randolph, comp., *Roll Me in Your Arms,* ed. Legman.

38. Hodgart, *The Ballads,* 27, borrows the term from Eisenstein, *The Film Sense.* It is one of the most apt to be applied to ballad style in the twentieth century. Bronson insists on the strategic and psychological role of the tunes in the formation of ballad dialogue; see *The Traditional Tunes of the Child Ballads,* 1:ix–xiii.

39. See Folk Legacy Records *The Traditional Music of Beech Mountain, North Carolina,* vol. 1 (FSA-22), side 1, band 3.

40. Hawes, "Folksongs and Function," 140–48.

41. John Bierhorst, ed., *A Cry from the Earth,* Folkways Records FC-7777, "Kiowa Gourd Dance with Captured Army Bugler."

Chapter 2: "One Morning in May"

1. Smith, *Virgin Land.*

2. For a discussion of this song and its vernacular meanings, see Toelken, "Folklore in the American West," in *A Literary History of The American West,* ed. Lyon et al., 40–42.

3. Bell, "'No Borders to the Ballad Maker's Art.'"

4. Nygard's study of "Lady Isabel and the Elf-Knight," in *The Ballad of "Heer Halewijn"* is an example. It traces all known versions of the ballad in many more languages and versions than any singer could possibly have commanded.

5. Logsdon, *"The Whorehouse Bells Were Ringing."*

6. See Wilgus, *Anglo-American Folksong Scholarship,* ch. 4, for a historical overview of the field of scrutiny.

7. Buchan, "Tale Roles and Revenants"; Buchan, "Talerole Analysis and Child's Supernatural Ballads," in *The Ballad and Oral Literature,* ed. Harris; Porter, "Jeannie Robertson's 'My Son David'"; Porter, "Context, Epistemics and Value"; Long, *"The Maid" and "The Hangman";* Renwick, *English Folk Poetry.*

8. Porter, "Ballad Explanations," 120.

9. For an extended discussion of high context groups, see Hall, *Beyond Culture,* esp. chs. 6, 7, and 8.

10. For example, see de Saussure, *A Course in General Linguistics,* 65–70. I am indebted to Rebecca Wheeler, a linguist, for bringing the relevance of this passage to my attention.

11. A leader in the discussion of performance has been Richard Bauman. See his "Verbal Art as Performance," as well as an updated version with supplementary essays, *Verbal Art as Performance.* A persuasive and sensible discussion of intertextuality is provided by Stewart in *Nonsense.*

12. Reeves, *Idiom of the People* and *The Everlasting Circle.*

13. Graves, *The White Goddess.*

14. S. Richards, review of Renwick's *English Folk Poetry,* 127.

15. Renwick, *English Folk Poetry,* 15, 37.

16. Wilgus, "The Text Is the Thing."

17. Renwick, *English Folk Poetry,* 13.

18. For the concept of "cultural scene," see McCarl, "Occupational Folklore," in *Folk Groups and Folklore Genres,* ed. Oring. McCarl defines "cultural scene" as "a recurrent social situation in which two or more people share some aspect of their cultural knowledge or folklore" (72).

19. Renwick, *English Folk Poetry,* 57.

20. Ibid., 11.

21. Other versions of this song can be found in Logsdon, *"The Whorehouse Bells Were Ringing,"* xix–xx, and in Thorp, *Songs of the Cowboys,* ed. Fife and Fife. The Fife American Collection (cited hereafter as FAC) in Utah State University's Fife Folklore Archive also holds three other variants (FAC 1:72, 73, and 837).

22. FAC 1:837.

23. FAC 1:838.

24. Partridge, *Shakespeare's Bawdy,* 41ff.

25. Antti Aarne and Stith Thompson, *The Types of the Folktale* (Folklore Fellows Communication no. 184, 1961). This research tool categorizes traditional narratives by the similarities among whole plots; it is refered to as the *Type-Index,* or as Aarne-Thompson.

26. McMahan, "The Two Things in Life That I Really Love," in *New Cowboy Poetry,* ed. Cannon, 39.

27. Wiggins, *Fiddlin' Georgia Crazy,* 186–87. Wiggins's account of his grandmother's "mishearing" of "Sugar in the Gourd" (84) confirms that not all members of the culture register the same sets of meanings when sexual innuendo is in the air.

28. Randolph, comp., *Roll Me in Your Arms,* ed. Legman.

29. This anecdote was kindly shared by my otherwise circumspect friend Jim Griffith of Tucson. In "Folklore as a Means of Getting Even," Orso notes that riding a horse is often a metaphor for coitus in Costa Rica, and that men often use *yegua* (mare) to refer to their female lovers. She also calls attention to the parallel "easy rider" in blues tradition.

30. "Young Hunting" is number 68 in Child, *English and Scottish Ballads;* numbers of subsequent citations from this book are given in the text.

31. Toelken, "An Oral Canon for the Child Ballads." For more on rose symbolism, see Heinz-Mohr and Sommer, *Die Rose*. Their study ranges from religious uses of the rose in connection with the Virgin Mary to the rose garden as the symbolic location of lovemaking (including the plucking of roses, which they equate with defloration).

32. See Olrik, "Epische Gesetze der Volksdichtung." The essay is presented in free translation by Steager in *The Study of Folklore*, ed. Dundes.

33. Reeves, *The Everlasting Circle*.

34. Krapp and Dobbie, eds., *The Exeter Book*, 204.

35. Porter, *Singing the Changes*, 45–59.

36. Purslow, ed., *The Wanton Seed*, 53.

37. Baring-Gould is quoted by Reeves, *The Everlasting Circle*, 250, in reference to "Strawberry Fair": "They [the words] turn on a *double entendre* which is quite lost—and fortunately so—to half the old fellows who sing the song," which only brings into question whether the *other* half of the old fellows understood but were careful not to acknowledge the metaphors in front of a proper clergyman.

38. See Benstock, *Textualizing the Feminine*, 127, 221n; DuBois, *Sowing the Body*, 55–56; Belenky et al., *Women's Ways of Knowing*, 18–19; Coates, "Gossip Revisited," in *Women in Their Speech Communities*, ed. Coates and Cameron, 94–95 and passim; Irigaray, *je, tu, nous*, trans. Martin, 29–36; Cameron, *Feminism and Linguistic Theory*; Radner and Lanser, "The Feminist Voice"; Kodish, "Absent Gender, Silent Encounter"; and Stewart, "Wishful Willful Wily Women," in *Feminist Messages*, ed. Radner. The entire Radner book is a landmark of clarity, wit, and insight.

Chapter 3: "It's dabbling in the dew where you might find me"

1. Moreover, as Renwick observes in "On the Interpretation of Folk Poetry," in *Narrative Folksong*, ed. Edwards and Manley, strictly denotative approaches to folksongs and ballads yield little more than a restatement of manifest content and overlook elements of poetic power, whereas excessively connotative treatments tell more about the abstractions in the critic's imagination than about the poetic abilities of everyday people. Both avoid the recognition that normal people have a capacity for using metaphors that can actually be discussed intelligently.

2. Edmonson, *Lore*, 51, 52.

3. Del Giudice, "Erotic Metaphor in the Nigra Ballads," provides an appendix of examples, 36–39.

4. Tax, "Can World Views Mix?" 280.

5. "The Cherry-Tree Carol" is number 54 in Child, *English and Scottish Popular Ballads*; numbers of subsequent citations from this book are given in the text.

6. Not only does the connotation fit the action, but it also does so in two different ways (virginity, sex) that are united by the story; it is a good example of the multivalent metaphors to be discussed in chapter 5.

7. Stewart, in *Nonsense*, 16, suggests that "the concept of intertextuality relies upon two basic assumptions: first, that various domains of meaning are contin-

gent upon one another, and second, that the common-sense world may be considered as a base from which other provinces of meaning are formed."

8. Excerpted from a whole ballad sung for me by Vivian Simmons Fendrick in Eugene, Oregon, several times during the 1970s. She had grown up in Scotland and had learned many of her songs while visiting relatives on the North Coast. She often used the river name "Fyvie" in place of "Virgie." My preference for the latter in this citation is probably based on my sense of its irony in the ballad story, but the ballad's metaphorical force does not depend on this detail.

9. See Toelken, "An Oral Canon for the Child Ballads," 93–97.

10. A fuller description of this event and its possible meanings can be found in "Context and Meaning in the Anglo-American Ballad," in Wilgus and Toelken, *The Ballad and the Scholars,* 37–40. The riddle song and its relations to other similar metaphors will be discussed more fully in chapter 6.

11. Another version of this song can be found in the Library of Congress recording *American Sea Songs and Chanteys* (AFC-L 26/27, 27B); see also Doerflinger, *Shantymen and Shantyboys,* 155–60. The song has always been a favorite among North German sailors, who sing it in a mixture of English and Plattdeutsch, ending with the line, "Rolling home, Hamburg, zu Di."

12. Renwick discusses Broadwood's early essays (1915 and 1923) in *English Folk Poetry,* 21–53. Laws, *American Balladry,* is an organized guide to ballad plots.

13. See, for example, Hymes, "Breakthrough into Performance," in *Folklore: Performance and Communication,* ed. Ben-Amos and Goldstein, and Bauman, *Verbal Art as Performance.*

14. Long, "'Young Man, I Think You're Dyin.'"

15. Buchan, *The Ballad and the Folk,* 171.

16. Röhrich and Brednich, eds., *Deutsche Volkslieder,* 2:444–59.

17. Sung by four members of the Klappacher-Fuchsberger family, joined by two members of the Koessner-Erlbacher families in Niederalm, September 12, 1991.

18. Sung by Margot and Martin Kuske, Bremen, December 20, 1985.

19. Baskerville, "English Songs of the Night Visit."

20. Cattermole-Tally, "The *Tagelied,"* 15–35; see also Shields, *"The Grey Cock,"* in *Ballad Studies,* ed. Lyle, 70–71, 90–91, 188, 196–97.

21. Cattermole-Tally, "The *Tagelied,"* 22.

22. For examples, see Partridge, *Shakespeare's Bawdy;* Brunvand, "The Taming of the Shrew Tale in the United States," in Brunvand, *The Study of American Folklore,* 304–16. The essay does not appear in the third edition of this helpful book. See also Brunvand's more exhaustive *"The Taming of the Shrew:* A Comparative Study of Oral and Literary Versions," Ph.D. diss., Indiana University, 1961.

23. For confirmation of the wide use of "cock" as a symbol of death, fertility, and sex, see M. Leach, *Standard Dictionary,* 239–40; for *Hahn,* see *Handwörterbuch des Deutschen Aberglaubens (HDA),* ed. Hoffman-Krayer and Bächtold-Stäubli, 3:1325–346; for *cock-penis,* see Partridge, *A Dictionary of Slang,* 232–35.

24. Davies, *Medieval English Lyrics,* 153–54. The poem is in the British Library in MS. Sloan 2593, f.10b, and was reprinted for public display in London subway trains in the series "Poems on the Underground." I am indebted to Diana Spencer of Snow College for providing a liberated exemplar of the underground poster.

25. The Dance of Death in its various guises from early times to the present has been used as an ongoing theme by the German artist Horst Janssen; see Fest, *Der tanzende Tod*. The figure shows up in Shakespeare's *The Winter's Tale*, the medieval German *Jedermann*, and many other early pieces, and is depicted in stained glass windows, murals, headstones, and church door handles all over Europe.

26. White, ed., *The Frank C. Brown Collection*, 2:95–101.

27. See, for example, Reeves's discussion of "dew" in his analysis of "The Foggy, Foggy Dew," *The Idiom of the People*, 45–57.

28. A standard version of this poem, also from MS. Sloan 2593, f.10b, is given by Davies, *Medieval English Lyrics*, 155. On the sensual and religious ambiguities of the dew image, see Raw, "As dew in Aprille," and Manning, "I syng of a myden."

29. Hufford to the author, July 17, 1988.

30. Stewart, *Nonsense*, 15.

Chapter 4: "üba d'Alm"

1. Thompson, *Lark Rise*, 62–69. The event took place in North Oxfordshire in the 1880s; the pub is actually called The Fox.

2. Alan Jabbour and Carl Fleischhauer, *The Hammons Family: A Study of a West Virginia Family's Traditions*, Archive of Folksong, Library of Congress, AFS L65–L66 (Washington, D.C., 1973).

3. In subsequent years, I have revisited the Koessner, Erlbacher, Polacek, Klappacher, and Fuchsberger families regularly and have continued to ask analytical (and no doubt impertinent) questions about the connotations of texts, music, and occasion. Their enthusiastic responses have made this particular area of research one of the richest parts of my academic and personal life.

4. A number of short descriptive studies and texts are available: Helmuth Pommer, during the 1920s and 1930s, produced a considerable number of commentaries, and there are brief pieces on yodeling throughout the pages of *Jahrbuch des deutschen Alpenvereins* and *Jahrbuch des österreichischen Volksliedwerkes*. Also see Senn, "Jodeln," and Deutsch, "Der Jodler in Österreich." Zemp has included yodeling as an aspect of "Filming Music."

5. See Wilgus, ed., Special Issue on Hilbilly Music, *Journal of American Folklore*, which features influential articles by Archie Green, Norman Cohen, L. Mayne Smith, Ed Kahn, and Wilgus. See also the massive discussions since that time by Malone, *Country Music U.S.A.*, Malone and McCulloh, *Stars of Country Music*, and Rosenberg, *Bluegrass*.

6. *Heimatpflege*, literally the nurturing or maintenance of the homeland, is understood as a kind of grass-roots movement, more ethnically and regionally nostalgic than it is political but nonetheless bothersome to some intellectuals for its similarity to chauvinistic passions of the 1930s. But it is rooted in a real identification with locale expressed, for example, in open reluctance to sing songs from areas other than where one was raised and in the assumption that songs from one's home area are so deeply familiar that they can be recognized by locals even when

played on a *Maultrommel* (jew's-harp). Hobsbawm and Ranger cover many of these issues in *The Invention of Tradition,* as does Bendix in "Tourism."

7. Pietsch has written an extensive essay on the monumental repertoire of *Gelegenheitslieder* (songs about special events) commanded by this talented and energetic singer.

8. "Easy for *you* to laugh—you don't have to buy any lard"—that is, it's easy enough for you to feel fortunate; you're not in need.

9. For an indication of the direction of these studies, see Porter, "Parody and Satire" in *Narrative Folksong,* ed. Edwards and Manley, 305–38, especially notes 26, 27, 32, 74; and Gower, "Analyzing" in *The Ballad Image,* ed. Porter, 131–47, especially notes 5 and 18.

10. This version was sung for me on September 10, 1991, by Hermi Polacek and Anneliese Erlbacher (the Koessner sisters) and Franz Fuchsberger at Hermi's home in Salzburg in answer to my question about whether they knew other songs with double meanings.

Chapter 5: "I sowed some seeds all in some grove"

This chapter grows out of a paper read at the Arbeitstagung of the Kommission für Volksdichtung (S.I.E.F.) in Freiburg im Breisgau, May 2–6, 1989. I would like to thank Jürgen Dittmar for his efforts in organizing the meeting, as well as Natascha Würzbach and Klaus Roth for their incisive and helpful suggestions on the role of metonymy and on diachronic-synchronic dimensions of the subject.

1. Renwick discusses larks, cuckoos, thrushes, and other meaningful birds in his chapter, "The Semiotics of Sexual Liaisons," in *English Folk Poetry.*

2. "Young Hunting" is number 68 in Child, *English and Scottish Popular Ballads;* numbers of subsequent citations from this book are given in the text.

3. Wimberly's views, common in his era, appear throughout *Folklore in the English and Scottish Popular Ballads.* He was also convinced that folksong generally "is not given to figurative language" (104n).

4. Child, *English and Scottish Popular Ballads,* 1:96. Bell makes it quite clear from a close reading of Child's famous (but seldom read) essay on ballads in *Johnson's Universal Cyclopedia* that Child did not consider poetic "fancy" among ballad singers to be debased or limited, however. See Bell, "No Borders to the Ballad Maker's Art."

5. See Partridge's entry for *thorn* in *Shakespeare's Bawdy,* for example; see also chapter 6 of this book.

6. White, ed., *The Frank C. Brown Collection,* 6:624; Frisk, *"Macer Floridus,"* 97–98.

7. *As You Like It,* III:ii:112–13; see the entry for *rose* in M. Leach, *Standard Dictionary.*

8. Reeves, *Idiom of the People,* 131–32. That the German and English traditions use many of the same plant metaphors with essentially the same meanings becomes abundantly clear in Meinel's perceptive essay, "Pflanzenmetaphorik im Volkslied," in *Jahrbuch für Volksliedforschung,* ed. Brednich and Dittmar; see also Röhrich, "Liebesmetaphorik im Volkslied," in *Folklore International,* ed. Wilgus,

and the entry for *rose* in such works as the *Handwörterbuch des Deutschen Aberglaubens* (*HDA*) and Röhrich's *Lexicon,* 2:777–78.

9. Long has discussed the twining plants thoroughly in "'Young Man, I Think You're Dyin.'" Despite her masterful argument, I do not believe it is provable that the image in the English language tradition descends directly from the Tristan materials, partly because of the widespread appearance of related imagery all over Northern Europe. It seems even more likely that both references come from a European metaphoric constellation that associates roses with women (see Meinel, "Pflanzenmetaphorik im Volkslied").

10. Hodgart, *The Ballads.*

11. Holzapfel, "Scandinavian Folk Ballad Symbols," in *Ballads and Ballad Research,* ed. Conroy; see also Holzapfel, "Towards a Ballad Definition," 86ff.

12. Because "Captain Wedderburn" and three other riddle ballads have no complete plot structure, Coffin calls them "black sheep" among Child's 305 ballads, but it is likely because he overlooks the extent to which the metaphors can function as plot. See Coffin in *The Ballad Image,* ed. Porter.

13. These and other possible meanings for the song are discussed in Toelken, "Ballads and Folksongs," in *Folk Groups and Folklore Genres,* ed. Oring.

14. The oral texts of this song demonstrate relatively little variation. This one was learned from Herb Arntson of Pullman, Washington, in June 1958. I have virtually identical texts from Clarissa Mae Judkins of Eugene, Oregon, (see *Dynamics of Folklore,* 382) and from Thomas J. Easterwood, also of Eugene (see T. J. Easterwood MSS. Collection, Archives and Special Collections, University of Oregon).

15. Coffin, *"Mary Hamilton."* Coffin's idea of an emotional core is closely related to the argument of this chapter, except that instead of positing a hypothetical core in the text of each ballad, I focus on the possibility of a system of metaphors in the culture, which functions to produce a recurring impact. We both see lineal plotting as subordinate to other factors in the establishment of this impact.

16. This is the same version noted in chapter 3, collected in Eugene, Oregon, from Vivian Fendrick.

17. See Child's extensive treatment of the story type in *English and Scottish Popular Ballads,* 1:171–73.

Chapter 6: *"Riddles Wisely Expounded"*

1. deCaro, "Riddles and Proverbs," in *Folk Groups and Folklore Genres,* ed. Oring; Burns, "Riddling: Occasion to Act."

2. An entire issue of the *Journal of American Folklore* (89, 1976) was devoted to the riddle; in addition, see Messenger, "Anang Proverb-Riddles"; Harries, "The Riddle in Africa" and "Semantic Fit in Riddles"; and Haring, "On Knowing the Answer" are prominent among the studies that have concentrated more on meaning in context than on structure. See also Abrahams, "The Literary Study of the Riddle."

3. Abrahams, "The Literary Study of the Riddle," is a cogent and articulate statement on metaphor. Abrahams's theoretical claim that folk metaphors are phrasings of culturally shared experience and imagination is central to the thesis of this book.

4. "King John and the Bishop" is number 45 in Child, *English and Scottish Popular Ballads;* numbers of subsequent citations from this book are given in the text.

5. The *Vafþrúðnismál* (Song of Vafþrúðnir), is one of several dramatic songs or lays that make up the Old Norse *Saemundar Edda,* often referred to as the "Elder Edda." In it, Odin defeats and kills a giant in a combat of intellectual strength using riddles.

6. From *The Merry Muses of Caledonia,* reprinted in *The Common Muse,* ed. Pinto and Rodway, 430.

7. See Prior's translation of "Gátu Rima" in *Ancient Danish Ballads,* 1:336–41.

8. Davies, *Medieval English Lyrics,* 158; the poem is found in MS. Sloan 1593, f.11b.

9. Reeves, *Idiom of the People,* 31. Although it is certainly possible—especially during Victorian times—that there was a good deal hidden in the emotional lives of British people, there is nothing much hidden about the metaphors they used in their vernacular songs and poems.

10. Cited in Bronson, *The Traditional Tunes of the Child Ballads,* 1:378. Other variants listed by Bronson have "apple" for "cherry" (note that what the image loses in its connection with virginity it gains in the connection between apple and temptation). In Bronson's variant number 12 there is another indication that the singer's knowledge of the underlying theme resulted in more of an obvious reference than that which usually appears. As an answer to "How can there be a baby with no cryin'?" most versions have "A baby when it's sleepin'," but here there are no questions, and the "answers" are given as outright statements. In the case of this line, "And when the baby's a-making / There's no squalling" (Bronson, *The Traditional Tunes of the Child Ballads,* 1:380).

11. See, for example, Wentworth and Flexner, eds., *Dictionary of American Slang,* 96, where the definition is given as "3. taboo. Virginity; lit., the hymen." Both Partridge, *Dictionary of Slang,* and the *Oxford English Dictionary* assign the appearance of this usage to the late nineteenth century, but surely the fifteenth-century *i have a yong suster,* which features a cherry without a stone, a briar without bark, and a dove without a bone—all in connection with love and longing— as well as the early sixteenth-century term *cherry-ripe* to indicate a woman who is sexually ready would indicate an earlier familiarity with and use of the image. The ring in this sequence of riddles might easily refer to the wedding ring bestowed after impregnation, but in his *Dictionary of Slang,* Partridge gives "the female pudend; cf., 'cracked in the ring'" (i.e., no longer virgin). Reeves notes in discussing a Sharp variant, "Pery Mery Winkle Domine," that Partridge lists "periwinkle" as a mid-nineteenth-century low colloquialism for "the female pudend" (Reeves, *Idiom of the People,* 170); and M. Leach lists the periwinkle plant as an aphrodisiac (*Standard Dictionary,* 857).

12. Taylor, *English Riddles from Oral Tradition,* 687.

13. Mackie, *The Exeter Book,* Part 2, 114–15, 126–29, 140–41, 146–47, 202–3.

14. Farr, "Riddles and Superstitions of Middle Tennessee," 318.

15. White, ed., *The Frank C. Brown Collection,* 1:301. The widespread currency of such riddles is attested to by studies of non-Western folklore genres. See, for

example, Maung and Dundes, "Riddles from Central Burma," especially two riddles on 72: "a pineapple" and "a cheroot (small cigarette)."

16. Gregor, *Notes,* 76.

17. Randolph and Parler, "Riddles from Arkansas," 256.

18. It is also conceivable that the analogy with "needle," aided by the actions noted, would suggest "penis," in which case the feminine designation would provide the discrepancy or discontinuity.

19. Peachy, ed., *Clareti Enigmata,* 27, 39. About 40 percent of Claret's riddles fall into this sexually suggestive arena in spite of his clerical status.

20. Ibid., 22.

21. Child, *English and Scottish Popular Ballads,* 1:8–14.

22. See, for example, Thistleton-Dyer, *The Folklore of Plants,* 160; and Wimberly, *Folklore in the English and Scottish Popular Ballads,* 350. Thomas Hardy uses thyme in this connection as a means of foreshadowing a death in *Return of the Native;* before she dies, Mrs. Yeobright lies back on a soft bank of thyme, watches a bird fly overhead toward the West, and has a thought like a falling star.

23. See Child's discussion of this cluster, *English and Scottish Popular Ballads,* 1:172–73.

24. Gregor, *Notes,* 79; Reeves, *Idiom of the People,* 203–4. Reeves's note on the line is "the wooden breeches: the coffin."

25. Northall, *English Folk-Rhymes,* 112; for love divination using sage, see also White, ed., *The Frank C. Brown Collection,* 6:261.

26. M. Leach, *Standard Dictionary,* 957.

27. Wedeck, *Dictionary of Aphrodisiacs,* 234; Douglas, *Paneros,* 45–46; Sharp, "Rosemary Lane," in Reeves, *Idiom of the People,* 181–83.

28. Frisk, *"Macer Floridus,"* 97–98.

29. Child, *English and Scottish Popular Ballads,* 1:261.

30. Röhrich and Brednich, eds., *Deutsche Volkslieder,* 2:555.

31. Of the kenning, Brodeur wrote, "Creation and apprehension of such a strained metaphor require an act of intellectual exercise not unlike that required by a riddle." *The Art of Beowulf,* 253.

32. See also Bronson, *The Traditional Tunes of the Child Ballads,* 2:130, no. 87.

33. White, ed., *The Frank C. Brown Collection,* 6:600–601.

34. Skeat, *An Etymological Dictionary of the English Language.*

35. Partridge, *Dictionary of Slang,* gives for *horn* "the male member." In *Shakespeare's Bawdy,* Partridge offers a parallel etymology of the word *yard:* "penis, usually with the implication of *erectus* . . . from M.E. *yarde,* O.E. *gerd,* 'a rod, staff,' which is cognate with L. *hasta,* 'a staff, a shaft; hence, a spear.'"

36. McPherson, *Primitive Beliefs in North-east Scotland,* 49–50.

37. White, ed., *The Frank C. Brown Collection,* 6:621, no. 45677; Randolph, *Ozark Superstitions,* 262–63.

38. Harry Wenden, Ohio State University, to author, August 12, 1960.

39. "The Mower," in *The Common Muse,* ed. Pinto and Rodway, 289.

40. Ibid., 417–20.

41. See Röhrich and Brednich, eds., *Deutsche Volkslieder,* 2:386–90, for six versions of this song.

42. Peter Kennedy, *The Folksongs of Britain,* vol. 4 (Caedmon Records).

43. Heine, *Luthers Flob,* 101.

44. O'Grady, ed. and trans., *Silva Gadelica,* 2:86.

45. In other versions in Child and elsewhere the most frequent reference is to the ram's horn. In nine out of eighteen versions in Bronson, *The Traditional Tunes of the Child Ballads,* for example, the ram's horn (its ancient connection with fertility and the cornucopia can hardly have been forgotten) is used. In five of the remaining versions it is simply "thy horn"; in the other four versions one is unspecified and the others are ambiguous: horse horn (two) and ox horn (one). In most of the American versions available to me, singers have either dropped their concern with ambiguity or have opted for discrepancy of another sort, for many of them assign tasks that are whimsically impossible; they use "muley cow's horn," "hog's horn," or "deer's horn." In Simon and Garfunkel's popularized version of the song, "Scarborough Fair," virtually all the tasks have become beautifully wispy impossibilities with no traditional coherence of delicious ambiguities. On the other hand, in bawdy songs the horn image is not rare, as Randolph and Legman point out in "I Blowed Her with My Horn" (*Roll Me in Your Arms,* 40–41), which has the lines "Right beneath her petticoat / I blowed her with my horn."

46. Also see "He plough'd her, and she cropt," in *Antony and Cleopatra,* II:ii:240–42, and Partridge's entries in *Shakespeare's Bawdy* under *crop, tillage, plough, unear'd.*

47. Reeves, *Idiom of the People,* 128.

48. Ibid., 156.

49. Nork, *Mythologie der Volksagen,* 301–2 (I translated the passage). The term *Vermehlung,* obviously a pun on making flour by grinding, is apparently Nork's coinage; the thirty-three-volume Grimm, *Deutsches Wörterbuch,* does not list it.

50. Röhrich and Brednich, eds., *Deutsche Volkslieder,* 2:556. The German Folksong Archive at Freiburg lists a ballad, "Die Müllerin" (The woman miller), which uses the same imagery for humorous purposes. A miller's wife whose husband is away from home decides to mill by herself and spends the whole night "milling" with lusty soldiers. The Miller returns and demands to be let in, but she refuses to rise because she's so tired. When he threatens to sell the mill, she says she will set up her mill on the Lüneburger Heide, where the water is purer. He will withdraw the threat if she lets him in. I am indebted to David Engle for calling this ballad to my attention.

51. Empson, *Seven Types of Ambiguity,* 3.

52. For a lengthy discussion of this theme, see Couliano, *Eros and Magic,* especially 151.

53. I am indebted to my colleague Leonard Rosenband, a social historian, for bringing this related set of possibilities to my attention.

Chapter 7: "My golden cup is down the strand"

1. Nagler, *Spontaneity and Tradition,* chs. 1 and 2.

2. Holzapfel, "Scandinavian Folk Ballad Symbols," in *Ballads and Ballad Research,* ed. Conroy, 118.

3. Toelken, "An Oral Canon for the Child Ballads," 101.

4. Andersen, *Commonplace and Creativity*, 34, 294–96.

5. "The Twa Brothers" is number 49 in Child, *English and Scottish Popular Ballads;* numbers of subsequent citations from this book are given in the text.

6. Andersen, *Commonplace and Creativity*, 105–222.

7. Nicolaisen, "Names and Narratives," 265–66.

8. Reeves, *Idiom of the People,* 55–56.

9. Because I possess no competence at representing Scots dialect, I asked Norman Kennedy to write out the text of this song. I have reproduced it here as he wrote it, adding only the quotation marks. I wish to thank him for his kindness in allowing me to use his version of the song. Randolph and Legman provide texts and discussion for several related songs, including "I Reckon You Know," which is very close to "The Wee Staggie" in phrasing and refrain (*Roll Me in Your Arms,* 44–52).

10. David Buchan to author, October 1991. The imagery here is identical to the horse-rider metaphor discussed in chapters 1 and 2. See Legman's comments on the horse as metaphor for penis in his notes to "A Soldier Rode"/"The Trooper and Maid," *Roll Me in Your Arms,* 210–212.

11. Cattermole-Tally, "The *Tagelied."*

12. Child, *English and Scottish Popular Ballads,* 1:231.

13. Buchan, "The Maid, the Palmer, and the Cruel Mother"; the version discussed in this piece was collected in Glenbuchat, Aberdeenshire, before 1818.

14. For an illuminating discussion of this theme, see Davis, *Society and Culture in Early Modern France,* 124–51 (the chapter is entitled "Women on Top").

15. See Dundes's classic characterization of this topic in "The Devolutionary Premise in Folklore Theory"; for a persuasive rejoinder that the decay theory was not so central to folklore theory, see Oring, "The Devolutionary Premise."

16. Hubbard, *Ballads and Songs from Utah,* 1–4.

17. Randolph, *Ozark Folksongs,* 41–47.

18. Nygard, *The Ballad of "Heer Halewijn,"* 200–316.

19. *HDA* 5:1306ff, 3:1527ff.

20. Nygard, *The Ballad of "Heer Halewijn,"* 283.

21. Ibid., 285.

22. Propp, *Morphology of the Folktale.* This is not to suggest that there are not many structural sequences and constellations in the ballads, as Buchan has fully illustrated.

23. Stewart, "Wishful Willful Wily Women," 68–69.

24. Buchan, *The Ballad and the Folk,* 41.

Epilogue

1. Bob Beers sang the song for me on numerous occasions; it appears on the Columbia record *Dumbarton's Drums* (CS 0472) and was—according to Beers— the most requested song in his family's repertoire when they sang on tour.

2. Randolph, comp., *Roll Me in Your Arms,* ed. Legman, 97–104.

3. Goldstein, "Bowdlerization and Expurgation," 381.

4. For example, del Giudice, in "Erotic Metaphor in the Nigra Ballads," calls attention to a variety of applications for the distaff/spool/spindle cluster as sexual metaphors (25–26).

5. Lloyd, *Folk Song in England,* 301–2. For a book-length treatment of such metaphors, see Porter's *The English Occupational Song,* which unfortunately came to hand too late to be exploited for its excellent perspectives in this discussion.

6. These and other bawdy songs may be found in Cray, *The Erotic Muse,* Logsdon, *"The Whorehouse Bells Were Ringing,"* and Randolph and Legman, *Roll Me in Your Arms.* A mechanical parallel given in the latter work is "Boring for Oil," 58–60.

7. This enthusiastic verse was supplied by James Griffith, who heard Seamus Ennis whoop it on several occasions over liquid refreshment in Ireland.

8. Ives, *Joe Scott,* 436. Ives has dedicated a long, productive scholarly life to the proposition that the imagined opposition between "learned" and "folk"—as a basis for qualitative judgment—is foolish and unproductive. I hope that this book has provided some support for this view.

9. Joyner's subsequent work has continued to focus on the idea of shared history and shared meaning in African-American communities.

10. Reddy, "The Moral Sense of Farce," in *Work in France,* ed. Kaplan and Koepp, 364–392; Mason, "Singing the French Revolution," Ph.D. diss., Princeton University 1990; Darnton, *The Great Cat Massacre.*

11. Takeshi, *Minasoko-no-Uta.*

12. "The Baffled Knight" is number 112 in Child, *English and Scottish Popular Ballads;* numbers of subsequent citations from this book are given in the text.

13. Lord discusses the "tension of essences" in *The Singer of Tales,* 97; Buchan, *The Ballad and the Folk,* 53.

14. Andersen, *Commonplace and Creativity,* 288, 292.

15. Fest, *Der tanzende Tod.*

16. Hymes, "Toward Ethnographics of Communication," in *Language and Social Context,* ed. Giglioli, 29.

17. Hanson, *Patterns of Discovery.* Of course, many others, from Benjamin Lee Whorf to Edward T. Hall to Mikhail Bakhtin, have studied multiple ways in which cultural details external to given texts may nonetheless be central aspects of understanding what those utterances mean.

Works Cited

Aarne, Antti, and Stith Thompson. *The Types of the Folktale*. Folklore Fellows Communication no. 184. 1961.

Abrahams, Roger, and George Foss. *Anglo-American Folksong Style*. Englewood Cliffs: Prentice-Hall, 1968.

———. *Deep Down in the Jungle*. Hatboro, Penn.: Folklore Associates, 1964.

———. "The Literary Study of the Riddle." *Texas Studies in Literature and Language* 14 (1972): 177–97.

Andersen, Flemming G. *Commonplace and Creativity: The Role of Formulaic Diction in Anglo-Scottish Traditional Balladry*. Odense: Odense University Press, 1985.

Bakhtin, Mikhail. *The Dialogic Imagination: Four Essays*. Translated by Caryl Emerson and Michael Holquist. Austin: University of Texas Press, 1981.

———. *Rabelais and His World*. Translated by Helene Iswolsky. Bloomington: Indiana University Press, 1984.

Baskerville, Charles Read. "English Songs of the Night Visit." *Publications of the Modern Language Association* 36 (1921): 565–614.

Bauman, Richard. "Verbal Art as Performance." *American Anthropologist* 77 (1975): 290–311.

———. *Verbal Art as Performance*. Prospect Heights: Waveland Press, 1984.

Belenky, Mary Field, Blythe McVicker Clinchy, Nancy Rule Goldberger, and Jill Mattuck Tarule, eds. *Women's Ways of Knowing: The Development of Self, Voice, and Mind*. New York: Basic Books, 1986.

Bell, Michael J. "'No Borders to the Ballad Maker's Art': Francis James Child and the Politics of the People." *Western Folklore* 47 (1988): 285–307.

Ben-Amos, Dan, and Kenneth S. Goldstein, eds. *Folklore: Performance and Communication*. The Hague: Mouton, 1975.

Bendix, Regina. "Tourism and Cultural Displays: Inventing Traditions for Whom?" *Journal of American Folklore* 102 (1989): 131–46.

Benstock, Shari. *Textualizing the Feminine: On the Limits of Genre*. Norman: University of Okalahoma Press, 1991.

Brednich, Rolf W., and Jürgen Dittmar, eds. *Jahrbuch für Volksliedforschung* 1982/83. Berlin: Erich Schmidt Verlag, 1982.

Brodeur, Arthur G. *The Art of Beowulf*. Berkeley: University of California Press, 1960.

Bronson, Bertrand. *The Traditional Tunes of the Child Ballads.* 4 vols. Princeton: Princeton University Press, 1959–72.

Brunvand, Jan Harold. *The Study of American Folklore: An Introduction.* 3d ed. New York: W. W. Norton, 1986.

Buchan, David. *The Ballad and the Folk.* London: Routledge and Kegan Paul, 1972.

———. "The Maid, the Palmer, and the Cruel Mother." *The Malahat Review* [Victoria, B.C.] 3 (1967): 98–107.

———. "Talerole Analysis and Child's Supernatural Ballads." In *The Ballad and Oral Literature,* edited by Joseph Harris, 60–77. Cambridge: Harvard University Press, 1991.

———. "Tale Roles and Revenants: A Morphology of Ghosts." *Western Folklore* 45 (1986): 143–58.

Burlakoff, Nikolai, and Carl Lindahl, eds. *Folklore on Two Continents: Essays in Honor of Linda Degh.* Bloomington: Indiana University Press, 1980.

Burns, Thomas A. "Riddling: Occasion to Act." *Journal of American Folklore* 89 (1976): 139–65.

Cameron, Deborah. *Feminism and Linguistic Theory.* London: Macmillan, 1985.

Cannon, Hal, ed. *New Cowboy Poetry: A Contemporary Gathering.* Salt Lake City: Gibbs Smith, 1990.

Cattermole-Tally, Frances. "The *Tagelied* and Other Dawn Songs: The Parting of Lovers, Living and Dead." *Folklore and Mythology Studies* 11–12 (1987–88): 15–35.

Child, Francis James. *The English and Scottish Popular Ballads.* 5 vols. 1882–98. Reprint. New York: Dover Press, 1965.

Coates, Jennifer. "Gossip Revisited: Language in All-Female Groups." In *Women in Their Speech Communities: New Perspectives on Language and Sex,* edited by Jennifer Coates and Deborah Cameron, 94–122. London: Longman, 1988.

Coates, Jennifer, and Deborah Cameron, eds. *Women in Their Speech Communities: New Perspectives on Language and Sex.* London: Longman, 1988.

Coffin, Tristram P. "Four Black Sheep Among the 305." In *The Ballad Image: Essays Presented to Bertrand Harris Bronson,* edited by James Porter, 30–38. Los Angeles: Center for the Study of Comparative Folklore and Mythology, 1983.

———. "*Mary Hamilton* and the Anglo-American Ballad as an Art Form." *Journal of American Folklore* 70 (1957): 208–14.

Cohen, Norm. "Robert W. Gordon and the Second Wreck of 'Old 97.'" *Journal of American Folklore* 87 (1974): 12–38.

Conroy, Patricia, ed., *Ballads and Ballad Research.* Seattle: University of Washington Press, 1978.

Couliano, Ioan P. *Eros and Magic in the Renaissance.* Chicago: University of Chicago Press, 1987.

Cray, Ed. "'Barbara Allen': Cheap Print and Reprint." In *Folklore International: Essays in Traditional Literature, Belief, and Custom in Honor of Wayland Debs Hand,* edited by D. K. Wilgus, 41–50. Hatboro, Penn.: Folklore Associates, 1967.

———, ed. *The Erotic Muse: American Bawdy Songs.* 2d ed. Urbana: University of Illinois Press, 1992.

Creighton, Helen. *Songs and Ballads from Nova Scotia.* 1933. Reprint. New York: Dover Publications, 1966.

Darnton, Robert. *The Great Cat Massacre*. 1984. Reprint. New York: Vintage, 1985.

Davies, R. T., ed. *Medieval English Lyrics: A Critical Anthology*. Chicago: Northwestern University Press, 1964.

Davis, Natalie Zemon. *Society and Culture in Early Modern France*. Stanford: Stanford University Press, 1975.

deCaro, F. A. "Riddles and Proverbs." In *Folk Groups and Folklore Genres,* edited by Elliott Oring, 175–97. Logan: Utah State University Press, 1986.

del Giudice, Luisa. "Erotic Metaphor in the Nigra Ballads." In *ARV: Scandinavian Yearbook of Folklore 1989,* 17–41. Stockholm: Royal Gustavus Adolphus Academy, 1990.

de Saussure, Ferdinand. *A Course in General Linguistics*. 1959. Reprint. New York: McGraw-Hill, 1966.

Deutsch, Walter. "Der Jodler in Österreich." *Handbuch des Volksliedes* 2 (1975): 647–67.

Doerflinger, William Main. *Shantymen and Shantyboys: Songs of the Sailor and Lumberman*. New York: Macmillan, 1951.

Douglas, Norman. *Paneros*. New York: R. M. McBride, 1932.

DuBois, Page. *Sowing the Body*. Chicago: University of Chicago Press, 1988.

Dugaw, Dianne M. "Anglo-American Folksong Reconsidered: The Interface of Oral and Written Forms." *Western Folklore* 43 (1984): 83–103.

Dundes, Alan. "The Devolutionary Premise in Folklore Theory." *Journal of the Folklore Institute* 6 (1969): 5–19.

———, ed. *The Study of Folklore*. Englewood Cliffs: Prentice-Hall, 1965.

Edmonson, Munro S. *Lore: An Introduction to the Science of Folklore and Literature*. New York: Holt, Rinehart and Winston, 1971.

Edwards, Carol L., and Kathleen E. B. Manley, eds. *Narrative Folksong: New Directions*. Boulder: Westview Press, 1985.

Eisenstein, Sergei. *The Film Sense*. Translated by Jay Layda. 1942. New York: Harcourt, Brace and World, 1970.

Empson, William. *Seven Types of Ambiguity*. New York: New Dictions, 1947.

Farr, T. J. "Riddles and Superstitions of Middle Tennessee." *Journal of American Folklore* 48 (1935): 318–36.

Fest, Joachim. *Der tanzende Tod: über Ursprung und Formen des Totentanzes vom Mittelalter bis zur Gegenwart*. Lübeck: Kunsthaus Lübeck, 1986.

Foster, John Wilson. "A Descriptive Nomenclature for the Study of Folklore, Part II: The Evolutionary Model." *Western Folklore* 28 (1969): 101–11.

Fowke, Edith. *Lumbering Songs from the Northern Woods*. Austin: University of Texas Press, 1970.

Friedman, Albert. *The Ballad Revival*. Chicago: University of Chicago Press, 1961.

———. "Counterstatement [to Jones]." *Journal of American Folklore* 74 (1961): 113–15.

———. "The Oral-Formulaic Theory of Balladry: A Re-rebuttal." In *The Ballad Image: Essays Presented to Bertrand Harris Bronson,* edited by James Porter, 215–40. Los Angeles: Center for the Study of Comparative Folklore and Mythology, 1983.

———, ed. *The Viking Book of Folk Ballads of the English-Speaking World*. 1956, 1977, 1978. Reprint. New York: Viking, 1982.

Frisk, Gösta, ed. *A Middle English Translation of "Macer Floridus de Viribus Herbarum"* in *Essays and Studies on English Language and Literature* 3 (1949).

Giglioli, Pier Paolo, ed. *Language and Social Context*. Harmondsworth: Penguin Books, 1972.

Goldstein, Kenneth S. "Bowdlerization and Expurgation: Academic and Folk." *Journal of American Folklore* 80 (1967): 374–86.

————. "Robert 'Fiddler' Beers and His Songs: A Study of the Revival of a Family Tradition." In *Two Penny Ballads and Four Dollar Whiskey: A Pennsylvania Folklore Miscellany*, edited by Kenneth S. Goldstein and Robert H. Byington, 33–50. Hatboro, Penn.: Folklore Associates, 1966.

Goldstein, Kenneth S., and Robert H. Byington, eds. *Two Penny Ballads and Four Dollar Whiskey: A Pennsylvania Folklore Miscellany*. Hatboro, Penn.: Folklore Associates, 1966.

Gower, Herschel. "Analyzing the Revival: The Influence of Jeannie Robertson." In *The Ballad Image: Essays Presented to Bertrand Harris Bronson*, edited by James Porter, 131–47. Los Angeles: Center for the Study of Comparative Folklore and Mythology, 1983.

Graves, Robert. *The White Goddess*. New York: Vintage, 1958.

Gregor, Reverend Walter. *Notes on the Folk-Lore of the North-East of Scotland*. London: The Folk-Lore Society, 1881.

Grimm, Jacob, and Wilhelm Grimm. *Deutsches Wörterbuch*. 1854. Reprint. Munich: Deutscher Taschenbuch Verlag, 1984.

Gumpel, Liselotte. *Metaphor Reexamined: A Non-Aristotelian Perspective*. Bloomington: Indiana University Press, 1984.

Hall, Edward T. *Beyond Culture*. Garden City: Doubleday, 1976.

Hanson, Norwood Russell. *Patterns of Discovery: An Inquiry into the Conceptual Foundations of Science*. Cambridge: Cambridge University Press, 1958.

Haring, Lee. "On Knowing the Answer." *Journal of American Folklore* 87 (1974): 197–207.

Harries, Lyndon. "The Riddle in Africa." *Journal of American Folklore* 84 (1971): 377–93.

————. "Semantic Fit in Riddles." *Journal of American Folklore* 89 (1976): 319–25.

Harris, Joseph, ed. *The Ballad and Oral Literature*. Cambridge: Harvard University Press, 1991.

Hawes, Bess Lomax. "Folksongs and Function: Some Thoughts on the American Lullaby." *Journal of American Folklore* 87 (1974): 140–48.

Heine, E. W. *Luthers Floh*. Zurich: Diogenes, 1987.

Heinz-Mohr, Gerd, and Volker Sommer. *Die Rose: Entfaltung eines Symbols*. Munich: Diederich, 1988.

Herrera-Sobek, Maria. *The Mexican Corrido: A Feminist Analysis*. Bloomington: Indiana University Press, 1990.

Hodgart, M. J. C. *The Ballads*. New York: Hutchinson's University Library, 1950.

Hobsbawm, Eric, and Terence Ranger, eds. *The Invention of Tradition*. Cambridge: Cambridge University Press, 1983.

Hoffman-Krayer, E., and Hanns Bächtold-Stäubli, eds. *Handwörterbuch des deutschen Aberglaubens*. 1930–31. Reprint. Berlin: Walter de Gruyter, 1987.

Holzapfel, Otto. "Scandinavian Folk Ballad Symbols, Epic Formulas and Verbal Traditions." In *Ballads and Ballad Research,* edited by Patricia Conroy, 113–21. Seattle: University of Washington Press, 1978.

———. "Towards a Ballad Definition. The Epic Formulaic Style." *ARV: Scandinavian Yearbook of Folklore* 36 (1980): 85–90.

Hubbard, Lester A. *Ballads and Songs from Utah.* Salt Lake City: University of Utah Press, 1961.

Hymes, Dell. "Breakthrough into Performance." In *Folklore: Performance and Communication,* edited by Dan Ben-Amos and Kenneth S. Goldstein, 11–74. The Hague: Mouton, 1975.

———. "Toward Ethnographics of Communication: The Analysis of Communicative Events." In *Language and Social Context,* edited by Pier Paolo Giglioli, 21–44. Harmondsworth: Penguin Books, 1972.

Irigaray, Luce. *je, tu, nous: Toward a Culture of Difference.* Translated by Alison Martin. New York: Routledge, 1993.

Ives, Edward D. *Joe Scott, the Woodsman-Songmaker.* Urbana: University of Illinois Press, 1978.

———. *Twenty-one Folksongs from Prince Edward Island, Northeast Folklore.* Volume 5. Orono: Northeast Folklore Society, 1963.

Jackson, Bruce. *Get Your Ass in the Water and Swim Like Me.* Cambridge: Harvard University Press, 1974.

Jones, James H. "Commonplace and Memorization in the Oral Tradition of the English and Scottish Popular Ballads." *Journal of American Folklore* 74 (1961): 97–112.

Joyner, Charles. *Down by the Riverside: A South Carolina Slave Community.* Urbana: University of Illinois Press, 1984.

Kaplan, Steven Laurence, and Cynthia J. Koepp, eds. *Work in France.* Ithaca: Cornell University Press, 1986.

Kodish, Debora. "Absent Gender, Silent Encounter." *Journal of American Folklore* 100 (1987): 573–78.

———. *Good Friends and Bad Enemies: Robert Winslow Gordon and the Study of American Folksong.* Urbana: University of Illinois Press, 1986.

Krapp, George Philip, and Elliott Van Kirk Dobbie, eds. *The Exeter Book.* New York: Columbia University Press, 1936.

Lakoff, George, and Mark Johnson. *Metaphors We Live By.* Chicago: University of Chicago Press, 1980.

Laws, George Malcom. *American Balladry from British Broadsides.* Philadelphia: American Folklore Society, 1957.

Leach, Geoffrey. *A Linguistic Guide to English Poetry.* London: Longmans, 1969.

Leach, MacEdward. *The Ballad Book.* New York: Harper and Brothers, 1955.

Leach, Maria. *Funk and Wagnall's Standard Dictionary of Folklore, Mythology and Legend.* New York: Funk and Wagnalls, 1949.

Legman, G. "'Unprintable' Folklore? The Vance Randolph Collection." *Journal of American Folklore* 103 (1990): 259–300.

Lloyd, A. L. *Folk Song in England.* London: Lawrence and Wishart, 1967.

Logsdon, Guy. *"The Whorehouse Bells Were Ringing" and Other Songs Cowboys Sing.* Urbana: University of Illinois Press, 1989.

Long, Eleanor. *"The Maid" and "The Hangman": Myth and Tradition in a Popular Ballad*. Los Angeles: University of California Press, 1971.

———. "'Young Man, I Think You're Dyin'': The Twining Branches Theme in the Tristan Legend and in English Tradition." *Fabula* 21 (1980): 183–99.

Lord, Albert. *The Singer of Tales*. Cambridge: Harvard University Press, 1960.

Lyle, E. B., ed. *Ballad Studies*. Cambridge: D. S. Brewer, 1976.

Mackie, W. S., ed. and trans. *The Exeter Book, Part II*. London: Early English Text Society, 1934.

Malone, Bill C. *Country Music U.S.A.: A Fifty-Year History*. Austin: University of Texas Press, 1968.

Malone, Bill C., and Judith McCulloh, eds. *Stars of Country Music: Uncle Dave Macon to Johnny Rodriguez*. Urbana: University of Illinois Press, 1975.

Manning, S. "I syng of a myden." *PMLA* 75 (1960): 8–12.

Mason, Laura Anne. "Singing the French Revolution: Popular Songs and Revolutionary Politics, 1787–1799." Ph.D. diss., Princeton University, 1990.

Maung Than Sein, and Alan Dundes. "Riddles from Central Burma." *Journal of American Folklore* 77 (1964): 69–75.

McCarl, Robert. "Occupational Folklore." In *Folk Groups and Folklore Genres*, edited by Elliott Oring, 71–89. Logan: Utah State University Press, 1986.

McMahan, Gary. "The Two Things in Life That I Really Love." In *New Cowboy Poetry: A Contemporary Gathering*, edited by Hal Cannon, 39. Salt Lake City: Gibbs Smith, 1990.

McPherson, J. M. *Primitive Beliefs in North-east Scotland*. London: Longmans, Green, 1929.

Meinel, Gertraud. "Pflanzenmetaphorik im Volkslied." In *Jahrbuch für Volksliedforschung* 1982/83, edited by Rolf W. Brednich and Jürgen Dittmar, 162–74. Berlin: Erich Schmidt Verlag, 1982..

Messenger, John. "Anang Proverb-Riddles." *Journal of American Folklore* 73 (1960): 225–35.

Nagler, Michael N. *Spontaneity and Tradition: A Study in the Oral Art of Homer*. Berkeley: University of California Press, 1974.

Nettl, Bruno. *Blackfoot Musical Thought*. Kent: Kent State University Press, 1989.

Nicolaisen, W. F. H. "Names and Narratives." *Journal of American Folklore* 97 (1984) 259–72.

Nork, F. *Mythologie der Volkssagen und Volksmärchen*. Volume 9, *Das Kloster*. Stuttgart: Verlag des Herausgebers, 1848.

Northall, G. F. *English Folk-Rhymes*. 1892. Reprint. Detroit: Singing Tree Press, 1968.

Nygard, Holger Olof. *The Ballad of "Heer Halewijn": Its Forms and Variations in Western Europe*. Folklore Fellows Communications 169. Helsinki: Suomalainen Tiedeakatemia, 1958.

O'Grady, Standish, ed. and trans. *Silva Gadelica*. London: Williams and Norgate, 1892.

Olrik, Axel. "Epische Gesetze der Volksdichtung." *Zeitschrift für deutsches Altertum* 51 (1909): 1–12. [A helpful free translation by Jeanne P. Steager is provided in *The Study of Folklore*, edited by Alan Dundes, 129–41. Englewood Cliffs: Prentice-Hall, 1965.]

Oring, Elliott. "The Devolutionary Premise: A Definitional Delusion?" *Western Folklore* 34 (1976): 36–44.

———, ed. *Folk Groups and Folklore Genres*. Logan: Utah State University Press, 1986.

Orso, Ethelyn. "Folklore as a Means of Getting Even: Mythical Legends from Costa Rica." *Southern Folklore* 47 (1990): 249–59.

Palmer, Roy. Review of Renwick. *TLS*, July 17, 1981.

Partridge, Eric. *A Dictionary of Slang and Unconventional English*. 8th ed. New York: Macmillan, 1984.

———. *Shakespeare's Bawdy*. New York: E. P. Dutton, 1960.

Peachy, Frederic, ed. *Clareti Enigmata*. Berkeley: University of California Press, 1957.

Pickering, Michael. "Popular Song at Juniper Hill." *Folk Music Journal* 4, no. 5 (1984): 481–503.

Pietsch, Rudolf. "'Gelegenheitslieder' im Repertoire des pongauer Sängers Hermann Kössner aus Goldegg Weng." In *Die Volksmusik im Lande Salzburg II,* compiled by Rudolf Pietsch, 113–55. Vienna: Schendl, 1990.

Pinto, Vivian deSola, and Allan Edwin Rodway, eds. *The Common Muse: An Anthology of Popular British Ballad Poetry, XVth–XXth Century*. New York: Philosophical Library, 1957.

Porter, Gerald. *The English Occupational Song*. Umea: Umea University, 1992.

———. *Singing the Changes: Variation in Four Traditional Ballads*. Umea: Umea University, 1991.

Porter, James. "Ballad Explanations, Ballad Reality, and the Singer's Epistemics." *Western Folklore* 45 (1986): 110–25.

———, ed. *The Ballad Image: Essays Presented to Bertrand Harris Bronson*. Los Angeles: Center for the Study of Comparative Folklore and Mythology, 1983.

———. "Context, Epistemics and Value: A Conceptual Performance Model Reconsidered." *Selected Reports in Ethnomusicology* 7 (1988): 69–97.

———. "Jeannie Robertson's 'My Son David': A Conceptual Performance Model." *Journal of American Folklore* 89 (1976): 7–26.

———. "Parody and Satire as Mediators of Change in the Traditional Songs of Belle Stewart." In *Narrative Folksong: New Directions,* edited by Carol L. Edwards and Kathleen E. B. Manley, 303–38. Boulder: Westview Press, 1985.

Prior, R. C. A. *Ancient Danish Ballads*. 3 vols. London: Williams and Norgate, 1860.

Propp, Vladimir. *Morphology of the Folktale*. Translated by Laurence Scott. Rev. ed. Austin: University of Texas Press, 1977.

Purslow, Frank, ed. *The Wanton Seed: More English Folksongs from the Hammond and Gardiner Mss*. London: English Folk Dance Society, 1968.

Radner, Joan Newlon, ed. *Feminist Messages: Coding in Women's Folk Culture*. Urbana: University of Illinois Press, 1993.

Radner, Joan Newlon, and Susan S. Lanser. "Strategies of Coding in Women's Cultures," in *Feminist Messages: Coding in Women's Folk Culture,* 1–29. Urbana: University of Illinois Press, 1993.

Randolph, Vance. *Ozark Folksongs*. 4 vols. Columbia: State Historical Society of Missouri, 1946.

————. *Ozark Superstitions.* 1947. Reprint. New York: Dover Press, 1964.

————, comp. *Roll Me in Your Arms: "Unprintable" Ozark Folksongs and Folklore.* Edited by G. Legman. Fayetteville: University of Arkansas Press, 1992.

Randolph, Vance, and Mary Celestia Parler. "Riddles from Arkansas." *Journal of American Folklore* 64 (1954) 253–59.

Raw, B. C. "As dew in Aprille." *Modern Language Review* 55 (1960): 411–14.

Reddy, William M. "The Moral Sense of Farce: The Patois Literature of Ille Factory Laborers, 1848–70." In *Work in France,* edited by Steven Laurence Kaplan and Cynthia J. Koepp, 364–92. Ithaca: Cornell University Press, 1986.

Reeves, James. *The Everlasting Circle.* New York: Macmillan, 1960.

————. *The Idiom of the People.* New York: Macmillan, 1958.

Renwick, Roger deV. *English Folk Poetry: Structure and Meaning.* Philadelphia: University of Pennsylvania Press, 1980.

————. "On the Interpretation of Folk Poetry." In *Narrative Folksong: New Directions,* edited by Carol L. Edwards and Kathleen E. B. Manly, 401–33. Boulder: Westview Press, 1985.

Richards, S. Review of Renwick. *Lore and Language* 3 (1982): 125–28.

Richmond, W. Edson. "Rhyme, Reason and Recreation." In *Ballads and Ballad Research,* edited by Patricia Conroy, 48–67. Seattle: University of Washington Press, 1978.

Röhrich, Lutz, and Rolf W. Brednich, eds. *Deutsche Volkslieder.* Dusseldorf: Schwann, 1965.

————. *Lexicon der sprichwörterlichen Redensarten.* Freiburg: Herder, 1973.

————. "Liebesmetaphorik im Volkslied." In *Folklore International: Essays in Traditional Literature, Belief, and Custom in Honor of Wayland Debs Hand,* edited by D. K. Wilgus, 187–200. Hatboro, Penn.: Folklore Associates, 1967.

Rosenberg, Neil V. *Bluegrass: A History.* Urbana: University of Illinois Press, 1985.

Russell, Ian. Review of Renwick. *Folk Music Journal* 4, no. 1 (1980): 291–93.

Senn, Walter. "Jodeln." *Jahrbuch des österreichischen Volksliedwerkes* 2 (1962): 150–66.

Sharp, Cecil J. *American-English Folk Songs.* New York: G. P. Putnam's Sons, 1918.

————. *English Folk-Songs from the Southern Appalachians.* Edited by Maud Karpeles. London: Oxford University Press, 1932.

Shields, Hugh. *"The Grey Cock:* Dawn Song or Revenant Ballad?" In *Ballad Studies,* edited by E. B. Lyle, 67–92. Cambridge: D. S. Brewer, 1976.

Skeat, William W. *An Etymological Dictionary of the English Language.* Oxford: Clarendon Press, 1910.

Smith, Henry Nash. *Virgin Land: The American West as Symbol and Myth.* Cambridge: Harvard University Press, 1950.

Stewart, Polly. "Wishful Willful Wily Women: Verbal Strategies for Female Success in the Child Ballads," in *Feminist Messages: Coding in Women's Folk Culture,* edited by Joan Newlon Radner, 54–73. Urbana: University of Illinois Press, 1993.

Stewart, Susan. *Nonsense: Aspects of Intertextuality in Folklore and Literature.* Baltimore: Johns Hopkins University Press, 1978.

Takeshi, Umebara. *Minasoko-no-Uta.* Tokyo: Shinchō-sha, 1983.

Tax, Sol. "Can World Views Mix?" *Human Organization* 49 (1990): 280–86.

Taylor, Archer. *English Riddles from Oral Tradition.* 1951. Reprint. New York: Octagon, 1977.

Thistleton-Dyer, T. F. *The Folklore of Plants.* New York: Singing Tree Press, 1898.

Thompson, Flora. *Lark Rise to Candleford: A Trilogy.* London: Oxford University Press, 1954.

Thorp, N. Howard ("Jack"). *Songs of the Cowboys.* Edited by Austin E. Fife and Alta Fife. New York: Bramhall House, 1966.

Toelken, Barre. "Ballads and Folksongs." In *Folk Groups and Folklore Genres,* edited by Elliott Oring, 147–74. Logan: Utah State University Press, 1986.

———. *The Dynamics of Folklore.* Boston: Houghton Mifflin, 1979.

———. "Folklore in the American West." In *A Literary History of The American West,* edited by Thomas Lyon et al., 29–67. Forth Worth: Texas Christian University Press, 1987.

———. "An Oral Canon for the Child Ballads: Construction and Application." *Journal of the Folklore Institute* 4 (1967): 75–101.

Wedeck, Harry. *Dictionary of Aphrodisiacs.* New York: Philosophical Library, 1961.

Wehse, Rainer. "The Erotic Metaphor in Humorous Narrative Songs." In *Folklore on Two Continents: Essays in Honor of Linda Degh,* edited by Nikolai Burlakoff and Carl Lindahl, 223–32. Bloomington: Indiana University Press, 1980.

Wentworth, Harold, and S. B. Flexner, eds. *Dictionary of American Slang.* New York: Thomas Y. Crowell, 1960.

White, Newman Ivey, ed. *The Frank C. Brown Collection of North Carolina Folklore.* Durham: Duke University Press, 1952.

Wiggins, Gene. *Fiddlin' Georgia Crazy: Fiddlin' John Carson, His Real World, and the World of His Songs.* Urbana: University of Illinois Press, 1987.

Wilgus, D. K. *Anglo-American Folksong Scholarship since 1898.* New Brunswick: Rutgers University Press, 1959.

———, ed. *Folklore International: Essays in Traditional Literature, Belief, and Custom in Honor of Wayland Debs Hand.* Hatboro, Penn.: Folklore Associates, 1967.

———, ed. *Journal of American Folklore* 78 (1965). Special Issue on Hillbilly Music.

———. "The Text Is the Thing." *Journal of American Folklore* 86 (1973): 241–52.

Wilgus, D. K., and Barre Toelken. *The Ballad and the Scholars: Approaches to Ballad Study.* Los Angeles: William Andrews Clark Memorial Library, 1986.

Wimberly, Lowry C. *Folklore in the English and Scottish Popular Ballads.* New York: Frederick Unger, 1928, 1959.

Zemp, Hugo. "Filming Music and Looking at Music Films." *Ethnomusicology* 32 (1988): 393–427.

Index

BARRE TOELKEN is past president of the American Folklore Society and a former editor of the *Journal of American Folklore*. He is the executive secretary of the International Ballad-Commission of the Société Internationale d'Ethnologie et de Folklore. His publications include *The Dynamics of Folklore, The Scholars and the Ballad* (with D. K. Wilgus), and a number of scholarly and popular essays on balladry, medieval literature, Native American narrative, and intercultural perspective. He is a professor of English and history at Utah State University, where he is director of the Folklore Program.

Books in the Series Folklore and Society